SPOKE

A Mother. A Son. Civil Rights. Vietnam.

COLEMAN

T0108095

LITTLE CREEK PRESS®
A DIVISION OF KRISTIN MITCHELL DESIGN, LLC

Mineral Point, Wisconsin USA

Little Creek Press®
A Division of Kristin Mitchell Design, LLC
5341 Sunny Ridge Road
Mineral Point, Wisconsin 53565

Editor: Carl Stratman
Book Design and Project Coordination: Little Creek Press

Limited First Edition
August 2013

Printed in Wisconsin, United States of America.

For more information or to order books:
www.spokesinthewheel.com or www.littlecreekpress.com

Library of Congress Control Number: 2013947337

ISBN-10: 0989643107
ISBN-13: 978-0-9896431-0-8

Dedicated to the grandchildren of Rosalyn Coleman Gilchrist:
Jennifer, Ginger, Greg, Jordan, Thomas and Lauren.

THE TASK
is not only to bind up the victims
BENEATH THE WHEEL,
BUT TO PUT A SPOKE
IN THAT WHEEL.

DIETRICH BONHOEFFER

Pampa, Texas — 1952

Jim and I lifted our heads at the sudden and familiar static in the air, the tang of ozone, the quickening of our own nerves. There, just on the horizon, a solid wall of dirt erupted from the featureless plain, quickly soaring to the edge of space itself, growing as it advanced and multiplying in its fury.

My twin and I headed indoors at times like these, without being called, and we boarded up the windows, closed the drapes, hung blankets over the doors, and stuffed the thresholds with wet towels.

In the kitchen, Mom brought out the candles, the flour, the baking soda, the chocolate chips, and the peanut butter. She struck a match and lit the gas stove. And as the storm overtook our house, and the dust crept in despite our precautions, and the electricity went out and the candles were lit, she baked cookies. Mom baked cookies by candlelight as the dust storm battered our house.

And then, we ate them.

Book One:
Nothing Left to Lose

FREEDOM'S
just another word for
NOTHING LEFT TO LOSE.

KRIS KRISTOFFERSON

Milan, Michigan — July, 1971

Prison wasn't so bad. Or so my mother taught me.

She hadn't wanted me to go to prison. But once I'd set my footsteps in hers, she was resigned and, I hope, a bit proud.

Bit by bit I discovered that prison *wasn't* so terrible—especially on days like this, as I passed the time in my cushy job tending the warden's flower beds. In June I'd planted both sides of his hundred-yard-long driveway with red and white petunias. Yesterday I weeded the south bed, and I had to say it looked damn good.

The warden's wife thought so too. I called her "Mrs. Warden." That afternoon she invited me into her kitchen for a cold glass of iced tea and a chat. She said I looked awfully hot out there in the sun, digging in the dirt. I said I didn't mind, that it beat sitting in the block all day, or working one of the mind-numbing jobs in prison industries, like making metal lockers for the Army while earning a whopping ten cents an hour. Digging and hoeing in the warden's gardens passed the time, and I had a lot of time that needed passing.

Mrs. Warden had difficulty smiling, but she did her best. A modest woman with a modest disposition, she presented a patina of happiness that I wasn't buying. Isolated in her faux-regal home set apart from any community, she was visibly, desperately lonely. During the many days that I worked as her gardener, I never saw anyone visit her home, and I never saw her leave it.

I served as a welcome and rare distraction. She evinced mild curiosity about my situation and never pried too deeply, but she hadn't invited me in so that I could talk about myself. She needed someone to listen as she talked about her children. Her daughter had recently married a man she didn't esteem and lived far away, and her son was in college back east. She worried about her daughter's happiness. She both anticipated and dreaded her daughter having children with this less than acceptable partner. But mostly she worried about what her son would do when he graduated next year. She feared he'd be drafted.

We sat at her kitchen table and she grew smaller as we talked, her hands tightly clasped in her lap, a sweating glass of iced tea sitting untouched at her place. After a time I thanked her and returned to my assigned task.

Today I was weeding the north bed. I was half done. I was in no hurry. I luxuriated in tilling the dry soil—good dark, rich loam—freeing it from weeds of any kind, transforming it into a welcoming plot of sweet black earth that would nourish the spread of my patriotically hued petunias. By midday I'd removed my shirt and was soaking in another Michigan summer day. I was lean and fit and I knew it, in the best shape of my life, thanks in no small measure to my prison routine. I relished the dirt under my nails, the sun blistering my back, and the sweat dripping down my forehead. Mostly I relished the solitude of working alone in the shadow of the front gun tower.

I was convinced that in my own way I was freer than the hawk-eyed guards in the tower, with their shiny, polyester uniforms, their skinny ties, their thermoses of tepid coffee, and their ever-ready rifles. All day long they stood and watched. They stood and watched me scratching in the dirt, progressing up one row of petunias and down the other. I wondered what they'd thought when Mrs. Warden had invited me into her house, whether they'd reported this to the Warden or whether they'd even noticed.

Bop pulled up in the prison-blue Ford pickup. Bop—his real name was Ken Baumann—was my hack, the head of the prison lawn detail. We called him Bop because of the way he bounced when he walked. At six-foot-three, he seemed to be all legs. Bop was a hack, but he wasn't like the other hacks. He was careful never to cross the line, but he managed to maintain a warm arms-length friendship with the handful of carefully screened inmates he supervised. I was lucky to be on his crew and I knew it. Bop treated his men with candor and respect, and they returned the favor. There was never any trouble on Bop's crew.

"Get in," chirped Bop, characteristically peering over the tops of his mirrored sunglasses with one hand and tugging at his handlebar mustache with the other. "The Chaplain wants to see you. Pronto."

He looked quizzically at me, as if expecting me to explain to him the odd summons. Bop knew of my disdain for the prison clergy, a dislike I suspected he shared though he never said so. No priest or pastor ever chose prison ministry. Rather, the church assigned the post to a lackluster servant of God with whom the church didn't know what else to do. Normally the chaplain in question would have no more desire to see me than I'd have to see him, so Bop's puzzlement made sense.

I didn't explain anything, but a peace settled over me. I already knew the reason for the summons. I'd known for a while it was coming, and last night, in the darkness of F block, surrounded by the nocturnal groans of the one hundred nineteen other inmates in my ward, somehow I'd felt her passing.

The Coleman family can be traced a long way back to a sturdy people who convinced themselves they controlled their own fate. Tough Scottish immigrants, they braved the rough Atlantic seas in the early 1700s and landed in an unknown, wild frontier, which would eventually become North Carolina. They became settlers in the New World, and they brought with them a much needed trade.

They were surveyors. They marked out the land, redefining wilderness as farms and towns by the simple acts of drawing lines on paper and pounding stakes into the ground. They were the instruments of change, the arbiters of possession, the progenitors of the White Man's westward progression.

As the land was surveyed and settled, the Colemans moved inland. By the turn of the century, they were established in Georgia. Half a century later, during the Civil War that pitted brother against brother, they fought for the Confederacy. They were slave owners.

In their time there was no need for my great-grandparents to conceal their contempt for all things "Colored." This disposition they passed to their children (my grandparents), who in turn passed it on to their children (my parents).

To them, Negroes were savages. They were no more human than the native "savages" whose land they surveyed, platted, and claimed. And "savages" could be civilized only to a point, after which their white masters needed to look after them and keep them in their place.

William Henry Coleman and Ellen Thrailkill Coleman

My great-grandfather, William Henry Coleman, served in Company E, 1st Texas Regiment, Infantry, Hood's Division, Longstreet's Corp., Army of Northern Virginia. He enlisted in New Orleans on June 6, 1861, and served until the surrender at Appomattox Court House in 1865. After the war William Henry settled in East Texas, continuing his work as a surveyor, and in 1870 he married Ellen Thrailkill.

Following Texas's independence from Mexico in 1836, there came about a kind of land grant known as a "head right." In order to obtain a clear title to a piece of land, all a settler had to do was hire a surveyor, who with his levels, chains, and compasses would "certify" the claim. Often the land being "certified" had previously been given to native tribes in peace treaties, which were routinely ignored. The Comanche were fighting to hold onto their buffalo plains, and they quite naturally hated the surveyors and went out of their way to hunt them down. Consequently, surveying was perhaps the most dangerous job in North America at the time.

William Henry's son and my grandfather, Henry Lee Coleman, was born in the piney woods of East Texas in 1872. By then the plains buffalo were gone: millions and millions of them slaughtered, leaving nothing behind but piles of sun-bleached bones on the very land where majestic herds had roamed free for millennia.

A hundred miles to the west, the U.S. Army sent three thousand soldiers against the Comanche, the largest force ever sent to hunt down hostile Indians. They crushed the one remaining band that hadn't already surrendered. The band was headed by Quanah Parker, the son of a chieftain and a white woman who'd been kidnapped off a Texas farm. With the plains Indians out of the way, the rush to settle West Texas and beyond was on.

The Coleman family was one of the first to settle in the heart of Comancheria, in a little crossroads called Vernon in what would become Wilbarger County. There my great-grandparents built a home on a hard-scrabble acreage of land that was to stay in the family for barely two generations. In 1881 Vernon was named the county seat. There were only fifty-six registered voters in the whole county. William Henry brought his son into the business, and young Henry Lee took up the sextant and the ruler. There was still plenty of land that needed surveying.

At the very ripe age of twenty-four, Henry Lee Coleman married Ara Bell Clarkson, and they did what all young families did back then. They had babies.

More kids meant more hands to till the soil, to break the horses, to bring in the harvest, to milk the cows. By the time my mother was born in 1910, there were five siblings waiting to greet her. She was a triplet, which brought the count to eight.

Five years later Ara Bell died while giving stillbirth to twins, and a hard plains life got harder. There were a lot of mouths to feed, and not much to put in them.

But my mother never revealed a hint of self-pity or bitterness about her beginnings. Her life was just her life, and was as filled with wonder and possibility as any child's, rich or poor.

During her last months, Mom wrote me a number of letters about her childhood. She knew she was going to die, I think, and I think this was her way of sharing a piece of herself that I'd always have.

January 19, 1971

Dear Joe,

Some things have been told to me about this era of family life.

We seemed to have plenty of food and things we needed as I look back on it. I made this remark once to your Uncle Floyd and his expression was incredulous. He decided it must have been my third and fourth years that were so bleak. Hard times were on in the whole town of Vernon. No farmer needed to know where his fence was to be placed separating him from his neighbor. Few if any were buying real estate so no lots were located in town. Business was off with Papa's title business.

Papa owned the Wilbarger [C]ounty Title Company. My sister Ona ran the office in the courthouse with Papa. Since there was little business, she became acquainted with the little Bailey girl who took art and painting. The Bailey's ran the hotel across the street. It was through this relationship that she became interested in painting, poetry and music. The Bailey girl died while quite young.

We were poor. My mama made most all the clothes, even Papa's shirts. We girls wore bloomers (not panties in those days) out of Belle of Vernon flour sacks. I remember having a pair where some of the blue printing had failed to bleach out of the sack.

Floyd said that Mama was very proud. He loved her like you love me. All his life he felt she had the harder role in the family—so much harder than Papa. She knitted, sewed, canned, crocheted.

Floyd said she depended too much on my sister Irma. Ona was older, but she was never there. Irma didn't have pretty clothes like Ona. Floyd blamed Papa for this. Irma helped with us kids; cooked, washed dishes. She was prettier and much more sociable but had the hardest time.

It was a matter of great pride to Floyd that Mama would dress us all in fresh starched clothes, making us look as nice as possible to go to church. Then after our hair ribbons and everything was in place he said she'd come out in her every day black cotton stockings and work shoes to get in the car. He said Mama's beautiful shining hair made up for it and when she got there her voice was the prettiest in the church. He told me this part of the story more than once. All he wanted of Mama's things was a pair of her cotton stockings.

When I was in high school, Floyd told me this story about Mama and those hard years. I was so ignorant or something it made me ashamed but I didn't tell him it did.

We weren't farmers, only had an acreage, but most of our neighbors farmed. Close to us was a little shack that was used for cotton pickers in the fall. J Marvin and I were infants at this time. Word got to Mama that the family was ill, so she put on her coat and head scarf and went over to see what they needed. She found a very ill mother with a tiny baby.

It was quite a distance from our house but regularly until this lady recovered, Mama went over and nursed the little baby. Now, why was I ashamed when Floyd told me this? Was it because she was already nursing twins?

On another occasion, soon after I married, I was at some social function at our church. A lady that was a stranger to me came up to me and said, "Your mother was my neighbor when you were a baby. You had the sweetest, best mother I ever knew." She didn't tell me who she was. It shook me up. I turned quickly so she wouldn't see the tears.

Love, Mom

The letter isn't clear on this point, and I never had the chance to ask her about it, but I've always wondered if the "cotton pickers" in her story were former slaves. Had my mother's mother nursed a black baby? Is that why she was ashamed?

These several letters were the only occasions when my mother shared with me any reflections on her own upbringing. She wrote about her family's first telephone, about a Fourth of July parade when Buster Brown himself rode in the lead car, about her fascination with reading as a child, and about her own mother's death. When I first read the letters, I was struck by how little I'd previously known about her. When I was a child, our relationship had always been about me, never about her, until the accident anyway. After the accident, it was about her recovery, which wasn't the same, I was learning, as being about her.

My mother (holding the board) with her brothers and sisters. Vernon, Texas

How did my mother meet my father?

Certainly they knew each other growing up. Vernon wasn't a large community. But they never spoke of their early years together. My father rarely spoke at all, and when he spoke it was never about his childhood. And although my mother eventually shared stories of her childhood with me, there was never any mention of my father.

My father grew up in or around Vernon. He might have been a farm kid or a town kid or a little bit of both. I know nothing about his father, but as a child I spent time with his mother and his two sisters.

When I was very young, we used to visit Dad's older sister Bennie in her small wooden frame home on the edge of Wichita Falls. There my twin brother and I would sleep on blankets on the back porch with Bennie's older, mischievous son, who always frightened us a little. He liked to fight and play with knives, and he considered any kid different from him to be a sissy. Well, if not fighting or cutting things made one a sissy then fine, I was a sissy, and I spent my dreaded visits to Benny's house doing my best to remain invisible to Bennie's scary son.

In a small dark stuffy bedroom lay the wrinkled, frail body of my expiring grandmother Sarah, my father's mother, whose daily activities were limited to dipping snuff and wetting her sheets. I never saw Grandma Sarah out of her bed, and there was no having a conversation with her. Presumably she spoke once upon a time, but I never heard her voice.

On other occasions we visited Dad's younger sister, Bessie, who lived in a little crossroads town called Electra. There wasn't much there: three or four houses, some oil pumps, one cow, and a succession of rolling tumbleweeds. Bessie was as taciturn as Dad. We'd sit in her sweltering home, drink sweetened iced tea in sweating metal glasses, swat the flies, and listen to the chugging of the oil pump in her front yard. Time would pass and no one would say a thing. Eventually someone would bring out a cribbage board or a deck of cards, but we never seemed to finish a game. After a day or two we'd go back home. Bessie didn't own the pump or the oil, or much else for that matter. She had a husband who didn't say much, a blue glass coffee table covered with doilies she'd crocheted, and a feisty Pekingese no one could safely approach. Her bathtub was always filled with her cow's milk, so no one was allowed to bathe.

Why did my parents wait so long to get married? They met back in the first years of the twentieth century, when men and women married young. Did my mother have suitors before my father? Did my father have girlfriends before my mother? Had they always had an eye for each other? Did they come to marriage out of desperation? Or love? How did they each get through the Depression and the Dust Bowl years? Did my mother live with her own father until she was married, or did she once have her own place? Did she have a job? What happened to all of my mother's brothers and sisters? There were so many of them. What happened to her father? He was dead before I was born, but how did he die and when?

However it happened, my parents married and made their home initially in Vernon—the town where they both grew up. There, in 1935, my mother gave stillbirth to two boys, John and Floyd.

In 1941 my parents moved to Amarillo, where my father took a job as a door to door salesman peddling life insurance with nickel-a-week premiums for National Life & Accident Insurance Company, which was based in Nashville. I was told he'd worked as a butcher in Vernon for some years before that, but it's always been hard for me to imagine my father doing anything as physical as cutting up a side of beef. It's even been hard for me to imagine that he ever had the stamina to walk door-to-door selling life insurance. I knew my father as a man who liked to be waited on. He didn't like to do things.

In Amarillo, in 1943, my brother Gordon was born.

At this time all the young men in the panhandle had either joined or been drafted into the military. My father had been too old for the draft and too timid to enlist. He was about the only man under forty still walking the streets of Amarillo. But as the war dragged on, the draft pool widened and they called him up. He went into the Navy and was posted to San Diego. He worked in a warehouse. He stocked shelves. He loaded ships. But he never left port.

John, Rosalyn, and Gordon Gilchrist — 1944

A family portrait survives from these years. Perhaps it's just an accident of timing that my mother looks unhappy in this photo. My father, on the other hand, looks well pleased, sharing a warm expression with the camera that I can't recall ever seeing during my own childhood. In other photos from the same period my mother looks peacefully happy. In the foreground of most of these lurks the shadow of the picture-taker, presumably my father. There's something about the way the camera captures her in these pictures that tells me that in spite of what came later, he once loved her.

By the time I was born, four years after this photo, my mother was already somewhat heavier and on her way to being plump. Her face and body became round. She accumulated several chins and loose flesh on her arms. (There was a lot of Mom to hold onto.) But because of the way she's depicted in this wartime portrait, I can believe my mother had aspirations of being a pretty woman. There's the stylish way she wore her hair, in the fashion of the Andrews Sisters. There's something in the attitude of her mouth, the angle of her eyebrows, the correctness of her posture. Even though I never knew her like this, whenever I think of her, this is how I see her in my mind.

This period of my parents' lives raises questions for which I have no answers. Something happened in San Diego. Any mention of their time there was always met with dark hostility and silence, and my parents retained no mementos from those years other than a handful of faded photographs that they kept sequestered away, and which I discovered only after their deaths.

His was a generation that has long been noted for its reluctance to speak about the war, but for my father, it was more than reluctance. Was it just that he hated the service? Or was it something else? Something between my mom and him? My twin brother recalls our mother speaking obliquely about my father's abuse of alcohol while in the Navy, but neither my older brother nor I have any memory of this. All three of us are sure, however, that something came between them—something that was never repaired.

After the war, my father returned to selling insurance, but this time in the small, struggling, Texas panhandle town of Pampa, which was a fraction of the size of Amarillo. There, in 1948, Jim and I were born. We were a surprise. We weren't planned for or particularly wanted, especially by my dad. But Mom—well, she seemed to like the idea of having twin boys.

My memories of Pampa are in black and white, like the few faded photographs I possess of those days, taken by my mother's precious Brownie camera. One short street downtown made up the entire business district, with uninteresting one-story frame buildings pretending some element of enterprise. My father's office was in the middle of these nondescript edifices. My older brother Gordon went to the Horace Mann Elementary School, a squat red brick building that competed unsuccessfully with the First Baptist Church to be the largest structure in town. A few dusty blocks of struggling homes and one dry patch of a city park abutted the meager commercial district. Outside of town there were rumored to be some people of wealth living in large mansions commanding many thousands of acres of panhandle scrub, home to armadillos and rattlers, dried up clay riverbeds, roaming herds of beef cattle, and armies of chugging oil wells. In the midst of the scratching poverty of the Texas panhandle, there was—and still is—great wealth. John Paul Getty. T. Boone Pickens.

Our family lived in a squat frame house with a tilted picket fence on a dusty dirt road named Dwight Street. I remember large flower beds filled with thirsty zinnias in the summer and dry dirt laid bare in the winter, and I remember an old wooden hutch filled with skinny brown rabbits we raised for food. It may be that my father had once been a butcher, but it was my mother who took a knife to the bunnies. Bunny harvesting time was no more traumatic to us kids than the harvesting of zinnias for a nice flower arrangement. That's what they were for.

The twins in the backyard. That's me with the hose.

I remember entire summers spent without putting on shoes. I remember running through a crude sprinkler on hot Texas days and spraying my brothers with a long garden hose. I remember a lawn where grass wouldn't grow, only dandelions and stickers. I remember tumbleweeds stacked high up against the fence and then gathered into bonfires on hot August nights. And I remember the dust storms and the carbon black and my mom baking cookies by candlelight.

In the summer we'd drag old, thin, and stained army-surplus mattresses out of our attic to the back yard, where the whole family slept under an avalanche of stars. In the kitchen an old rusted icebox stood sentry, and daily a tall, thin man delivered a large block of ice. Sometimes he'd let Jim and me into his truck, and we'd take turns sitting on his frozen cache until we couldn't stand it any longer. In the evenings we'd fill old mayonnaise jars with the magic of fireflies, and then employ hours sitting on our old wooden ice-cream freezer while my father and older brother took turns cranking it.

And I remember annual twin parties in the city park, organized by my mother. Pampa, it seemed, had a fair number of twins, most of them sets of identical girls, tall and pretty, dressed in matching print dresses.

Everything changed, as everything always does.

In 1954 my father was promoted and transferred to a new branch in Oklahoma City. In a low, flat, red brick building at 911 N. Harvey he got his own office, from which he managed younger men who went door-to-door. He had a big steel desk, file cabinets, leather chairs, official forms for writing things down, and shiny sales plaques that emblazoned words like:

Have You Heard?

Five Million's the Word!

At home he listened to recordings by Norman Vincent Peale, practiced the "Power of Positive Thinking," and rehearsed sales pitches with a machine that projected images from fragile film loops onto a little pop-up screen. He bought shiny suits and skinny ties, brown and maroon leather briefcases, and wing tip shoes, which his sons kept polished to a fine shine. He wore silver cuff links and jeweled tie clips, straw hats with small feathers in the brim, and stiffly-starched white shirts, which came from the cleaners folded around sheets of white cardboard that he discarded and I rescued and used for whatever project came to mind—a drawing or a model airplane or something intended to be a replica of our house.

We settled in Warr Acres, an outlying Oklahoma City suburb, and into a cramped two-bedroom frame home with casement windows, brown linoleum floors, and a leaking septic system. Outside there was a flower box lurking beneath the living room window and a single sprawling mimosa that never grew very tall but had fantastic exploding little red flowers all over it in the spring. To the north and west was nothing but cracked red earth and rolling dusty plains. It felt like the end of the earth, which suited me fine.

My brothers and I played in puddles from sudden downpours; painted our initials on the backs of turtles with red nail polish and raced them with the neighbor kids' turtles; captured horny toads and tarantulas and tied strings around their necks and kept them in matchboxes as pets; and built toy guns from scraps of wood and slices of discarded inner tubes and clothes pins. We played hide-and-seek, tag, and backyard football, running "Old Faithful" again and again until it was too dark to see the ball. We erected old sheets in our garage and performed pirate plays with homemade scabbards. In the empty lot at the end of the street we each dug our own cave, lined it with cardboard and newspapers, and stored there our comic books and precious objects we'd found. We begged pop bottles from the neighbors and hauled them in our rusted, red wagon to the corner store two blocks away, where we exchanged them for coins, which we spent on more pop that we drank before we got back home. We all had used Raleigh bikes, which we took apart and put back together again and again. Although we never locked up our bikes, they were stolen only once, which didn't really matter because the Sheriff found and returned them the same afternoon.

There was one tree big enough to climb a few blocks away in a grassy field. We built rafts in that tree, each of us having our own, and we initiated a complex set of rules governing who could sit where or climb where and do what and when. And there were the sand pits: several acres of moon-like terrain where earth-moving machines had carved out craters that became full of rain water. The murky water was a home for water moccasins, frogs, and dragonflies. We were forbidden to go to the sand pits, so of course we did, and we swam there on days when the men and their machines were somewhere else.

There were no TVs and I'm glad for that. When I was a kid I didn't watch adventures on a tube. With my brothers and my friends I created a new adventure every day. I was a pirate. I was a pilot. I was Davy Crockett. I was a boy.

All this time our home had a dark flaw, and the flaw was my father. I don't know what troubled him. I never knew. But whatever it was, it led him to torment his family.

I have no recollection of my father laughing. He never hugged or kissed. I can't recall a single instance of his showing affection to my mother or to any of his kids. If any of us violated some petty rule or interrupted his solitude, he was quick to shed his belt and apply it to our backs or legs. A day didn't go by without one or all of us getting hit. Sometimes, if he was angry enough, he couldn't bide the time it took to remove his belt, so he'd use his open hand, his fist, or whatever was handy: a rolled up newspaper, a book, a shoe.

And that's the only kind of touch I remember from my father.

In 1956 Dad was promoted and transferred again, this time to the home office in Nashville. To celebrate, he traded the rusted brown Hudson for a turquoise and white Bel Air. Then rather than move his family with him, he made the decision to commute. Twice each month he flew to Nashville, and twice each month, on alternate weekends, he flew back to Oklahoma. He reluctantly allowed my mother to learn to drive because he didn't want to pay to leave the car at the airport.

Every other Friday night we'd hop in the car and drive sixty blocks south to Will Rogers Airport, where we'd wait behind a chain link fence for his silver prop plane to land. On Sunday we'd drive him back there and watch as he flew off. He never waved from the plane like other people, but we always waved anyway. He was away from home twelve days out of every fourteen.

It proved to be a blessing. With Dad away, Mom was free to make new friends. She spent time with neighbors: with Ethel Flood, who ran a beauty salon of sorts in her garage; Mrs. Butler, who designed a new kind of kitchen cabinet and had all white furniture covered with thick plastic; Myrtle Bommer, whose husband always seemed to be away on a fishing trip; and Edna Pevehouse, whose husband had one eye, drank too much, and made his living collecting junk that piled up all around his house.

My mother's friendship with Edna Pevehouse spoke volumes about her character. People in our community shunned the Pevehouses. Their home was little more than a shanty; their yard was a junkyard. The old man was bent, unshaven, and unkempt. Edna kept herself clean, but in the hand-me-down men's clothes she wore, she seemed poor and pitiable to most people. They had a battered truck held together with coat hangers and spit, and they drove it around Warr Acres looking for cast-off junk they could turn into treasure. They had a son named John, a year younger than me. Tall, gangly, and smarter than people gave him credit for, John moved through the world under the dark shadow of his parentage.

The Pevehouses were members of our church. The old man never showed up for anything, but Edna was there every Sunday, though one never saw her in the sanctuary where the services were held. She hid in a small room in the back, where she prepared the communion trays for the service and cleaned them afterward. She never socialized with the other women. She didn't have a pretty dress to wear, or white gloves or a church hat.

It made me proud that my mother was Edna's friend. While other women passed Edna by, my mother always stopped to chat. And Edna's home was only a couple of blocks away from ours, so Mom was always walking over to Edna's, taking her an apple pie or dropping in to have a cup of coffee. Edna was no stranger to our home either, often dropping in unannounced for a glass of iced tea and a short visit with my mom.

Mom filled her life with volunteering. She chaired the PTA for Gordon's, Jim's, and my homerooms. And when my big brother Gordon was in high school and his friends wanted to form a golf team because the school didn't have one, she started one and "coached" them by driving them to tournaments and cheering them on. She was a coach on paper only. She never picked up a golf club herself. But without her, there would have been no team.

When she learned about a little boy who badly needed glasses but whose family had no money for them, she found an optometrist who'd examine him and an optician who'd provide him glasses. Afterward it seemed as if every other week the school nurse would call and tell my mother about another boy or girl who needed glasses, and she'd take care of it. And when Gordon's friend Phil Ratcliffe, who didn't have a father, needed a winter coat, Mom came up with a coat. Soon she was providing coats to a lot of kids.

When my father was away, our house was filled with friends. There was always an extra plate for dinner; usually for some kid Gordon dragged home, often someone from his golf team. But on those alternate weekends when Dad was home, none of us was allowed to have any friends over, and we all had to bear his anger that during his absence "strangers" had invaded his home. He preached the dictum, *"You can't trust other people in your home; you never know what they'll do."* This never made any sense to us. We knew exactly what they'd do. They'd be our friends. They'd eat a good meal, tell stories, play games, make us laugh. On his visits, we'd bear our father's unceasing wrath for two miserable days, and then we'd promptly forget he was ever there when he boarded the plane on Monday to return to Nashville. Eventually, we stopped waving goodbye.

Saturday, June 6, 1959

At sunset we piled into our shiny Bel Air and headed to a drive-in movie. Jim and I sat in the back seat, Mom and Dad sat in the front, and Gordon was, well... somewhere else. At sixteen, Gordon was mostly on his own, and he tended to make himself scarce when Dad was in town.

Dad seemed in an unusually charitable mood as the evening began. He wasn't given to watching movies in general, or drive-ins in particular, and it was extremely rare when he'd want to do anything when he was home other than sleep or yell. I don't recall what movie we saw, but this I remember: There was a trailer before the movie about some natives on some South Pacific island. Their life was hard. They lived in grass huts. They fished with spears and nets. They wore little more than rags. Everyone worked: the women, the men, and the children.

At home in bed, sometime after midnight, I awoke. My parents were having a terrible fight. I think he was hitting her. Eventually the wailing and shouting turned to sobs, and then whimpers. My mother was repeating something about the people on the island. "I didn't know…" she said. "I didn't know."

I'd learned not to listen to my parents' fights. I'd learned not to see them when I saw them; not to hear them when I heard them. It was none of my business. It wasn't happening. But something this night was different. I lay still in the dark, my eyes and ears wide open, trying to decipher the hurt and bitter signals from the next room.

It grew quiet. Eventually I fell asleep.

The next morning, Jim, Dad and I dressed for church and waited for Mom to get ready. Gordon was getting ready to go to the golf course, where he worked every weekend, grooming the fairways and greens and helping out in the pro-shop. Jim was fiddling with the piano, annoying everyone but himself. I was reading the Sunday comics, annoying Jim who was waiting his turn to read them.

Suddenly there was a loud *whump*—a sound like something huge falling from a great height—and the air was rent with a deafening shriek. I turned toward the sound and saw flames leaping from under the bathroom door down the hallway.

"The bathroom's on fire! The bathroom's on fire!" I shouted. But it wasn't the bathroom. It was my mother.

Gordon ran to open the bathroom door, but it was either jammed from the heat or locked from the inside. I ran outside to the backyard and turned on a garden hose. I stood on my tiptoes and peered in the closed bathroom window at the flames encircling my mother. She was turning slowly around and around as she screamed, her arms over her head beating uselessly against the flames. "Open the window," I whispered in a quiet voice that I could barely hear myself.

I saw the door cave in. Then Gordon and my father smothered the flames with a blanket, and doused them with water from a nearby vase.

I was back in the house in time to see my father warning Gordon not to lay Mom down on the bed until he could cover it with an old blanket to protect the chenille bedspread. Then Jim and I were ordered to sit in the rusty lawn chairs in front of the house, and to wait for the ambulance under the watchful eyes of the startled neighbors, who stared from across the street.

In the next few minutes, as I sat in the steel chair, the world itself seemed to grow older and darker. I was conscious of being on display, of being marooned in a capsule of time from which I might never escape. Gordon appeared at my side, mumbling something about how he wanted Jim and me to come inside to say goodbye to our mother.

Her charred face. Her unseeing eyes. The few blackened and brittle curls of her hair. The skin peeling like birch bark from her arms. The ghastly smell. Her horrible wheezing. I didn't know what to do with my hands.

Gordon told Mom that Jim and I were there, that we were standing there beside her. "Always believe in God," she said. "Always believe in God."

"I will, Momma," I replied. "I will."

It was nine days before my eleventh birthday.

She should have died. No one understood why she didn't, except perhaps Hubert M. Anderson, M.D., a young surgical intern at the shiny new Oklahoma Baptist Hospital on 63rd Street, which had opened only months earlier. Anderson had been looking for the opportunity to try some experimental treatments he had in mind for severe burn patients, and since no one else had a better idea, he was allowed to try.

My mother had third degree burns over ninety percent of her body. Only her feet and portions of her legs were untouched. She lost her ears, her nose, her eyelids, and most of her fingers. Her breasts. Her lips. Part of her tongue.

Dad didn't return to Nashville that Monday. He didn't board a plane for several months. His company was good about that, and transferred him back to the Oklahoma City office. Meanwhile Jim and I were ushered out of town. Mom's older brother Floyd and his wife Sue drove up from Odessa in their dusty Rambler, and they took us back to live with them for the rest of the summer.

They were kind people. Sue especially. Childless herself, she seemed to enjoy having kids around, and she baked a fresh blueberry pie or up-side-down pineapple cake pretty much every day of the summer, swatting flies with one hand and rolling out a pie crust with the other.

Their house wasn't much to look at—just a couple of rooms, a cramped kitchen, a closet of a bathroom with an outdoor shower, and a tiny, unfinished addition that looked as though it'd been slapped together out of someone else's discarded building material. Every now and then something new appeared: a window where there hadn't been one before, or a door instead of a hole in the wall. Jim and I slept on a mattress on the floor in the unfinished addition.

For some reason, everyone in Odessa called Uncle Floyd "Oscar." Bald and imposing, he was possessed of that West-Texas male inability to say much. He went to work every day, selling classified advertising for the *Odessa American*. He stopped off at his favorite bar each night for a few JAX beers, and then had a few more when he got home. He was most at ease with his three big dogs, mangy mutts all of them. They'd crowd around his feet at night, slavishly devoted to their master, who sank into a monstrous chair with the springs and stuffing sticking out. Surrounded by empty beer cans and contented dogs, Uncle Floyd smoked his Chesterfields and cut out ads from that day's newspaper with pinking shears, and then sorted them in colored folders. Uncle Floyd had lots of folders.

In this new and strange land, Jim and I lost no time finding things to do,

and those things mostly involved an abandoned house trailer in an over-
grown field choked with tumbleweeds behind Floyd and Sue's make-
shift home. Missing a door and some windows, it'd been violated by a
succession of dogs and coons and crows. But we cleaned it out enough
to make it our clubhouse, our getaway, our refuge. When it got too hot,
we'd tramp into Aunt Sue's kitchen and pump cold well water into a jug
from the pump that jutted out over the kitchen sink. Then we'd dump
a packet of Kool-Aid in the water and mix it up, and we'd drag the cold
jug back out with us to our clubhouse and place it in the shade. It must
have been one hundred ten degrees in that old trailer, but we didn't care.
Every weekend Floyd took us to the miniature golf range while Sue had
her hair done, and we'd try to knock little white balls past the slowly
spinning blades of a windmill that needed a coat of paint.

At the end of the summer, just before the start of school in September,
Floyd drove us home and life continued pretty much as usual, except
without Mom. Jim and I started the sixth grade in separate classes.

After school we'd walk home and stay there just long enough to change
clothes before walking to work. Jim and I had taken jobs working the
concession stand at the Coronado Theatre, a dark narrow box that
smelled like rancid butter, and which everyone called "The Roach" for
reasons which were obvious enough. We earned the princely sum of
forty cents an hour and all the pop and all the popcorn we could
consume. Each Friday we received our wages in cash in small brown
envelopes, which we turned over to our Dad to help pay the bills.
Sometimes he'd let us keep enough for a comic book or two.

These days it's a criminal offense to give an eleven-year-old a job.
I understand the need to protect children from exploitation, but I'm
glad that when I was eleven my employment was legal. In some
ways—perhaps in many ways—that job saved me. It gave me a focus, a
purpose. It gave me something to do other than being at home and
miserable. It gave me a way to contribute, to help make things better.

When I was working at the Roach, I wasn't a sad kid whose mother was in the hospital, whose father was mean, and whose home had been torn apart. I was just a worker, a kid selling Dots and Junior Mints and keeping track of the inventory of paper cups in which I dispensed Coca-Cola and Dr. Pepper. I loved my job.

My dad never had any friends. He never had any buddies, no one he went fishing or golfing with, or to a bar (not that he'd ever go to a bar). There was no one he went to a ball game with, or played cards with (not that he'd every play cards either). Of course, his life in Nashville was (and is) a mystery to all of us. Perhaps he had friends there. But more likely Nashville was just another version of his life at home. I imagined he went to work in the hulking National Life headquarters in downtown Nashville, and when work was over, he found some place to eat, and then he went to his hotel to watch television. Then the next day, he'd do it all over again.

Still, I wonder. Was there ever anything more in his life? His company owned the Grand Ole Opry. The call letters of the Opry's home station, WSM, stood for the company's motto: "We Sell Millions." Dad must have gone to the Grand Ole Opry, but if he did, he never talked about it. Did he ever meet Minnie Pearl or Roy Acuff? If he had, it seems probable that he'd have told us. But maybe not.

After Mom's accident, Dad did seem to change a bit at home. He was no more approachable, but he was perhaps less aggressively mean. He took less interest in what Jim and I were doing, and he seemed to forget to use his belt on us on occasions that would have surely prompted a spanking before. He walked around us, and we around him. After the accident, we all led our separate lives.

The *accident*.

That's what we all called it, and perhaps it was. There's no way I can be certain about what happened that morning. On the day after the accident, the *Daily Oklahoman* carried a short front page notice which, in its entirety, read:

> Fluid Ignites, Woman Hurt
>
> A Warr Acres woman was critically burned in her home early Sunday morning after a cleaning fluid ignited while she was cleaning her dress.
>
> Mrs. John T. Gilchrist, 5416 NW 44 was taken to Baptist hospital shortly after 9 a.m. Bethany police officer John Sharp, who answered the emergency call, said the woman apparently was cleaning her dress when the fire erupted. Police were unable to determine what caused the fluid to ignite.
>
> Sharp said the victim suffered burns over 50 percent of her body and was listed in critical condition in the hospital.

So that was it—the official version of the fire, and as much as I can determine, it's the version that today is accepted by anyone connected with the event. And yet from the beginning I had my suspicions. How was it that a can of gasoline (not cleaning fluid as the newspaper erroneously reported) that was normally kept in the garage was with her in the bathroom on a Sunday morning? (Does anyone really use gasoline to clean a spot on a dress?) How did the gas get all over her, and how did it ignite? (There was a small gas heater built into the wall in the bathroom which had a pilot light going year round, so maybe it's possible that…)

I was ten years old when it happened and it was best to believe what I was told. It was an "*accident*." Even a decade later, when my cynical adult self knew better, I still pretended to think of it as an accident. And for several more decades, long after I'd acknowledged a different truth to myself, whenever I spoke of that day, I talked about her accident.

Anyway, after the accident Dad got religion, or at least the semblance of religion. Maybe he had it all along, but he'd always before seemed a reluctant, if regular churchgoer. By the time Jim and I had returned from Odessa, Dad was investing a lot of time and energy in the Putnam City

Christian Church. He became a deacon, which meant that he was one of the select men who passed the communion and the offering plates at church on Sunday mornings.

It was always men, of course, never women. Grim faced, silent, and wearing dark suits and wide ties, the deacons stood at the end of the rows of wooden pews, passing the velvet-lined aluminum trays that held little shot glasses of grape juice and tasteless wafers the size of a child's thumbnail.

To see my Dad serving communion was unnerving. I wasn't sure what to make of it. I'd always assumed the men who were deacons were good men, holy men, devout men. I knew enough about my Dad to know that wasn't true of him. So what might that mean about the other men?

Once a week the deacons got together to read their Bibles and talk about deacon business. That's how Dad got to know the minister, Reverend Garrell Dunn, and the head deacon, Eldon Lawson, who was a realtor and homebuilder and also the mayor of the rapidly expanding Warr Acres. Perhaps Dad found some solace with them. Or friendship. Perhaps he talked with them about what happened to his wife.

Jim and I didn't see much of Dad that fall after our return from our summer in Odessa. In the mornings, before the sun was up, he'd wake us and we'd all get our own breakfast, and then he'd drive to work, back to his old office at 911 N. Harvey, and Jim and I would walk to school. Most nights after school Jim and I went to work at the Roach, and Dad went straight from work to the hospital to pull a shift there. There was no money for round-the-clock private nurses for my mother, so Dad and Gordon pitched in.

Gordon was a junior in high school and after school he worked at the golf course until dark, taking care of the greens and scooping golf balls out of the ponds and traps. After work he went to the hospital where he took the midnight nursing shift. Jim and I saw little of Dad; we saw Gordon even less.

Jim, Gordon, and I all bore scars from this period of our childhood, and we all wore them differently. I struck out on my own, becoming self-reliant, independent, and ambitious. I liked being happy and I was determined to be just that. So I declared myself content in my own mind and went about my life, engaged in just about any activity that would have me.

Jim wanted stability. He clung to my father. And the more he held fast to Dad, the less I understood my twin brother. Up to this point in our lives, Jim and I had been practically inseparable. But now, suddenly, we had little in common.

And Gordon? Gordon had cast off our family before the accident, but the accident pulled him back in. He had it the worst. Here he was, sixteen years old, living most of the time out of a shack on the golf course where the golf pro, Woody, brought him cases of beer and moonshine, which he resold to his high school friends. He was barely making it in school and was frequently in trouble with the Warr Acres police. But every day, after he finished his work at the golf course, he went to the hospital to take the third shift nursing our mother through the long night. Hour after grueling hour he sat there in the presence of her ruined flesh, her gasps and moans and cries, and he tended to her needs.

During the five months when Jim and I were not allowed into the hospital to see our mother, she asked for a photo of us to place by her bed. Dad decided we needed a formal portrait, so Jim, Gordon, and I were given new shirts and new haircuts, and we sat to have our picture taken for our mom. You never saw three sadder boys than the three in this Kodachrome portrait. There's not a glint of happiness anywhere in the frame. Of the three  hangdog visages, it's Gordon's that draws me in. I remember him as being so old and mature during this period, but as the portrait attests, he was not. He still had a baby face.

Jim and I were shielded from the horrors Gordon endured every night. As a result, Jim and I at least had a chance to escape permanent damage. But not Gordon. For the rest of his life Gordon was haunted by demons he never conquered. Given what he went through, it's a wonder he did as well as he did.

I can imagine what their exchanges were like when Dad's shift ended and Gordon's started. Gordon would have walked in and put down his books. Dad would have stood. One of them would have muttered, "Good night," and the other might have muttered it back.

Without Mom, conversation had become a lost art in our family. Talking was something we did with other people but not with each other. Even Jim and I stopped talking. We walked to and from school without a word between us. Even when we worked the same shift at the Roach, crammed in behind the concession counter, we talked only when other people were present, but only with them and not with each other.

Back at home we had a succession of housekeepers, all of them foreign women, Estonian or Latvian. Some were young, some were old, and all had an unfamiliar accent and the occasional difficulty finding the right word. None of them lasted too long on the job. They were hired to help with the laundry and cleaning, and to cook dinner for the three boys. Dad always ate his dinner at the hospital, so he never had to suffer through their meals the way Jim and I did.

Our mother had been a simple cook. We always knew what food would be on the table on what day of the week. On Friday nights we had brown beans and cornbread; on Saturdays we had meatloaf, whole kernel corn, and Jell-O; and on Sundays we ate crispy fried chicken with mashed potatoes and gravy. Now we ate whatever was put in front of us, and we often didn't know what it was.

There was one imposing Estonian whose name was Mrs. Bowman. Behind her broad back we called her Bow-Woman, because of the funny way she stood and walked. She had a more commanding presence in the house, but she didn't last any longer than the others. It was never clear whether the housekeepers all left of their own accord or whether Dad fired them. They were just a blur of foreign women who wore too much makeup, talked funny, and whose dinners of boiled meats and strange vegetables never tasted right.

In October Jim and I started having short, scheduled phone conversations with our mother. Her voice sounded wrong, but it *was* our mother and talking with her was reassuring. In November, five months after the accident, Dad came by the school and picked us up. We drove to the hospital and got out in the parking lot. Standing on the asphalt, Jim and I looked where Dad pointed, up to room 536. Then he went inside and left us waiting in the lot, our eyes straining to see something. After a while, we saw a curtain part, and we saw him standing at the window. Someone beside him was waving at us. Afterward, he said it was our mother.

The next day she came home.

I don't know what I'd been expecting. That she'd be healed, I suppose. But if it bothered me that she hadn't, it only lasted for a moment. When I looked at her I didn't see her burns. I just saw my mom. That's how it was from then on. I never could see her scars. Maybe it was because of her eyes, which hadn't changed. She looked out at me with the same eyes, and I found her in them and in her voice, which had become softer, deprived as it was of certain consonants, like D and B and P.

Gordon taught Jim and me to share the nursing duties he'd learned and had been performing for months. Mom slept in a hospital bed that had been moved into our parents' bedroom, the kind with metal sides that swung up to prevent her from falling out, with cranks and handles at the foot of the bed that changed its shape so she could rest sometimes in a lying position and sometimes in a sitting. We bathed her in her bed with sponges soaked in a solution of hydrogen peroxide and water. We fed her liquids and mashed food through a turkey baster with a curved rubber tube at the end, one small swallow at a time, taking care not to let the rubber tip of the baster come in contact with her still raw lips. We coached her to exercise what was left of her hands, encouraging her to hold and squeeze tennis balls. We changed her dressings, applied salve to her lidless eyes and petroleum jelly to her burns, and removed from the surgical wounds stitches the doctors had missed. We changed her nightgown and her sheets. We sat with her.

She never complained, at least not to me. She must have been suffering, but she did so in silence. When we talked it was about our lives: what we did in school that day, did we have any homework, what was the movie at the Roach. She was interested in news about people she knew and about the neighbors, who never came to visit her, except for Edna Pevehouse. And she was interested in her Dodgers.

While she was in the hospital, Gordon had brought her a small transistor radio. She couldn't operate it herself, but on game days she asked the nurses to tune it to the Dodgers game. Mysteriously, the Dodger broadcasts all the way from Brooklyn came through clear on the tinny speakers of her small plastic radio. In the summer and fall of 1959, while she lay on her back unable to do anything for herself, she listened to the Dodgers and fell in love with Mickey Mantle and Roger Maris.

After my mother returned home, we saw our father even less. I don't know where he was or what he was doing, but he wasn't around much. He'd drop in once a day or every other day, to pay the housekeeper, to water the plants in the flower box, or to collect the money Jim and I had made selling popcorn. He walked through the house as if it belonged to someone else. In my parents' bedroom there were now two beds: their marriage bed and my mother's new hospital bed, but only the hospital bed was occupied. When my father slept at home he slept on the sofa. He took no interest in Jim or me and we returned the favor. His clothes disappeared from the closet.

And I remember this.

It was a Wednesday in late November. The day began like other days. Jim and I changed into our school clothes and went through our separate ministrations in the bathroom, which still retained the smell of burning flesh in spite of the modest renovation following the fire. We scrabbled up something to eat. We embarked in silence on our six-block walk to school. It was the day before Thanksgiving, and we each carried a can of peas to put in the basket for the poor people who otherwise wouldn't have a happy Thanksgiving.

School that day was routine, which means enjoyable enough. Once Jim and I parted into our separate classrooms, we didn't see each other again until it was time for our walk home at the end of the school day. Not having Jim around helped me forget the tragedy that was our family. I was just another kid in school, just one kid in a classroom of kids.

We were in sixth grade, where I excelled in all things academic but especially in reading and math. I was the kid who always raised his hand to answer questions, the kid who always finished the reading assignment first. In the classroom I competed, even at that early age, with a kid named John Kinney, on whom I had a secret crush, and whom I suspected to be smarter than me. At recess I played foursquare and tether ball.

That day, after walking home, Jim and I found the street in front of our house lined with cars. The front door was open, and after we entered we coursed through a swarm of murmuring and contented women, most of them unknown to us. Our mother was sitting in a chair in the living room. The neighbor women had given my mother several elegant nightgowns and robes upon her return home—identical except for their varying shades of pastel. This was the first time I saw her dressed in one of them. She hadn't wanted to wear them before for fear of staining them, so normally she remained in her plain cotton hospital gowns.

The school nurse was standing next to my mother with her hand on my mother's shoulder. The assembled women ignored Jim and me as we entered. Jim turned to go into our bedroom to escape the gathering— whatever it was. I had the same idea, but I turned to the right, rushing through the kitchen on my way to pass through the garage to the backyard to greet our dog, Jingles. But I never made it to the backyard.

The garage was filled with boxes. End to end. Row upon row. Box piled upon box of canned and dry goods. I looked for the box from Mrs. Naifeh's room and found it quickly. Amid cartons of Jell-O, powdered milk, and cans of candied yam and tomato soup, I found my can of peas.

I was mortified. We were poor. We were the poor family who wouldn't enjoy a happy Thanksgiving without the charity of schoolchildren, and we received the charity of not only Jim's and my classrooms, but of the entire elementary school, some forty or fifty classrooms altogether, which had gathered more than a hundred boxes of food.

There had to be other families who needed food at Thanksgiving, I thought. All of this food can't come to us. But it did. That's how poor we were. All of the pie filling, condensed milk, and pickled beets from the entire school was sitting in our garage. And everybody knew it. All those women in the living room. And all the teachers at school. And all the neighbors who must have been watching as all these boxes were delivered.

I made a silent vow to myself that when I grew up I'd never be poor again. What I felt at that moment I never wanted to feel again. I was not a helpless child. I didn't need any one's help. I could (and would) help myself.

A year later, we were still eating food from those boxes.

When I became an adult, I was always the provider. It was never a goal of mine to make a lot of money, but it was always important to have enough to take care of myself, with some left over to take care of other people in need.

There was a time in Chicago in the 1980s when I hosted these giant Thanksgiving parties that started early and went late. Anybody and everybody was invited, but mostly I sought out what I called "Thanksgiving orphans"—people who didn't have anywhere to go on Thanksgiving. I insisted that the orphans I knew should invite other orphans. Fully half of the people who packed my home each Thanksgiving were strangers to me. Some people came for a noontime feast, others a mid-afternoon; still others came at the dinner hour and others at the witching hour. There was always a core of friends who were present from start to finish.

These events were always raucous, bountiful affairs, with mountains of food and wine, and a hodgepodge of people of all ages, backgrounds, and interests. I always had my son with me on Thanksgiving, and that contributed to my opinion that this holiday was my favorite.

Some homeless friend was always crashing at my place in the 70s, 80s, and 90s—someone between jobs or between relationships or just between. Like stray dogs, they'd arrive and stay for a week, or in the case of my older brother, for four years. It never seemed an imposition, and no one seemed to take me for granted. I always felt that this was something that people should do for each other.

It was extremely hard for my mother to accept charity, and even harder, I think, for my father. They both had a stubborn, go-it-alone nature that was honed on the Texas plains, through the deprivations of the Dust Bowl and the sacrifices of the war. What distinguished them was that my mother was as generous as my father was stingy. I seem to have been born with my mother's genes when it comes to matters of giving, and I'm glad for that.

Over the next two years my mother returned to the hospital for more than two dozen operations—various plastic surgeries attempting reconstruction or repair of this or that part of her body. It was in the later operations that Dr. Anderson attempted to rebuild her face, making up his technique as he went along.

In one operation, while doing other work on her hands or arms, he made two long incisions along an unburned portion of her inner thigh, and rolled the flesh in such a way as to create a curved tube connected at either end to her leg. It looked like a caterpillar of flesh. In subsequent operations he moved the tube up her body one end at a time, as if it were a living slinky, taking care each time to connect it to blood vessels and nerves to keep the flesh in the tube alive. When it eventually sagged from both sides of her chest, the next operation attached one end to the side of her face, and a second operation attached the other end to the other side. Now the tube hung from both sides of her mouth. In the final operation Dr. Anderson used the flesh in the tube to forms lips and a nose and to fill in her cheeks.

During the long months of this extended procedure, her appearance changed significantly with each operation, and while her face eventually began to take form again, it remained covered in thick, unyielding scars.

It was during these many visits to the hospital that my mother became friends with the black nurses who dressed the suppurating wounds of severe burn patients. In particular she was befriended by one nurse named Mrs. Fulbright, who was always there to direct the other nurses and to personally take care of her whenever Mom was at the hospital recovering from an operation.

Mom told me how she lay in agony those first weeks and months, wanting only to die, but Mrs. Fulbright wouldn't let her. "Your sons need you, Rosie," Mrs. Fulbright would say. "You can't die." And then she'd pray over my mom and assure her God still had a plan for her. Mom said at first Mrs. Fulbright annoyed her. But eventually she began to believe her. Maybe not that God had a plan, for her or anyone else, but that her sons needed her, and that maybe there was something she was supposed to do.

If God had a plan, it didn't include my mother attending our home church. When she'd healed enough to walk, dress in church clothing, and sit in a chair for an extended period, she wanted to attend a Sunday service. She enlisted the aid of Mrs. Flood, who came over and did her hair, and of Mrs. Bommer, who found her a dress to wear. None of my mother's dresses from before the fire fit her anymore. She'd lost all her weight, and Mrs. Bommer was about the same size.

We arrived at the church just before the service was set to begin. The back rows were already full so we took seats toward the middle. There was a palpable uneasiness in the church as, throughout the duration of the service, people snatched glances at Mom and us. I could feel their stares crawling over us, but as soon as I looked up, their heads snapped forward.

That afternoon Reverend Dunn called my father and asked him not to bring Mom to church again. It was too disruptive, he said. She scared the children and some of the adults. He didn't want to seem uncharitable, but he had to think of his congregation first. She couldn't come back. He was sure my father would understand.

My father understood. My mother didn't. Frankly, neither did I.

This initiated a long period when all things religious confused me. I'd liken my reaction to the church's heinous rebuke of my mother to the situation a faithful dog might find itself in when, after years of affection from a loving master, the dog finds itself suddenly kicked to the curb.

I should have severed all ties with this church, and perhaps all churches for all time, on the instant, but I didn't. Like that faithful dog, I went back to that door seeking entrance, again and again.

My flirtation with religion in subsequent years was largely habitual. I'd been weaned on Sunday School lessons and Bible verses. I knew my Psalms and I could sing nearly any hymn that was on the program without looking at the Broadman Hymnal. I was scrubbed, purified, and born-again. In short, I believed.

Today I'm astonished and embarrassed that I forgave the un-Christian behavior of Reverend Dunn; that I returned to that same church not once, not twice, but every Sunday for a number of years. I can't imagine how I reconciled the church's rejection of my mom with the teachings of Jesus, which leads me to believe that I simply didn't reconcile them at all. I filed it all in a never-to-be-opened drawer in the back reaches of my mind; a drawer labeled *Things to be Ignored*.

It may be that this cushion was necessary for my survival and growth. Perhaps if I'd allowed myself the luxury of indignation and anger, I wouldn't have had time or space for what was left of my childhood. I wouldn't have had room to be happy. And I was determined to be happy.

It would be years before my confusion would come to some resolution.

Despite Dr. Anderson's best efforts, Mom remained horribly disfigured. Dr. Anderson wanted to continue his work on her, but she'd had enough—enough of the pain, enough of the stupor, enough of the helplessness. For three years she'd been a full-time patient, and she was tired of it. She decided she'd rather look the way she did than have even one more operation. Freed from the ordeals of the surgeries, she started to regain her strength and independence. She began to awaken each morning with a sense of humor.

The last housekeeper was dismissed from our home. Painfully and slowly, hour by hour, alone in her home while the kids were at school and her husband was AWOL, she relearned basic skills: how to sweep the floor, to iron a shirt, to wash a dish, to comb her hair, to button her own buttons, to cook a meal. She started visiting the neighbors and having them over for coffee. She started thinking about herself.

In January 1962 my mother filed for divorce. It was a courageous act for a crippled woman. Somehow following the protracted three years of her painful hospitalizations, my mother found the will to do what she should have done years before.

I've wished many times that she might have found such courage earlier—some time before 1959, before the "accident." But I understand how it would have been so difficult; how it would have seemed so impossible to her. In our community in those years, divorce practically didn't exist. Today it's difficult to imagine that women had so few resources, but back then, her options were limited to the point of being nearly nonexistent. There were no organizations she could have turned to for help. There were no women's shelters, no counselors, no assistance of any kind. There was no example to follow. All of the churches in our ultra-religious community preached that divorce was a mortal sin, and if that weren't enough, the law was stacked against her.

In that time and place obtaining a divorce was very difficult, very expensive, and very humiliating, especially for a woman filing against her husband. And there was the added complication that my mother had no means of support. Since her marriage to my father, her only role had been housewife. Not many women held jobs back then, other than teachers, nurses, sales clerks, or housekeepers. She had no training to be a teacher or nurse, and clerks and housekeepers didn't make much money.

My father had by this time taken an apartment in the Siebert Hotel on Hudson, a half a dozen blocks from his office. He'd removed himself from all of our lives some time before, but once a month, if he remembered, he'd take Jim and me to an inexpensive cafeteria for an early dinner.

Although my parents' divorce was a relief to me, in town the divorce was a new source of scandal and served to isolate my mother even further from the community that had already retreated from our family. Aside from Edna Pevehouse, my mother had no friends left. No white friends, that is.

Mrs. Fulbright became a frequent visitor to our home. One day she invited my mom to attend her church, the Calvary Baptist Church. This African-American church on Oklahoma City's east side knew all about my mom. They'd been praying for her recovery since the day Mrs. Fulbright first cared for her. They'd prayed for her every time she had an operation, and they'd prayed for her when she came back home.

Mom started having more frequent visits from Mrs. Fulbright and others from the church, adults and kids. These visits stigmatized and isolated my mother even further in our community. They'd pick her up and take her to church or to meetings, and occasionally small groups would visit for a while in our home. For some reason the kids in the church especially seemed to take to her, and most likely all of them were members of the Youth Council of the NAACP. The Youth Council had quite a reputation, and in all-white Warr Acres, it was feared and hated.

There was nothing extraordinary about the morning of Monday, August 18, 1958. School was out for a few more weeks, and kids still needed something to do. For the twelve children and one intrepid advisor who made up the Oklahoma NAACP Youth Council, that meant coming together routinely at the advisor's home. They said a prayer and the pledge of allegiance, and then the talk turned to what they'd learned that summer. These were good kids, kids who wanted to make a difference, but they had no inkling that they were about to fundamentally change their lives, and the lives of a lot of other people, too.

Earlier that summer the Youth Council presented an original play at the annual convention of the NAACP in New York City. Traveling to New York had been a very big deal for these kids, as had been the opportunity to perform before the leaders of the increasingly visible NAACP.

During the trip the kids experienced first-hand how blacks were treated in different states. On the way to New York they took a northern route and it was never difficult finding a place to sleep, a place to eat, or a place to use the restroom. But on the way back to Oklahoma they took a southern route, and it was a struggle to find accommodations and service. Everywhere they traveled there were signs warning "whites only," and even where there were no signs, it was still "whites only."

In 1958 there wasn't a single integrated restaurant in Oklahoma. There were no integrated schools, movie theatres, swimming pools, amusement parks, hotels, motels, or houses of worship.

The situation at the popular lunch counter at the downtown Katz Drug Store was typical. At Katz Drug Store blacks were allowed to shop and order food to go but were not allowed to sit at the counter. Their food was served in a brown paper bag, and they had to leave the store to eat it.

And so, on Monday, August 18, after a lengthy discussion about the discrimination the group had faced on their trip and the injustice they faced every day in their own hometown, a ten-year-old girl, Marilyn Luper, surprised everyone with a motion to adjourn to Katz Drug. Marilyn was the daughter of Clara Luper, a high school history teacher and the advisor of the Youth Council. The vote passed unanimously, without much discussion.

Clara Luper and the twelve children walked to Katz's Drug Store, sat down at the counter and ordered thirteen Cokes. Mr. Masoner, the manager, was incredulous and quickly ordered the children and Mrs. Luper to leave his store.

But Clara Luper and the children did not move, and when outraged customers threatened the children, Mr. Masoner called the police. The police arrived in due order, and although they did nothing, their presence averted an escalation of violence. At closing, the group left quietly. No one was served, and remarkably, no one was arrested.

On Tuesday the children returned to the lunch counter to continue their sit-in, and they brought more friends with them. On Wednesday Katz Drug Store conceded and announced that henceforth *all* people were welcome to eat-in at all thirty-nine Katz Drug stores in Oklahoma, Kansas, and Missouri.

On Thursday the Youth Council moved their protest to other segregated lunch counters. First they desegregated the service at Veazey's Drug Store, and later that same day at S.H. Kress. On Friday they initiated a sit-in at John A. Brown, the largest department store in Oklahoma, covering a block and a half of the downtown business district.

In 1958 I was ten years old, the same age as Marilyn Luper. While Marilyn Luper and her friends passed intimidating hours waiting for Cokes that were never served, I was playing hide-and-seek in my front yard with the neighbor kids and sneaking out my bedroom window at night to swim in the forbidden sand pits.

As a child in Warr Acres—an all-white suburb northwest of Oklahoma City—I knew nothing of segregated lunch counters. I had no concept of what it might feel like to be a denied a Coke because of my skin color, or of what it might feel like to demand one anyway and to remain seated surrounded by an angry crowd and in the presence of unfriendly police. While Marilyn Luper was engaging in acts of great courage, I was simply being a child.

At the start of the Oklahoma City sit-ins, only two white establishments in the state allowed blacks to order food, but only as take-out. By 1961, thanks to the NAACP Youth Council, one hundred seventeen restaurants and lunch counters had ended segregation. However, the job of desegregation was far from over.

One night in the late spring of 1963, a rusty church bus parked in front of our modest Warr Acres house, and several black teenagers stumbled out to visit with my mom. This greatly alarmed the neighbors. It was bad enough that Mom had been receiving black visitors one at a time, but now they were coming by the bus load. And they were teenagers.

Warr Acres was as white as a suburb could possibly get. Black faces just weren't seen in our part of town, not even in menial jobs. Therefore their presence in our neighborhood made a lot of people very uncomfortable.

My mother became a different person during these visits—more alive, more youthful, more hopeful and happy. But these visits confounded me. Until my mom started receiving black visitors, I'd met few adults of another race, and none my own age. I didn't know what to make of it. I didn't know how to talk to them. I felt alien in my own house. During these visits, after saying hello, I went to my room and stayed there until they left.

There were no blacks in our school, none in our church, none on the streets of Warr Acres. None anywhere at all, except in the papers and now, occasionally, in my living room, visiting with my mom.

During the spring and summer of 1963 things got worse (or better, depending I suppose on how you look at it). My mom joined the Oklahoma NAACP and participated actively with the Youth Council. While my twin and I earned money at the Roach, where we both now worked as projectionists, she was off to meetings, demonstrations, rallies, and sit-ins with her new friends.

Now, all these years later, I can't explain why I didn't join her, why she didn't invite me, or why I didn't invite myself. For the most part, I ignored what was happening and focused on my own life: school, homework, and my work at the Roach. I was aware of what Mom was doing, but remained apart from it, watching it from a great distance. It was, to my unending regret, something we didn't talk about. I can plead ignorance, and there is more than a measure of truth to that. But such a plea is hardly satisfying. What my mother was engaged in was foreign and frightening, and there was nothing in my limited experience to explain it. To my shame, I chose not to ask questions. I chose not to be a part of it.

Perhaps my mother's reticence to involve her children is not so hard to understand. Lots of people were arrested at these events, both adults and children. Far worse, people were being injured and killed, not yet in Oklahoma but throughout the South. The killing of the field secretary of the Mississippi NAACP, Medgar Evers, made big news that summer of 1963.

Most likely my mother was just trying to protect us. And given what eventually happened as a result of her Civil Rights involvement, she'd been right to exclude us.

June 1963 was a busy month for the Oklahoma NAACP Youth Council, and my mother was in the thick of it. On June 1 the *Daily Oklahoman* reported: "Negroes Remain in Cafe 9 Hours." After five years of Youth Council sit-ins, many Oklahoma City restaurants had been integrated, but not Bishops Restaurant. The very stubborn owner insisted that, although he had nothing against "colored people," he had to do what his customers wanted. Demonstrations at Bishops Restaurant had been going on for two years, and yet not a single African-American had been admitted through the front door as a customer—though several entered the back door each day to perform their jobs as dishwashers.

On June 2 Clara Luper and forty supporters demanded service at the lunch counter of the Hotel Black, and after only thirty minutes, they were given service when the hotel management decided to change their policy. This hadn't happened all at once. The group had been there the previous Saturday night, at which time they'd been refused entrance. They'd demonstrated outside for over three hours.

On June 3 sit-ins at Anna Maude Cafeteria and the Huckins Hotel ended with both establishments dropping the racial barrier. On June 4 the paper reported that the picketing at Bishops Restaurant had gone on for three and a half days, with signs the restaurant owner was considering a change in policy—but not before an unidentified man "unleashed a snarling chimpanzee on the crowd. Both the man and the chimpanzee were admitted into the restaurant. But the door was closed on Negroes and newsmen."

On June 5 headlines read: "Negroes 'Test' 20 Businesses." On that one day the Youth Council sent supporters to twenty different Oklahoma City hotels and motels to challenge their policies of segregation. Clara Luper said, "Demonstrators couldn't find one that wouldn't serve them." The walls of segregation in Oklahoma City were, one by one, falling. The article went on to say, "The next aim of the anti-segregation leaders is being permitted to attend the city's two major amusement parks, Springlake and Wedgewood… When told Maurice Woods, owner of Wedgewood, had said he would not allow Negroes to enter, Mrs. Luper replied, 'We have heard the word *no* before.'"

One of the great pleasures of my childhood was idling away countless weekends at Wedgewood Amusement Park, a massive pleasure garden with a giant swimming pool, daring rides, and an addictive penny arcade. Wedgewood was only a mile or so away from our house, easily within walking distance. For only a few nickels, dimes, and quarters, I gained admission and lost myself in the games and rides of Wedgewood. I came to know every nook and cranny of the place, every lane of the swimming pool, every bump and hairpin turn of the Wild Mouse, every smile of each employee, every dip of the giant gleaming white roller coaster called the Tornado.

It'd never occurred to me that Wedgewood was segregated. It was just a place where I disappeared to have fun.

In those years my father's life insurance company sold lots of policies to African-Americans in Oklahoma City. I knew this because occasionally, while my brother and I were visiting his office, our father would show us where he and his agents had their routes in the slums on the east side of Oklahoma City, where the "colored people" lived. "Shanty Town," he called it, for reasons which seemed obvious enough to me at the time.

Of course, I knew of this part of town only through my father's eyes. The truth is that like any other section of town there were good and bad neighborhoods, and there were more good than bad. In many parts of what my father called Shanty Town there were manicured lawns and well-tended rose beds in front of tidy little houses filled with loving families. But to my father the neighborhoods were all one and the same: just another part of Shanty Town. By labeling them as such he—and everyone else in our white affluent community—could dismiss the families that lived there as somehow unimportant, as failures, and as unworthy of consideration.

For a nickel or dime each week, the residents of Shanty Town could protect their families with insurance policies that would pay out at their death. One or two hundred dollars—enough to pay for a modest funeral, with perhaps a bit left over. Those scant premiums might not seem like much, but added up, they made the National Life Insurance Company a lot of money, and they kept my father employed.

On June 22 my mother climbed on board a church bus that had stopped in front of our house. It was loaded with black kids who wanted to enter Wedgewood Amusement Park. They just wanted to ride the roller coaster and bumper-cars like the white kids, like my mother's sons. Mom stood at Wedgewood's gates with those kids. They were turned away, but they didn't leave. Of the sixty-three demonstrators, fifty were arrested: thirty black children and twenty adults. Among the adults arrested were ten black men, seven white men, and three black women. Their names and addresses all appeared in the paper the next morning. My mother was one of two white women who demonstrated at Wedgewood that morning, but without explanation, they weren't arrested.

NAACP
FREEDOM RALLY
Celebrating 5 Years of Progress
in
Oklahoma City, Oklahoma

Held In
Fifth Street Baptist Church
801 N.E. Fifth St.

Friday August 23, 1963
8:00 P.M.

A church bulletin found in my mother's belongings after her death. The Freedom Rally commemorated and celebrated five years of sit-ins.

I have memories of my mother being arrested that summer, but I don't remember where and when. Calvin Luper, who was seventeen in 1963, recalls demonstrating with my mother. He remembers her visiting his home frequently and coming to Youth Council meetings. He remembers her demonstrating at Bishops Restaurant. He remembers her being arrested at Anna Maude Cafeteria. He remembers her on a trip to D.C., the significance of which he wouldn't realize until he was some years older. And he remembers an event she attended celebrating the fifth anniversary of the first lunch-counter sit-in, and the progress made in those five turbulent years.

Early one August morning, my mother's friends picked her up and together they drove to the parking lot of Douglas High School, the all-black high school on Oklahoma City's east side. There they boarded two chartered buses filled with seventy passengers, all black except for my mother. A United Press International photographer named Johnny Melton captured an image of my mom sitting in the seat assigned to her by Clara Luper.

The photo shows my mother surrounded by the people who knew her best, who accepted and loved her. To her right, a kind-looking woman leans in toward my mother in conversation. An older man on her left nods in consideration of her words. Perhaps they were talking about the ride, the weather, or her scars. Perhaps they were talking about the sit-ins, about the restaurants, hotels, and businesses that wouldn't serve people because of their race. Perhaps they were just getting to know each other like people do—where they came from, whom they knew in common, what they liked to eat. Perhaps she was talking about her children. More than likely, she was talking about her beloved Dodgers.

Behind her some kids are having fun, showing off, and chatting up a storm. She'd have gotten to know these kids on this trip. Every one of them. And they'd have loved her.

Rosalyn Coleman Gilchrist (front row in sunglasses and scarf) Photo courtesy Oklahoma Historical Society. Johnny Melton Collection.

I didn't meet Clara Luper until 2009.

I must have met her before, but introductions to my mother's NAACP friends in the 1960s were hurried, and there were just too many people for me to remember. I also wasn't especially interested in meeting them at the time. Mrs. Luper's name wouldn't have meant anything to me anyway, as removed as I was from what was happening. But by 2009 I'd long known who she was, how important she'd been to the Civil Rights Movement, and how important she'd been to my mother.

I'd suspected that she might not still be alive, but if she was still breathing, I wanted the opportunity to thank her. I wanted to thank her for what she did for Oklahoma, what she did for America, and what she did for my mother.

And remarkably, without great effort, I found her phone number.

I dialed it. It rang. Once. Twice. A man answered. "Hello," he said.

"Hello," I said, not quite sure where to begin. "Forgive me for intruding, but I'm trying to locate Clara Luper."

"You've dialed the right number," the voice replied. "This is her son, Calvin."

My heart skipped several beats. "Mr. Luper," I said, "you don't know me, but my name used to be Joe Gilchrist. My mother was Rosalyn Gilchrist, and she rode on the bus with you to Washington, D.C., in 1963."

"Joe who?" Calvin asked.

"Joe Gilchrist. My mother's name was Rosalyn Gilchrist. Some people called her Rosie. She also participated in several sit-ins and demonstrations, including Anna Maude Cafeteria and Wedgewood Amusement Park. She was a white woman, from Warr Acres, heavily scarred from an accident."

"Rosie?" said Calvin. "Sure, I remember Rosie. How is she? My, I haven't thought of her in a mighty long time."

I briefly told him my mother's history after 1963, and asked him if it might be possible for me to visit with his mother and himself sometime soon.

"Sure," he said, and then he paused our conversation for a moment to talk with his mom. "Mom, it's Joe Gilchrist on the phone. Rosie Gilchrist's boy. You remember Rosie? She went with us to hear Dr. King."

I waited on the other end of the line, hoping to hear a response from Mrs. Luper.

"My mom's not real well these days, Joe," Calvin said. "But she nodded when I said your mother's name. I'm sure she'd be real glad to see you."

A few weeks later I had the opportunity to spend several afternoons in the living room of Mrs. Luper. Confined to a wheelchair, she suffered from an ailment that was not disclosed to me, and which left her occasionally too weak to talk. Some of the time during my visits she'd be lucid and verbal, and at other times she'd appear to doze off.

But like Calvin said, she remembered my mom, and so did Calvin, his sister, and several of their friends who dropped in while I was there.

That week Calvin invited me to appear on his weekly radio show to talk about my mother, and Clara invited me to a meeting of her beloved NAACP Youth Council at the Freedom Center. Both encouraged me to visit the exhibit at the Oklahoma Historical Society Museum, which includes a replica of the Katz Drug soda counter where the first sit-in took place.

I shared the photo of my mother and the others on the bus with Mrs. Luper, who said she hadn't seen the photo before. She and Calvin and Marilyn laughed and smiled as they recalled the names of the others in the photos. Mrs. Luper told me my mother was seated in the front of the bus to and from Washington because she was one of five adults who made the journey, and she assigned the adults to sit in the front. This was where Mom sat for all four days of travel.

In the photo my mother is wearing her signature sunglasses and headscarf, which she was rarely without in public. The sunglasses helped protect her sensitive eyes from dust. The headscarf kept her hair in place and disguised the absence of ears.

The buses stopped at a motel in Pittsburgh on the way to and from Washington, D.C., and they had motel accommodations in D.C. as well. Through the national NAACP, Clara Luper had arranged for a small group of the Oklahoma contingent to meet President Kennedy at the White House. She told me how her son Calvin had held up his hand after shaking the President's. He'd looked into his mother's eyes and said, "Mom, I'm never going to wash this hand again."

On August 28, 1963, my mother was at the National Mall on that most historic of days when Mahalia Jackson, Marian Anderson, and Joan Baez sang; when Josephine Baker introduced Rosa Parks; and when Martin Luther King proclaimed his prophetic dream.

I wish I could tell a story about how proud of her I was when she came home. I wish I could write that my only regret is I hadn't gone with her. But my regret goes much deeper.

When she took off for Washington and left Jim and me at home, I felt hopeless, deserted, and angry. I didn't understand where she was going or why. I only knew things weren't right at home. Mom had asked my brother Gordon and Beverly, his pregnant wife, to move into our home to look after us while Mom was away. Gordon had enough on his mind without worrying about his younger twin brothers, and Beverly, who was very kind, had plenty on her mind too.

I remember waking up to Beverly's cries. Her baby was coming. Gordon was rushing around, gathering whatever they might need at the hospital, and issuing instructions to Jim and me. Then the front door opened and Mom was standing there, suitcase in hand, exhausted and exuberant from her cross-country bus ride. She was bursting at the seams with what she'd experienced, and she wanted to share it with us. Gordon had to yell at her to shut up, to get out of the way, that Beverly was having her baby.

I never did hear from her the story of that trip. What was it like being on the bus? Where did they stop for meals? How close was she to Dr. King? Could she hear his words?

Who hasn't seen photos of the crowd on the Mall that day? When I see the photos, I always have the same reaction. Where other people see a mass of people on the Washington Mall gathered around the reflecting pool, I'm looking for just one person.

Times were tough. My father had been ordered to pay two hundred dollars a month in child support. That amount barely met the mortgage payment, and therefore didn't help put food on the table. During the first months after the divorce, the checks had arrived late, but they'd arrived. But then, beginning in the summer, the checks stopped coming.

Gordon, now in college, was on his own, struggling to pay tuition while supporting his wife and baby daughter. Mom had started taking in ironing and performing odd housekeeping jobs around the neighborhood, but the work was spotty and didn't pay well. Jim and I were working every evening after school and weekends, and our money went to pay the bills. I'd taken a job stocking the shelves at Rost Drugs in a new strip mall in Warr Acres. I didn't like it as much as the job at the Roach. It wasn't really much fun. But it paid better—a few more dollars a week. Still, it wasn't enough. The phone was shut off. Then the lights. And there was little food.

Through Mrs. Fulbright's efforts, my mom found a job cleaning offices downtown, but it meant we had to move since she had no car (which she wouldn't have been able to drive anyway because of her crippled hands), and there was no public transportation from Warr Acres.

Moving would mean changing schools, and I didn't want to change schools, especially not to one of the rough schools in the center of the city. Everyone knew our school was one of the best, if not *the* best in the state, and everyone knew the inner city schools were the worst. Then Mom told us she was preparing to sell the house to a man named Dr. James West, a young professional with a wife and a newborn child.

They were black.

And the wagons started circling in Warr Acres.

People began picking Jim and me up at school, calling us out of our classes for private meetings. First there was our dad. Then Chief Beckett, the Warr Acres police chief. Then Eldon Lawson, the town mayor and its leading real estate developer. Finally Garrell Dunn, our minister.

The chat with Dad was short and confusing. "Your mom's not well and she needs help," he told us. "When you're ready to do something about it, let Chief Beckett know." This was neither more nor less coherent than any of my other conversations with my father, so I didn't think too much about it.

Chief Beckett was more direct. Sitting in his squad car in the school parking lot, he told us, "We need to do something about your mother, but your dad wants to wait until you kids are ready. When you're ready, you just come see me, but don't wait too long."

Mayor Lawson seemed to dance around what he wanted to say, and was never quite able to say it, but his appearance alerted us to the town's concern.

Reverend Dunn was the last to recruit us. He picked us up from school and took us to Whit's Drive-In at the corner of Ann Arbor and 39th Street, which was Highway 66. He bought us burgers, fries, and chocolate malts. Over lunch we talked about things other than our mother—about the church, the youth group, the new youth minister he was hiring named Bill Reid, and his plans for a church teen basketball team—none of which was of any interest to Jim or me. He talked about his two young daughters. He asked about our classes.

In Reverend Dunn's dark sedan on the way back to the school, he told us that he and a lot of other people were watching out for us. "When you're ready," he said, "when you can't take it anymore, just go see Chief Beckett. We'll take care of it."

I didn't know what "taking care of it" meant, but I did know that life was not getting easier, and I was tired of it.

The house had to be inspected before the sale, and my mother became obsessed with cleaning it, keeping it clean, and cleaning it again, and she enrolled Jim and me in her efforts. She had us scrub the kitchen linoleum floor until there was no wax left on it, and then she had us wax it. Then, unsatisfied, she had us scrub it again and wax it again. When she wanted it scrubbed one more time, I made my decision.

I got up from the floor. I told my mother what I was going to do. I told her I was sorry. I took my twin by the hand and we walked out the door, across the lawn and down the street. We didn't stop until we reached the Warr Acres police station.

Chief Beckett picked up our mother. He put her in the back of his police cruiser and took her to the county jail.

Ruby Dunn, our piano teacher and the reverend's wife, set up some cots in their cramped music room where that night Jim and I slept. The next morning, a Monday, we didn't go to school. Reverend Dunn drove us to the Oklahoma County Courthouse. He said we needed to be present at the proceedings. When we arrived, we found Gordon there awaiting us.

Gordon, Jim, and I sat in straight-backed wooden chairs against the wall—not in a courtroom, but in the private chambers of Judge

Harold Theus. Around the judge's walnut desk, Reverend Dunn, Mayor Lawson, and Chief Beckett made their case.

"Rosalyn Gilchrist is crazy," they said. "She's consorting with colored people. She attends a Negro church. She's had colored people over to her house. She's been arrested at Negro protests. She has gatherings of Negro children in her home. She rode a bus filled with coloreds night and day all the way to Washington and back. She's trying to sell her house in Warr Acres to a nigger doctor."

My mom sat alone against a far wall, ignored, silent, dazed, and disbelieving. There was no opportunity for me to speak with her, and if there had been, I don't know what I would have said.

The judge put her away. She went back to the county lockup, then to the state mental hospital in Norman. Her house, all of her belongings, her children—they gave to my father.

At least that's what I thought for more than forty years. In many later conversations with my brothers, especially with Gordon, we often talked about how Dad had taken everything that had belonged to our mother. In 2002, in a much-abbreviated written history, I recorded that version of events and shared it with Gordon and with his children and grandchildren, and Gordon never corrected me.

After her commitment, Gordon, his wife, and child moved into our house on 45th street, where they continued to live for almost a year until it was sold. This I clearly recalled, but I always assumed Gordon was paying rent to our father. (I certainly never imagined Dad let him live there for free.)

But a search of the real estate records of Oklahoma County presents a different picture. They show that on June 13, 1963, the deed to the house was transferred to my mother as part of a divorce proceeding. They next show that on August 18, 1964, some ten months or so after her commitment to Central State Hospital, the deed was transferred in a sale to a new buyer. The grantor on the transaction is my brother, Gordon Gilchrist, who is listed as "Guardian."

This makes sense. A prudent court would have made Gordon Mom's guardian and trustee rather than giving the house and everything in it to my father, my mother's ex-husband. It seems that for all these years I may have considered Judge Theus too harshly regarding the disposition of her property. But all this raises troubling questions. Why didn't Gordon correct me on the many occasions when he could have? Did my mother consent to the sale of her home, or was she even aware of it? What happened to the proceeds of the sale? Did Gordon keep them? Did our father get them? We know no money went to her. She was penniless throughout her hospitalization, and she was penniless when she was released. And what happened to her furnishings and personal possessions? Were they thrown away? Given away? Sold?

The easiest thing, I suppose, would have been for me to ask Gordon, to inquire what his specific memory of these events might be. But I've waited too long. The demons from his childhood fueled his twin addictions to alcohol and food. By the turn of the millennium, my handsome, charming, and highly intelligent brother had become his own version of Gilbert Grape's mother. Gordon had little liver function left, he was diabetic and disabled by extreme obesity, and, following a hospitalization from an infection that caused his brain to swell, he was mentally semi-lucid. In his last few years he rarely left his recliner, where he sat with his television blaring twenty-four hours a day. In 2009, after a lengthy debilitating illness, Gordon died.

So in the end I only know this: My mother was completely disenfranchised, and my father was complicit. It seems my older brother was as well. And though I may have been a minor at the time, my own complicity is regrettably apparent.

I sat in those chambers. I was not asked an opinion. I was not asked anything at all. I was not given an opportunity to speak. But I did nothing to help my mother either. After all, I was the one who set the ball in motion, who grabbed my twin brother Jim and walked to the police station, who informed Chief Beckett we were ready—ready for whatever it was they'd planned.

Jim and I slept on the canvas cots in Ruby Dunn's music room for the next month. During the day we went to school, and at night we joined the Dunn family around their table for dinner, before retiring to the music room to work on our homework. No one talked about what had happened to our mother.

John and Dolores Gilchrist

One night our father picked us up to take us out to Wyatt's Cafeteria for dinner. Along the way he stopped at the Siebert Hotel where he'd been living, and we picked up a matronly, heavily rouged woman with large sparkly stones on her several rings and a glistening fur coat. She had dyed red hair arranged in a Patricia Neal coif, sagging dark bags under her eyes, and a mouth that was permanently contorted into a grin. Or a grimace. I was never entirely sure. Her name was Dolores Roe. At dinner Dad told us she was going to be our new mom, a piece of news she seemed to digest with less enthusiasm than her steam-table dinner.

"That's great, Dad," I responded, not knowing what I really thought about it.

"We're going to be married next week. Just the two of us in front of a justice of the peace. Then we're getting a place to live and you boys will come live with us."

"Okay."

"And you'll have to obey her rules just like you obeyed your old mother."

Now I was confused for sure. Dad was always the one with rules. Mom was the one who broke them the moment he left town. I thought about how, before the accident, she'd taken up smoking—but only when he was in Nashville. My dad smoked like a chimney, but he didn't allow my mother to smoke, saying it was unladylike. She deferred to his command when he was home, but when he wasn't, she was like the rest of us and did what she wanted. She smoked. We had friends over. We broke his rules.

"Sure," I said. "Okay."

The next week we moved in with Dolores and Dad into a new two-story "luxury" apartment complex ostentatiously called The Normandie Apartments. Our new home was within sight of the hospital where my mother had been treated for her burns, and just down the street from the amusement park where she'd risked arrest trying to enter with a group of black kids. The Normandie was comprised of four large identical housing units, each of which enclosed a small but serviceable swimming pool.

Jim and I unpacked such things as we had, and Dad informed us he'd gotten us jobs in maintenance. Twice a week we went to each apartment in the complex, opened a little bin beside each front door, removed the garbage, and dumped it into a larger bin on rollers. This flotsam we then disposed into a dumpster in the parking lot. Twice a week we patrolled the grounds and the parking lots, stabbing litter with poles sprouting nails on the end and collecting it in sacks that we had slung over our shoulders. In warmer weather we mowed the grass, weeded the flower beds, and skimmed the leaves and detritus from the pools with nets attached to long handles.

We learned the new rules. We must come straight home from school. Dolores would cook and we must eat everything she put on our plates. Jim and I must do all the cleaning. Nothing could ever be out of place. A bed, having been sat on, must be straightened immediately so that it showed no sign of the sitter. A glass, having been drunk from, must be washed and tucked quickly out of sight; and there must be no sign of the washing: no errant drop of water left on the counter or unfolded dishtowel left displayed. A hand, having touched a face, required washing with soap instantly, lest it contaminate the toucher through an inadvertent journey to the mouth. A toilet must be sat upon for urination to decrease the possibility of splatter, and the bathroom door must remain open at all times to ensure this rule was obeyed. Bedroom doors must also always remain open, for as everyone knew, doorknobs were the surest path to infection.

At the first sign of a pimple, Dolores went to work. She strained into rubber gloves, and then seated Jim or me, whosever face was offending, on the closed toilet seat. She rubbed the angry spot with gauze soaked in alcohol, and then took up her instrument, a small metal device with an evil circular object at one end. This she used to purge the offending blemish by gouging it into my skin, pleased only when it resulted in a timid eruption of white pimple puss, followed by a satisfying sufficiency of blood. She'd staunch the blood with a tiny scrap of toilet paper.

The ritual was repeated until my face was populated with bloody TP fragments from chin to crown. Blackheads were attacked no less violently. Sometimes she wielded her instrument on my face when there was nothing there at all, except in her imagination. After her ministrations, as I viewed the wreck of my face in a mirror, I thought I looked as if I'd been peppered by buckshot. She was determined to find and drive out all pimples. They would not be allowed in her home. Dolores had been an RN, and she knew the importance of cleanliness.

And quiet. Children were to be seen and not heard (although it'd be preferable if they weren't seen, either). Therefore, aside from meals and our nightly card games, we were to stay in our rooms. And be quiet.

Dolores was a card player. Hearts, Canasta, Twenty-One. She loved playing cribbage. She said her favorite game was Bridge, but she quickly abandoned hopes of teaching it to her dull-witted new family. She was used to playing with people who understood the game, and she couldn't tolerate a stupid play.

She never lost an opportunity to remind us she suffered from arthritis, caused, she said, by her years of hard work as a nurse. And it's true her hands had a crippled appearance.

She'd been married once, to a doctor who died and left her well off. He was a Mason, she said, and we smiled, not having any idea what that meant. And she was a member of the even more mysterious Eastern Star, which explained the majesty of one of her rings: a large central diamond surrounded by a number of smaller blue and green stones. She never had children because, being an orphan herself, she'd never wanted any.

She agreed with Dad that there would be no visitors in our house. We were never to invite anyone over, and if anyone invited us to their house, we must politely refuse as well. That's how germs were spread. It was bad enough we had to be around other children at school.

Our family stopped eating at Wyatt's. Now we dressed up to frequent a shiny new revolving restaurant atop a modern twenty-story insurance building, which was within sight of our apartment. It provided spectacular views of the Oklahoma twilight, which seemed to justify the exorbitant prices. On weekends we went to the movies next door at the new Cinerama, where we saw *The Greatest Story Ever Told*, *Cleopatra*, and *How the West was Won* in 70mm and with stereo surround-sound. After the movies we'd stop at the Sonic Drive-In where carhops on roller skates would bring us root beer floats—depending, of course, on the state of blemishes on our faces.

In the summer of 1964 Dolores needed a break from her new children. So one day Jim and I found ourselves on a bus to Yates Center, Kansas, where Dolores had been raised. She'd been an "orphan train" baby.

Back in the early years of the Depression, unwanted orphans were crowded onto trains in New York and shipped west. Once they'd reached the plains, they disembarked in little towns along the way, and the infants, toddlers, and older kids would be inspected by farmers and settlers who either wanted an extra child or needed an extra hand. She'd been adopted by a childless railroad man and his barren wife in a desolate west Kansas town. After a grim month with Dolores's foster parents in Yates Center, I returned home with some understanding of what had made her so unhappy.

We were to call Dolores's foster parents "Grandma" and "Grandpa," even though the words didn't seemed to evoke any welling of familial affection on either their part or ours.

I'd always thought my Dad was taciturn until I met Dolores's foster father. In the course of our month in Yates Center, I probably heard no more than a couple dozen words from his mouth, and they were mostly the same two or three sounds—"mmm," "nnnn," or "uhhhh." "Grandma" waited on "Grandpa" as if he was helpless, and he probably had become so after years of having everything done for him.

Jim and I had nothing to do. I even longed for my job collecting trash and stabbing litter at the Normandie Apartments.

"Grandma" had an older and even frailer sister living nearby, whom we were to call "Aunt." On Sundays the two women took us to church, which was our only outing. Other than that, Jim and I sat in their cramped, uncomfortable home and played endless games of hearts and twenty-one. If there was a benefit to our trip to Kansas, it might have been that it forced Jim and me to talk to each other, if only for a little while.

In the fall Dad bought his wife a new, sprawling, pink brick ranch home on a rolling half-acre lot that bordered a wooded, gurgling creek. Equipped with all new furnishings, a stone fireplace, a two-car garage, two full bathrooms, and new carpeting wall-to-every-blessed-wall, it was the kind of house I'd always wanted to live in. I was astonished that I seemed to be a part of a family that was relatively well off.

Next door to our new house was a shell of a building, slowly taking an unusual shape. It was the first Pizza Hut opened outside of Lawrence, Kansas, and it took on a signature form that would be copied for decades in towns and cities around the country. I took a job there after school and on weekends, cooking ninety-nine-cent cheese pizzas in a four-hundred-degree oven, while dressed in a uniform of blue Bermuda shorts and a short-sleeve red-checked shirt. Jim took a job at Wyatt's Cafeteria. We gave our paychecks to our father who said he'd invest them for us.

☼

Milan, Michigan — 1971

It was customary in those days to award bereavement leave to inmates when members of their immediate family died, so long as there wasn't anything in the inmate's record that argued against it.

There was plenty in mine to argue against it, including most particularly a new indictment that had me awaiting yet another trial, this time on much more serious charges than what had landed me here. I decided to go for it anyway, and I had some help.

I stood in the warden's office to make my case. My mother had died alone in New York, I told him, while living and working at the Catholic Worker—a homeless shelter and soup kitchen in the Lower East Side. She hadn't been there long enough to make many friends, and her only other family—my brothers—lived hundreds of miles away and were strangers to New York. I knew the people there, I told him, and I needed to go there to take care of the arrangements.

Speaking against me was the captain of the guards, an imposing man who looked as impenetrable as I supposed a captain of the guards ought to look. Inmates generally had no contact with this man, unless they were in very serious trouble. I'd never had a conversation with him, and had only seen him on rare occasions from a great distance. He carried an aura of danger. You didn't want to mess with him.

Today he was oddly taciturn. In a flat, no-nonsense manner, he stated he opposed my release. "This is a dangerous man," he told the warden, "and he shouldn't be out on the streets."

The warden, I knew, didn't find me so dangerous. I'd had a couple of brief encounters with him as he made his rounds and I'd found him quite personable. I'd had even more conversations with his pleasant wife. I had the notion he was sensitive to the reasons I was in prison, though it'd have been impossible for him ever to say so. But I could have been wrong. Still, there was something in the way he looked at me, and in the way he shook my hand, that told me I had nothing to fear from him.

Two other people were in the room, and they spoke for me.

Bop was always careful not to show favoritism for any of his crooks, but I knew he really liked me and that he had a good heart. For whatever reasons of his own, he was determined I was going to go to my mother's funeral. "Dangerous?" said Bop. "He's no more dangerous than you or I. Probably less so. The man's a pacifist. He wouldn't hurt a flea."

"Anything else?" asked the warden.

"Yes," Bop said. "I'll tell you how much faith I have in him. I'll go with him if you want him to have an escort, and I'll pay my own way. I'll keep him cuffed the whole time and I won't take my eyes off him, not that that's necessary, but if that's what it takes, that's what I'll do."

I was surprised at Bop, at the forcefulness and generosity of his offer. He not only made it, but he made it in front of his boss, the captain of the guards. Either Bop felt secure in his job, or he didn't give a damn what the captain thought. I suspect it was a bit of both.

Trudy Huntington smiled. Trudy was the "prison visitor," a humble title considering the abundance of grace she provided to certain inmates. Back before the First World War, when Quakers and Mennonites were routinely imprisoned for being conscientious objectors, a deal had been struck with the Federal Bureau of Prisons allowing these pacifist churches to send one person to each federal prison, where he or she served as the official "prison visitor" to so-called "prisoners of conscience." For Trudy, the normal visiting rules didn't apply. She could come as often as she wanted, and spend as much time as she wanted with any inmate on her list. She could visit with multiple inmates at the same time. She could intervene in the affairs of these inmates. Unlike other visitors, she was never searched, but she'd never have abused this privilege. No "prison visitor" ever had.

Trudy provided other services as well, not the least of which was offering local housing and transportation for family and friends who came from afar to visit her inmates. My mother had stayed with Trudy, and my fiancée, and a number of friends. She lived in a rambling farmhouse (actually two old stone farmhouses joined together in the middle and sitting on the edge of the Ann Arbor Arboretum). Her comfortable but drafty home was filled with austere furnishings that had been in her family for generations. Her husband, who always wore dark slacks, a white shirt, a thin black tie, and a dark jacket with patches on the elbows, and who always kept his horse-shoe beard well-trimmed, was a professor of art at the University of Michigan, where Trudy also lectured on her research on the Amish way of life. They were both successful authors.

Picture in your mind a Quaker woman and you can picture Trudy. She wore sensible shoes and long, plain cotton dresses with high collars and long sleeves. Her graying hair was pulled back permanently into a bun. Her simple face was eager and open, and she never wore a trace of makeup. Her posture was positively perfect. But there was nothing boring, dull, or sanctimonious about Trudy. She was vibrantly alive, a little devious, and the very soul of compassion. She came to see me every week, and we visited on many of those occasions for an entire day. She was a phenomenal conversationalist and always came loaded with interesting things to talk about. During a visit with Trudy, the prison walls receded. It was time spent not locked up.

There was one other thing that was inexpressibly precious about my visits with Trudy: She was not male. The hardest thing for me about being in prison was not being in prison per se, but it was the absence of certain things I'd previously taken for granted. Especially women and children. I lived in a compound with several hundred testosterone-amped young inmates, (and at least a hundred male guards whose own testosterone was never in doubt). I knew how lucky I was occasionally to have the opportunity to be in the presence of a feminine mind, and what's more, I got this opportunity every week. It wasn't a sexual thing. It was a human thing. Trudy kept me human.

"Warden," she said, "you know yourself there's nothing dangerous about Joe or any of my boys. They are in here precisely because they are not dangerous. There's no reason to deny him his presence at his mother's funeral."

What was going on in the warden's mind as he considered his options? He must have been aware of my open indictment, but when nobody else brought it up, he didn't either. Did he think about what might happen to his own career if he let me go and something happened? Did the fact that his wife liked me inform his next question?

"Joe," said the Warden, "I'm going to ask you a question and I want you to tell me the truth. If I let you go, unescorted, to your mother's funeral, will you stay out of trouble, and will you come back here in three days?"

He looked me straight in the eye, and I looked right back at him.

"Yes," I said.

He paused before he answered, and we continued to regard each other.

"Very well," he said. "That settles it. You'll leave tomorrow. Be back in three days. Trudy, you'll be making the arrangements?"

"Yes, Warden," she said.

And she did.

Oklahoma – 1964

It'd been almost a year since I'd seen my mother. I was allowed to write her, and letters from her were allowed to reach me after, of course, they were first read by Dad and Dolores. I wrote mostly of school and work. She wrote of things she'd read, of conversations she'd had, of a garden she'd seen, and of memories. I wanted to visit her, but as far as Dad was concerned, that was out of the question. "She's crazy," he said.

So I hitchhiked.

The Interstate Highway system was still being built, and since it hadn't quite penetrated our part of Oklahoma yet, there were no on-ramps where I could seek a ride. We lived on the far northwest side of Oklahoma City, and Norman was some thirty miles past the southeast edge of town. First, I had to get across town, and that was ten or fifteen miles in itself. This meant my hitchhiking involved a lot of walking.

From our house south to Reno Street was about thirty long city blocks. There was little to no chance of a ride on those streets, but once I reached Reno, I could usually pick up a ride from a trucker entering the city from the west. Once in the city I'd walk past downtown, where I'd pick up a ride from another trucker on his way out of town, or if I was lucky, from an OU student on his way to campus.

Hitchhiking was common in those days and in that place. I felt safe, and I was. The drivers were always kind and respectful. They seemed glad to have the company, and I was glad to have the ride. The state mental hospital was only a mile or so northeast of the Oklahoma University campus, so I always told the drivers to drop me at the campus. After they deposited me, I'd walk the rest of the way to visit my mom. Coming home was always easier. If I hung around the student union with a sign saying I needed a lift to Warr Acres, I could usually find someone headed in that direction.

On my first visit, I wasn't sure what to expect. What I found was a logically laid out compound dominated by a gigantic smokestack, which grew out of the hospital's power plant. There were a dozen or so buildings scattered around. Half of them appeared to be housing units, made of brick and two stories tall; the other half were smaller, serving functions that weren't clear. The administration building had classical granite columns, a testimony to the power that resided therein.

Throughout the compound there was a modest attempt at landscaping that I later came to equate with litter-free government installations of various kinds: modest gardens at right angles, scattered tree saplings, well-trimmed curbs, and crack-free sidewalks.

From reception in the administration building, I was directed to a particular unit to see my mom. The door to the unit was open, and I entered a screened corridor that fronted the entire building. Scattered along the corridor were plain wooden chairs and a few rockers. Some of the chairs were occupied with patients, still in their pajamas, who paid me no attention. The corridor had interior doors that led to the sleeping quarters and to the utilitarian public spaces—a mess hall and a rec room—where the patients spent most of their time. I found someone who appeared to be working instead of residing there, and I asked for my mother. Eventually, she appeared.

We hugged for what seemed like years.

"You should have told me you were coming," she said. "I must look terrible." Perhaps she didn't look her best, but I only remember her looking wonderful. We sat for a while in the corridor, bothered occasionally by other patients. Most appeared normal enough, but some clearly were not. Mom suggested that we take a walk. "I have grounds privileges here. I can come and go as I want, so long as I stay on campus and am back at certain times."

We didn't talk much about her life there. Over time I learned a few things, but now I'd like to know so much more. She told me that in her first months she was confined behind bars in a heavily secured building, like a jail, which housed the criminally insane. She said she feared for her life there, and was witness to many acts of cruelty. She said during those first weeks she kept thinking that this all had to be a mistake, that eventually someone would figure it out and come to free her. It took a long time for it to dawn on her no one was coming.

She spent most of the rest of her confinement in this drab barrack where I'd found her. She said that the hardest thing was not the confinement itself but rather finding something to occupy her mind. There wasn't anything to do, and most of the patients were heavily drugged, which made meaningful conversation a rare thing. The nurses, who wore starched hats and white stockings, were kind enough, but they weren't allowed to socialize with patients, so her interactions with them were routine and sterile. And the doctors? Well, she didn't have anything good to say about the doctors. She said aside from her intake and her initial days there, she never saw them, which suited her fine.

She said in her first days there she'd been forced to take the same Thorazine pills that dulled most of the patients in the hospital, and made them easy to manage for the custodial staff. She said it was this drug that accounted for the odd behavior I'd witnessed in some of the patients: the glazed look in the eyes, the mindless rocking, the walking back and forth, the muttering. She said she'd learned to fake ingestion of the drug, until finally the nurses realized she'd stopped taking it. But since she hadn't been uncooperative, they'd stopped trying to force it on her.

She found solace and purpose where she could. She'd started assuming nursing duties when she saw an opportunity. If a patient next to her became ill and lacked water or clean sheets, she'd take care of it. Eventually the staff began to accept her intervention and even counted on her for it. When she got grounds privileges she joined a garden club sponsored by the Norman Junior League. She became friends with some of the Junior Leaguers, and she took on responsibility for certain flower beds. Roses were her favorite. She spent time in the sun, in the wind, in the rain, and in the dirt. She was proud of her cannas and her zinnias. Toward the end of her confinement, she obtained a job in the canteen on weekends, where she served patients and visitors soft drinks, candy bars, and hot dogs. She earned modest spending money for herself, which she kept tucked away in a small tobacco pouch in her bra. She became well known and universally liked. Whenever we walked across the grounds together, my arm draped across her shoulders, everyone greeted her. Everyone said hi to Rosie.

In the 1950s the University of Oklahoma produced a short documentary promoting the state hospital in Norman, Oklahoma, as a beacon of hope for the mentally ill. The film opens like a Hitchcock thriller, with dark and somber music underpinning shadowed close-ups of a harrowed man being driven through the snow to what he calls "the bughouse," where three guards with grim faces grab the patient by the arms and escort him through the vault-like doors to begin treatment.

The music shifts to a rheumy violin solo of "Let My People Go" (you can't make this stuff up). The camera pans across a row of old people in rockers, and the narrator explains that many of the patients are merely old and destitute, with nowhere else to go. Others, the narrator informs us, are deranged, and the camera provides a series of images defining for us exactly what derangement looks like.

The music shifts again, to a bright theme one might expect in a Shirley Temple comedy, as the narrator shares that "most" of the thirty-two hundred patients are well cared for and—yes—happy. Now the patients are cooking bread, doing laundry, herding cattle, and—wait for it—fishing off a dock. The message is clear: Who wouldn't want to go to the state mental hospital?

We watch the new patient being scrubbed by an attendant after he arrives, and then submitted to examinations of his blood, spinal fluid, and lungs to check him for gonorrhea, meningitis, and tuberculosis. We witness some bizarre interviews with elderly appearing psychiatrists and psychologists, and a series of rudimentary tests. Following these tests, the patient is paraded in a large room filled with nurses and doctors and attendants. And in this Kafkaesque setting the patient is informed of his diagnosis and proscribed treatment.

Ah. The treatment. The grainy black-and-white footage takes you inside the treatment rooms where doctors and nurses administer Thorazine, inject patients with insulin to shock their systems back to sanity, and attach electrodes to patients' heads. There's something called "hydro-therapy," where patients are subjected to confinement in crate-like devices pumped with steam with only their heads poking out.

The film neglects to mention that lobotomies were not infrequently performed at this hospital.

Now the music turns sweet again as we see inmates playing dominos, square dancing, and sewing. "What could be better," the narrator asks, "than an afternoon softball game?"

Much has been written about this hospital and others of this era, and how the primary means of "treatment" was heavy doses of Thorazine, which kept the patients dazed and dulled, making them docile and easy to lead around like sheep. Lobotomies were a close second in the short list of preferred treatments.

Altogether I find this a much scarier movie than, say, *Dawn of the Dead*. Zombies from the movies don't really exist, but the subjects of this mov-ie are real. All this really happened. And the people in charge boasted about what they were doing and documented their work so that we can enjoy it all these many years later.

If there was anything good about my mother's "treatments" at the hospital, it was simply that she didn't get any treatments at all, following her initial dose of Thorazine. Her five years of hospital records (all twenty-three pages of them) reveal in clear language that she was there to be confined, not treated. And confined she was.

When Jim and I were infants, we spoke a secret language of our own invention. We were slow to learn normal language because we didn't need it. Our own was sufficient. The rest of our family learned some of our words so they could communicate with us. They knew, for example, that Gordon's true name was "Ga-Ga," and no amount of encouragement could convince us otherwise. Eventually we learned to converse with other people, but we continued our own private conversation for many years.

Before Mom's "accident," Jim and I were so close we hardly knew we were two separate people. After the first grade our parents forced us into separate classrooms against our wishes because they feared we were too close, and they wanted us to form our own personalities—also because our first grade teacher had found teaching us difficult. When she asked one of us a question, the other would surely answer it. We walked, breathed, and lived with a single rhythm.

Until we were eleven, when Mom's "accident" happened, we remained tight. Outside of our separate classrooms, we did everything together. We'd find each other on the playground and at lunch, and our time together excluded anyone else. At home we never played separately, and when we went out in our neighborhood to play with friends, we went together. That we seemed to speak with one voice and act with one mind seemed natural to us, and our friends took it for granted as well.

All that changed after Mom's "accident." It was instant. We each now lived in our own heads. Neither of us disclosed to the other what we were thinking or feeling. That first summer, when we were in Odessa with Uncle Floyd and Aunt Sue, we still stuck together, but only because there was no one else around. Now, four years later, at the ripe age of fifteen, we were strangers to each other.

I can't say what went on in Jim's head, only in my own. I was struggling to survive in my own way. I wanted a normal life (whatever that was). I wasn't sure what I was striving for, but somehow it had something to do with being a great kid. I felt that I could perhaps survive all the crap at home, so long as my own life, outside of home, was exceptional.

I made straight As, except for an occasional (and no doubt unfairly administered) A-minus. I was class president and a member of the Latin club, debate team, and honor society. At church I was a Junior Deacon and was even occasionally called upon to deliver the sermon when the Reverend Dunn was unavailable. But nothing I did could please my father. Meanwhile everything I did sorely displeased my new stepmother. I kept thinking that eventually there would be some acknowledgement from either or both of them of just how good I was. Other people seemed to notice it. Why couldn't they?

An inventory of my life so far proves my point. I did very well at school. I came directly home from school as instructed. I worked hard and turned over all my money to my dad. I kept my bedspread tight enough to bounce a quarter, and I always peed sitting down on the toilet with the bathroom door securely open (when I was at home anyway). I was careful to make sure Dolores always won at cards, especially cribbage. I ate whatever she put in front of me, and I always said I liked it even when I didn't. (*Especially* when I didn't.) The moment I came home, I changed out of my "good" school clothes, which were not particularly good, and put on my "lounging" clothes, which were at least two years old and two sizes too tight. I let Dolores violate my pimpled face with her brutal instrument of pain, and then I thanked her for the wreckage she left behind with a kiss, which I deposited on her amply rouged and perfumed cheek. I spoke when spoken to. I removed myself to my room when required, which was most of the time.

No, I don't remember any praise, however slight. But I remember Dolores's sighs. She had an entire symphony of sighs. There were long, drawn-out sighs that seemed to come from some great depth and rise reluctantly into the open air, accompanied by sharp grimaces and mournful looks. Then she'd peek around to make sure someone had beheld her suffering. Oh, she was suffering! My, how she was suffering!

She also pulled from her song book a variety of short, quick sighs. Sometimes just one—a quick, audible gasp, followed by a sudden stillness as if she were insisting the sigh had never happened. And sometimes a staccato sequence of sighs, hopping out of her like frogs. And again the eyes, imploring reassurance that her suffering had been noted.

In the fall of 1964 I was cast in a leading role in the all-school production of *Look Homeward, Angel* by Thomas Wolfe. I was to play the alcoholic brother of a man who was dying of tuberculosis and part of a dysfunctional Southern family. I rushed home, bursting with excitement at the news. Our school had just constructed a new, ultra-modern, twenty-four-hundred-seat, state of the art auditorium, and this was to be the first production in it.

My father's reaction to the news was predictable. A play meant rehearsals, and rehearsals meant I wouldn't be coming straight home from school, and that was against the rules. After dinner he ordered me to my bedroom. He followed. He whipped off his familiar belt and started hitting me.

Of all the things which made my father proud, I think perhaps it was his spanking technique that most satisfied him. It'd been honed through a lifetime of spankings, stretching from the ones he'd received as a child, to the hundreds he'd delivered to his own sons. It usually involved a belt. The same belt. His spanking belt. But any object would do in a pinch. The swing was important, especially the backswing. A pause at the top of the arc, while maintaining eye contact with the target, provided an opportunity for the maximum accumulation of fear. Once fear of the impending pain was firmly established in the mind of the target, Dad's arm plummeted in one clean, graceful motion. The sounds were important. The sound of the whack. The sound of the cry. A spanking was not a spanking until the right sounds had been elicited. Exactly where the whack was to land was not particularly important. Any part of the back, buttocks, legs—or even arms—would do.

Over time Jim and I had learned that the faster we reacted with the right sounds, the sooner the spanking would stop. But I was tired of playing the victim. So this time I just stood, stoically and silently, staring at my father as he swung again and again. The quieter I remained, the angrier he became and the harder he swung. I'd decided this man had wrung his last tear from me.

Maybe his arm grew tired, maybe he grew frustrated at his failure to break me, maybe I spooked him a little, or maybe he was as tired of this ritual as I was. At any rate, eventually he stopped. We stared at each other across a very deep chasm. He turned and left the room.

And I left the house. I walked out the front door and kept walking. I never went back. Jim stayed behind.

Where was there to walk? I was sixteen and homeless (which is unfortunately a more common status for kids today than it was then). I had no destination in mind. The only place in my thoughts was the place I was leaving and would never return to again. I knew this to be the case. And I knew I was going to be all right. In fact, from the moment I stepped outside the door, I felt better, safer, and happier than I had in years. Maybe ever. Something would turn up. I'd figure something out.

At first I wandered the neighborhood, making ever-widening circles, wondering whether some option would present itself. If I were in our old neighborhood, I'd have felt comfortable walking into any of several neighbors' houses. Mrs. Bommer would have given me something to eat, maybe some iced tea and a peanut butter sandwich, but I had to admit she wouldn't have taken me in. Her gruff husband wouldn't have permitted it, and she'd have been too afraid of my dad. The Butlers and the O'Keefes barely took care of their own kids; they wouldn't have wanted any more. The Flood kids were grown and out of the house; the last thing they'd want was another kid. But I probably could have moved in with Richard Okoluk and his folks. They kept cheap wine in their fridge and let Richard come and go pretty much as he wanted. They'd hardly notice if someone new was sleeping in their house.

The more I thought about it, the more I realized I didn't have a clue what I was going to do. My only idea of a homeless kid was in an old Dickens novel. I might have preferred a Fagin over my father, but I was pretty sure there were no Fagins in Warr Acres. My dad had frequently threatened to send me to a military academy where they'd pound some sense into me, but a few weeks earlier, after an argument, I'd acquiesced and said, "Yes, please send me to the military academy!" He said no. He said that had been only a threat. He didn't have the money to pay for a military academy, and if he did, he wouldn't waste the money on me. He said I'd just have to "toe the line."

Night loomed. The sky darkened. I kept walking. I didn't know anyone in this new neighborhood. Since we'd moved in, Dad and Dolores had made sure we had no opportunity to get to know anyone, since we always had to come straight home from school and stay home, except for working our jobs. Besides, this new neighborhood was filled with large modern homes, with manicured lawns and new cars in every driveway. I didn't belong here.

Eventually I circled back to Dad and Dolores's house and continued past it. I wandered into the neighboring Pizza Hut. It was almost closing time, and Kenny, a fellow employee, was cleaning up alone. Ken was an okay enough guy (he was something of a greaser), but I knew whatever I needed that night, Ken didn't have it. The restaurant was almost empty, but there was one person there who might be a possibility. He was alone, finishing off a small cheese pizza by himself, having come from some school or sports function.

I didn't know Bob Pahlka very well. He and I had been in the second grade together, but we'd never had much to do with each other. Not for any particular reason. We just hadn't. After second grade I hardly saw him at all, until we got to high school. Then he started to date a girl named Glenda who went to our church, so I saw him at church occasionally. In our sophomore year he'd run against me for student council treasurer, and I'd won by a small margin. I'd always thought he was nice. But like I said, I didn't really know him.

"Hi, Bob," I said. "I don't have any place to stay tonight. Any chance I can stay over at your house?"

"I guess so," Bob said. "Let me call my folks."

It was that simple.

After he finished his pizza, Bob drove me to his folks' house in his mom's '58 pink Pontiac. We didn't talk much in the car on the way over. He didn't ask me why I needed a place to stay, and I don't recall that I told him. I'm not sure what I'd have said if he'd asked.

He lived in a part of town where I'd never been before, in a small development at the southwestern edge of our sprawling school district. Amongst the homes there were modest hills and not so modest towering oak trees. We pulled into his circular driveway and Bob took me into his house.

His mom and dad were sitting up in bed watching Johnny Carson. Bob showed me into their bedroom, and we met awkwardly. I briefly explained the situation: I was a good kid, but I wasn't going to let my dad ever hit me again, so I had to leave home. They instructed Bob to put me in the guest room, and we said good night. I'd never before been in a house that had an actual guest room. I slept well that night.

The next morning Bob loaned me some clean clothes. Esther, Bob's mom, cooked us a hearty breakfast. She said it was something she did every day for her boys before she went to work herself. Her oldest son, Bill, whom I knew slightly, was already away at college, a freshman at Yale. After breakfast Bob and I went outside to wait for the school bus.

That day at school was just like any other day. Jim and I didn't have any classes together, so it wasn't unusual that I didn't see him. When the school day finished, Bob and I took the bus back to his house.

Harlan, Bob's dad, had called my father that afternoon. When my dad told Harlan he didn't care where I was or what I was doing, it made Harlan mad. He couldn't imagine a father behaving that way toward his son for any reason. But what really got Harlan's goat was when my father said, without a request from Harlan, that he wasn't going to give Harlan any money to take care of me.

What my father didn't know, and what I didn't know until many decades later, is that during the Depression, Harlan's father had sold him as a young boy to a neighboring farmer who had no children of his own. Harlan never saw his own parents again.

Harlan's dad had needed money and the farmer needed cheap labor. Even though the farmer had a fine house with empty bedrooms, Harlan was made to sleep on straw in the barn. Every morning before dawn, Harlan performed the chores of feeding and tending the farmer's live-stock, and again every evening after school. For his work he was com-pensated with leftovers handed to him through the kitchen door and the barn roof over his head.

There's nothing that my father could have said that would have made Harlan angrier than suggesting some financial transaction in exchange for a boy. He'd lived through it himself.

That night Harlan and Esther said I could stay with them as long as I needed. Although we'd never met before, I wasn't a complete stranger to them. They knew by reputation that I was a good kid. Bob spoke well of me, and that was good enough for them.

And that's how I got my new family.

⚙

The Pahlkas never made a big deal about my living with them. It quickly felt as if I'd been a part of their family forever, even though their family was very different from mine, or any I'd imagined.

The first thing that struck me was they didn't argue. All families argued, didn't they? That had been my experience thus far in my limited years, and I had no reason to expect otherwise. Yet the Pahlkas simply didn't fight. They might disagree over something every now and then—though even that was rare—but they'd never argue about it. They would discuss things. Calmly. Intelligently. No doors were ever slammed, no voices were raised, and, hard as it was for me to imagine, no one was ever hit.

This not-fighting thing seemed to work pretty well. They loved each other, they respected each other, and they got along. I was fine with that. So I fell right in.

My two years with the Pahlkas passed quickly and were mostly filled with the humdrum activities common to any junior, and then senior, in high school.

One of the major benefits of living with the Pahlkas was that they enabled frequent, usually weekly, visits with my mother. Initially, before I got my license, Esther drove me to Norman. Later, they loaned me a car and I drove myself. But my visits with my mother weren't limited to the hospital grounds.

During that first Christmas with the Pahlkas I got permission from the hospital to sponsor my mother on a furlough to my new home. The Pahlkas welcomed her again at Easter, on Mother's Day, and during the occasional weekend as well. Usually she'd come for the day and stay for dinner, but now and then she'd spend the night in the guest room and I'd bunk with Bob.

My mother never burdened the Pahlkas or me with her problems. She was profoundly grateful to them for taking care of me and giving me a good home, and grateful for enabling our visits. She never asked anything for herself. And when there was a school event, like my performance my senior year as Harold Hill in *The Music Man*, Esther always made sure my mother was present.

There was something poetic about my mother sitting in the front row as I belted out "76 Trombones." It'd been one year since my father took his belt to me for being cast in a school play, and the irony of performing with the explicit blessing of my mother in the audience was not lost on me or her.

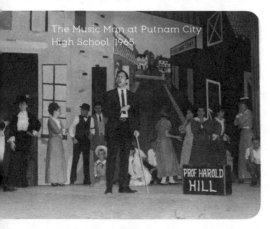

The Music Man at Putnam City High School. 1965

"I'm so proud of you," she said, and she was. And I was proud of her. I brought her backstage and introduced her to my friends and teachers. The next morning I drove her back to the hospital in Norman.

I was painfully aware that she'd been wronged and had no business being confined. Did I do nothing to change things out of helplessness, naivety, stupidity, or selfishness? All of them probably. But I did what I thought I could at the time. I wrote her. I visited. I got her out for a day or two. I included her in my world as often as possible and never looked too closely at hers. Her behavior toward me was always gracious, loving, and supportive; it was never seeking, plaintive, or beseeching. She never asked for my help. She bore her troubles on her own.

I didn't think my life with the Pahlkas was something I'd earned, or something special I deserved. At the time, their generosity felt so easy, so natural, so right that I never questioned how it came about, or examined it too closely. Looking back, I know how precious a gift the Pahlkas were to me and my mother.

But this too, I know: There truly is more pleasure in giving than in receiving. For all the joy and happiness the Pahlkas' love and assistance provided me in the two years I lived under their roof, I know their own joy and happiness was multiplied. I know this because I've learned in my adult life that in helping others I'm really helping myself. There's no satisfaction as great as providing a helping hand. I learned that from the

Pahlkas. And I'm so grateful for the lesson and the opportunity to pay them back by paying it forward.

Bob and I became fast friends. He and I were different. He tended toward sports and I did not. I tended toward academics and he did not. He was mechanically inclined and I was all thumbs at anything involving tools, even a screwdriver or a hammer. But we seemed to share a common outlook, a calm approach to things, and an irreverent look at life.

In our senior year I announced I was going to run for student council president. I'd been planning this for years. What I didn't know, because I was too self-absorbed to notice, was that Bob had been planning the same run. After all, his father had been student council president at our same school many years before. And his mother. And his older brother. But then, unknown to me at the time, Bob had had a quiet talk with his mother. He'd informed her he decided not to run because he thought I needed the office more than he did. Bob ran for vice president, and we both won.

Almost everyone I've ever known complains about high school and their high school years. I'm an aberration. I loved high school.

It didn't hurt that as student council president I had a permanent hall pass signed by the principal. No shit. This thing was like gold. When other students had to grovel for permission to get out of class to do anything, I had a reusable get-out-of-jail-free card. And I was involved in so many activities that I was out of class more than I was in.

The Pahlkas weren't the only adults who had an influence on me, or who took special care of me during those years. The teachers who had the greatest lasting effect on my life were Juanita Wood and Sue Dennis. They were night and day in temperament and teaching style, but they shared an affection for me. They watched out for me. They guided me and nurtured me. They both went beyond the normal duties of teaching to mentor and coach me. They honed my skills in writing, speaking, and communication, arming me with the ammo I'd need for my confrontation with the status quo a few years yet in the future.

Sue was fiery, spirited, and inquisitive. Juanita was stable, a rock, a fortress. Sue was focused on the world, the universe, the future. Juanita's gaze was turned inward and back in time. How their similar half-smiles, which sat permanently on each of their faces, expressed so perfectly their separate personalities, I do not know.

Sue Dennis taught forensics. A diminutive and attractive redhead who always looked great in her signature black high heels and tight skirt, she assembled a crack team of boys and girls that became a powerhouse at the many Oklahoma speech tournaments. The only thing Jim and I shared in high school was the pleasure of being taught and coached by Sue Dennis, though we took her class at separate hours and debated on separate teams. During our many tournaments, we never roomed together. We each won our debates more often than we lost.

Under Sue's coaching I gravitated toward extemporaneous speaking and original oratory, and in my senior year I won state in both, along with the opportunity to compete at nationals. My winning oration was titled "Stop for a Moment," and was purposely different from the style of most orations written and performed by high school students in 1966. The style of the times was bombastic and sincere, oratorical and sweeping, in the manner of Billy Graham or John Kennedy. My oration was quiet and thoughtful. It spoke of the quickening pace of life, the tumultuous demands of the times, and the gains to be wrought from stepping back, reflecting, and enjoying a moment of peace. The judges at nationals didn't get it, but I didn't care. It may not have been the winning speech, but it was the message I needed to deliver at the time, because it was the message I needed to hear myself, and it's a message that has stood me well for almost half a century.

Juanita Wood taught speech, which was somehow distinguished from forensics. She was also the drama coach and directed one play and one musical each year. She gifted me with the love of everything theatrical: watching it, reading it, reading *about* it, acting, designing, directing, lighting… all of it. She worked in tandem with Sue Dennis to guide me

SPOKE   85

through high school and then toward college. They were co-conspirators for my success.

One day Mrs. Wood and Mrs. Dennis asked me to meet with them after school. They told me Putnam City was about to get its first black student, a kid named Mike, a transferee from Douglas High on the city's east side. They didn't know a lot about him except that he played football and was supposed to be smart. They asked me to befriend him, and of course I agreed. I would have jumped off a cliff if they asked me.

I'm not sure how much of a friend I was to Mike. It might have helped had I been a football player, or even cared for the sport, which I didn't. Still, I attempted to seek him out each day, in the lunchroom or the halls. It wasn't hard to find him. He was always the one with the wide berth around him, the kid sitting alone when all the other tables were crowded. To my knowledge, no one at Putnam City ever gave Mike any trouble—they just never gave him anything at all. He lasted two months at Putnam City, and then one day he was gone.

There's another tale about Juanita Wood that bears, in a particularly satisfying and ironic manner, on a part of the story yet to come. She coached my entry into—ta-da!—the annual American Legion High School Oratory Contest.

Every spring, in thousands of high schools around the nation, tens of thousands of pimply-faced students wrote and memorized and practiced and recited ten-minute patriotic orations. These were performed at local, district, state, regional, and national contests, until the single most patriotic high school voice in the land was anointed by the American Legion. It was an exhausting and most serious business. The winners, at each stage of the contest, also walked away with a modest prize—always some denomination of U.S. Savings Bonds.

I mock the contest—and it surely deserves mocking—but it also did a lot of good. It did me good. While it reduced patriotism to a contest of flowery words, it also forced lots of kids onto their feet and made them talk in front of an audience (a notable accomplishment in and of itself). It also provided a lot of kids who needed some funds a little bit of cash.

In 1965, with the intensive coaching of Mrs. Wood, I won the local and district contests, and placed second at state. In 1966, with a new and improved oration, and the benefit of the previous year's experience, I won the local, district, and state contests, and then went on to regionals, where I took second in Kansas City. I lost to a very pretty girl. (I remain convinced her speech was written by her mother, who sat in the front row and silently voiced it word for word in sync with her daughter.)

But that's not the interesting part of the story.

While researching material for my speech, I'd discovered some words I liked from William Lloyd Garrison, the nineteenth century abolitionist. In one of his most quoted passages, he wrote:

> Tell a man whose house is on fire to give a moderate alarm; tell him to moderately rescue his wife from the hands of the ravisher; tell the mother to gradually extricate her babe from the fire into which it has fallen; — but urge me not to use moderation in a cause like the present. I am in earnest—I will not equivocate—I will not excuse—I will not retreat a single inch—and I will be heard.

It's a passionate and almost unbearably flowery passage, written by an eloquent and excited man in the center of his generation's fight against racial injustice. This quote resonated deeply with me. I built my oration around it and a quote from Henry David Thoreau—the quote everybody knows, about marching to a different drummer.

Each oration had to have a title reflecting its theme, and mine was "United Through Controversy"—the idea being that the American tradition of protest and civil disobedience is a core characteristic of what it means to be American, and that it ultimately unites us as a people. I spoke of how our country itself grew out of disobedience to an unjust government imposed by the British, and in particular, I pointed to our country's recent experience of civil disobedience during the Civil Rights Movement. I cited Rosa Parks's refusal to move to the back of the bus, and the 1960 lunch counter boycott in Greensboro, North Carolina. Regrettably, I failed to mention anything about Marilyn Luper, the Oklahoma

NAACP, or the 1958 sit-in at Katz Drug Store. It was as if I'd forgotten those events had ever happened. And I said nothing about my mother.

In those days and in that place, it was okay—good, even—to talk about the Civil Rights struggles and the advancements that had been achieved far away, in North Carolina or Mississippi perhaps, but one was not permitted to talk about the struggle for racial equality in white suburban Oklahoma. There was this weird hypocrisy that allowed people, me included, to blithely criticize racism in those "backward" states like Alabama, while giving no thought to the racism in our own backyard. We chose to believe that our community had no race problem. It made a perverse kind of sense. Racism was a problem that obviously existed elsewhere because blacks themselves existed elsewhere.

Whenever racism was discussed or thought about, it was always someone else's problem, someone else's struggle. It was someone else who was prejudiced or victimized. Racism was an issue to be considered from afar. Without knowing it, I'd become one with the collective consciousness, adopting the blindness of all those around me who made our own racist reality invisible.

In that spring of 1966 I delivered my oration praising and advocating the sacred right of Americans to disagree with each other, to protest, and to engage when necessary in civil disobedience. I delivered it to classrooms, at contests, and to a score of American Legion posts, which had invited me to potluck dinners in backwater towns. I delivered it at Kiwanis Club dinners and Optimist Club luncheons, to churches and to school assemblies. It seemed everyone wanted to hear it, not just in my own community but also all over the state. I delivered it dozens of times in dozens of communities and always to standing ovations. I became known throughout the state as a notable high school orator. (Okay, perhaps it wasn't the same as being regarded as the best high school quarterback in the state, but at least it was something. It was my own brand of notoriety.)

Not too many years later I learned that the universal appreciation of my oration—its embrace of free speech, disagreement, protest, and civil disobedience—was pathetically shallow. It was one thing to get audience after audience on its feet in a rousing defense of America's tradition of protest. It'd be quite something else when I became a dissenter myself, and those same people didn't like what they saw or what I had to say.

Milan, Michigan to New York City – July, 1971

W hat does a prisoner wear to his mother's funeral?

I considered this question as I rifled through the scant options available in the prison's A&D (arrival and departure) wardrobe. Everything on display had been previously worn and was uniformly drab, making me wonder about their origins. Perhaps they were castoffs from other inmates on their way in, or discards culled from the Salvation Army. Who knows? Anyway, even though the clothes might not have been to my liking, they were not the signature army surplus khakis that were the standard uniform of federal prisoners, so they felt good.

I chose a plain blue dress shirt, a pair of brown blended slacks, and brown oxfords (well broken in). No belts were available, belts being banned in prison. I was also allotted two pairs of ubiquitous white cotton socks and two pairs of briefs. My spare socks and briefs, along with my toothbrush and razor, went into a small duffle, also from the prison locker.

Then I changed my mind. I wasn't ashamed of being a prisoner. In fact, I was rather really proud of it. I asked if I could trade the blue dress shirt and the brown slacks for my prison-issue khakis, with the faded outlines of insignia and patches on the sleeves and pockets. The hack didn't care. It was all the same to him. So that's what I wore as I walked out the prison gates. My standard prison garb.

Trudy picked me up and we drove in her Volvo station wagon to the Detroit Airport. Along the way she regaled me with her usual perky banter, and I was surprisingly in a good mood to hear it. It occurred to me I should have felt despondent. After all, I was still a convicted felon serving my sentence, my mother had recently died, and I was on my way to her funeral. On the face of it, things didn't look so good. But truthfully, I felt great. The sun was shining. I was outside the prison compound for the first time in almost a year. I was going to ride on a plane, see my friends, and visit New York. Yes, I was devastated at Mom's death, but I was elated at the gift of momentary freedom that she inadvertently gave me.

At the gate Trudy gave me some pocket money to help with meals, taxis, or whatever else I might need. I put it in my pocket alongside two other items: my prison photo ID, which I'd been instructed to keep on my person at all times, and directions to the federal lock-up in Manhattan, where I was to bed for the next two nights. As a concession to the captain of the guards, the warden had agreed that between the hours of six p.m. and six a.m. I was to be jailed in Manhattan. But for the other hours, I'd be free to go about my business. It seemed like a peculiar arrangement, but any freedom was better than no freedom at all.

My twin brother Jim, my fiancée Susan, and my best friends from Cornell, Gretchen and Stephen, greeted me at the gate at JFK. How swell was this? The loves of my life, all gathered to welcome me into their arms. Stephen said, in a noticeably loud voice, "How's things in prison? What, no handcuffs? You mean they let federal inmates travel without chains?" This had been intended to get a rise from those around us, but no one seemed to notice—this was New York after all—and we soon fell into familiar conversation as we traded embraces and, hand in hand, walked along the concourse to the exit.

We drove in Stephen's car to Chinatown, where a few other friends joined us for an early dinner. This was my normal feeding time, but for everyone else it must have seemed awfully early to chow down. Nonetheless, we ordered with abandon and ate with gusto. Hot and sour soup, Peking duck, and cashew chicken were all items sadly missing from the menu in prison, and I exuberantly savored every bite.

The transition from a Michigan federal prison to New York's Chinatown is hard to capture in words. If prison was a broken instrument with no strings, Chinatown was an orchestra at full volume. The colors, sights, smells, and sounds were magical and overwhelming. The frantic rush of the never-ending traffic. The din of New Yorkers on the sidewalks. The gusts of aromas from the kitchens. The touch of Susan's hand on mine. Stephen's laughter. Gretchen's wink. A glass of cheap red wine.

New York City - July, 1968. Left to right: Jim Gilchrist, Joe Gilchrist (behind), Susan Smith, Stephen Katz, Bonnie Barnes, Fred Solowey of the Cornell Daily Sun, unknown, and Barbara Hawkins.

After dinner there wasn't much time before I was due at the federal halfway house in lower Manhattan, so we just made one hurried visit to the Catholic Worker, where my mother had lived and died.

In the middle of a tenement block in the heart of the Bowery, the Catholic Worker was many things, but institutionally it was a soup kitchen for the homeless. It also had a limited amount of sleeping quarters upstairs, mostly for permanent volunteer staff like my mother, many of whom were only a few steps away from being homeless themselves. Since the years of the Great Depression, the Worker also published a monthly newspaper, which was distributed worldwide and was a thorn in the side of whatever pope or president happened to be on the holiest of thrones or in the highest of offices. Dorothy Day, the Worker's founder, took Jesus's commands to heart and challenged the established Catholic Church at every turn—not only in her newspaper but also by example. No ornate temples and gilded chalices and palatial dwellings for her. She'd taken her own vow of poverty, and she took it seriously. Similarly, she challenged the seats of political power. In the 1950s, when I was participating in ridiculous "duck and cover" atom-bomb drills in my Oklahoma elementary classroom, Dorothy and her friends were being arrested in Times Square for refusing to "take cover" during Manhattan's Cold War nuclear air raid drills.

Her life was dedicated simply to helping others. The Catholic Worker at 36 E. 1st Street was the first of its kind, but it has since been emulated many times; now there are Catholic Worker Houses of Hospitality in scores of cities around the world. Long before there was Mother Theresa, there was Dorothy Day.

Because Dorothy herself was travelling at the moment, I couldn't thank her for her kindness to my mother, though Dorothy was never one to accept thanks graciously. She didn't do what she did to be thanked. Nonetheless, I took the opportunity to thank everyone present for being good to my mom, but they were more profuse in thanking me for the great help she'd been to all of them. They told of how she always went out of her way to help other people, how no task was too small or too big for her to take on, and how inspiring she was to so many people. They had a small suitcase with her things in it and wanted to know what I wanted done with it. Susan and I went through it. We donated the few items of clothing to the Worker. There were a small number of photos: yellowed prints of her brothers from decades ago, and a few Brownie photos from Oklahoma and Texas of Gordon, Jim, and me. There were a lot of letters, most of which were the letters I'd written her from prison. Susan took these scant belongings and promised to keep them for me until I got out.

Then it was off to jail. At the curb in front of the halfway house, Susan, Jim, Stephen, and Gretchen got out of the car and gave me big hugs and kisses. Stephen loudly proclaimed he hoped I'd have a nice night in jail. I entered the building, which seemed to dissolve into the fabric of the city itself. I felt a bit outside of my own body. None of this was real. This day—the flight, the touch of my friends, the death of my mother, this going in and out and back in to jail—none of this was what I'd ever had in mind for my life. But here I was. Here I was.

1965 – 1968

In the late winter of 1965 I got a postcard from my mother. She'd been moved far away to a remote state mental health facility in Vinita, Oklahoma. It was hardly a town, not much more than a dusty crossroads on the plains. She was allowed no visitors, and she said she wouldn't be allowed any more letters for a while. She'd write again, when she could. There was no further explanation of this mysterious move, and there was nothing I could do, it seemed, but go along with it.

I later learned she'd been writing letters to seek her own release. She wrote letters to the governor, to senators, and even the president. The transfer to Vinita was a punishment and a warning. She must stop writing such letters, and she must not do anything to seek her release.

After several months, having learned her lesson, she was returned to Norman where I could visit her again.

During these years of her incarceration, I visited my mother as often as I could, but we knew each other mostly through our letters. We wrote to each other every week, and usually several times a week. We wrote short, quick letters, frivolous and trivial. I wrote of the weather, of homework, of school assemblies and sock-hops, and of my job at the Pizza Hut. She wrote of the weather, of poetry and fiction, of roses and zinnias, and her work in the hospital commissary. Sometimes I'd enclose a clipping or a photo; she'd enclose a leaf or a poem she'd copied from a book. And once a week I'd send her a little cash, two or five dollars, which she could use to get her hair done at the hospital beauty parlor, or to buy magazines, candy, or cigarettes for her friends on the ward.

In the fall of my senior year, the Pahlkas guided my application to college. I knew if I'd stayed with my father, college would have been difficult, if not impossible. My older brother Gordon had been able to work his way through Central State College without any help from anyone, and perhaps I could have done the same. Just as likely, I'd have considered enlisting. There was a war on, and as every veteran in the state knew from my numerous appearances in their Legion Halls, I was one patriotic American.

My senior counselor, not having any vision beyond sixty miles or so, pushed me toward OU or OSU. Harlan and Esther urged me to look further, well beyond Oklahoma's borders. Ultimately I blithely applied to four schools: Princeton, Brown, Penn, and Cornell. I was woefully ignorant of all of them, not having ever met anyone who'd visited or attended any of these schools; but because they each presented full scholarships—an offer not possible within our state's borders—they were all irresistibly attractive.

One good effect of my college aspirations was that it shamed my father into agreeing to help pay for Jim's college tuition. My dad was not one to easily part with money, and not having been to college himself, he saw no use for it for anyone else. Nonetheless, he supported Jim's application to Oklahoma State, where Jim got a nice, but far from complete, scholarship. Oklahoma colleges just didn't have that kind of money to give out.

I lucked out. I received identical offers from three of the four schools: full tuition and fees plus a stipend for room and board. Only Princeton turned me down, which ticks me off to this day. I think it might have had something to do with an interview I'd had with a Princeton alum that hadn't gone too well. He'd interviewed me at a fancy restaurant that had more forks than I knew what to do with and a menu with selections I couldn't pronounce. Screw it. It was Princeton's loss.

I chose Cornell because a) it was in New York and I wanted to go to New York, and b) they had a program in Southeast Asian Studies that sounded interesting. I was leaning toward a career in government or politics, and, because of the war, this program might be the right thing for me to study.

Imagine my surprise when I arrived at Cornell in September 1966 and found it was in a rural, backwater town. I'd been expecting Rockefeller Center. That's how stupid I was, and how little I knew of geography in general and of the college I'd decided to attend in particular. I'd also arrived three days early and the dorms weren't open yet. A kindly janitor secreted me into my room early, after eliciting my promise to stay hidden for his sake more than mine.

My disappointment in the lack of skyscrapers and yellow cabs was short-lived. It was impossible not to fall in love with the majesty that was (and is) Cornell: the rolling hills of the Finger Lakes, the breathtaking views of the gorges that divided the campus, the waterfalls, and the stately gothic architecture. To my humble Warr Acres eyes, I'd landed in a little slice of heaven.

My ignorance of geography was only the first of many revelations that would pummel me during the first weeks of my matriculation. The food they served in the cafeterias was alien (smoked fish on sliced hard donuts—what was that all about?). The music my roommate and dorm-mates played was unsettling: James Brown, The Byrds, and Bob Dylan— a far cry from the Beach Boy vibe that filled my high school years. Everyone I encountered at Cornell—students, faculty, staff, and towns-people—spoke a regional language that was undecipherable to me. During the most casual conversations, I often felt as if I were a foreigner.

In Oklahoma I'd been a golden boy, a straight-A student, a wunderkind. At Cornell, I was a rube, a hick, an idiot. Even my roommate's *name* was intimidating—Dixon Spencer Kuhn III—not to mention his pedigree. His father was on the board of General Motors. Dixon had attended St. George's Academy in Providence, Rhode Island, where he played lacrosse (whatever that was), and he toured Europe every summer. He dressed in a preppy uniform of tattered khakis, penny loafers, no socks, and a frayed blue oxford shirt. I quickly learned it was chic to look poor, but not to be poor. He drove a new, cherry, red Mustang convertible. (Of course he did. What else would he drive?) Dixon was kind to me and, remarkably, not visibly condescending, but we were from different planets. He had no interest in my planet, and I couldn't comprehend his.

Classes were as intimidating as classmates. At my first Gov-101 lecture, I sat dumbfounded as Professor Clinton Rossiter led off with a discussion of Joseph McCarthy, HUAC, and Checkers. I noted with great alarm that everyone in the lecture hall—some two hundred students—seemed to know what he was talking about. Everyone, that is, but me. The only

McCarthy I was familiar with was a wooden dummy whose first name was Charlie. HUAC sounded like something one did to clear one's throat. And Checkers? What the hell was Checkers?

After class I scoured the assigned textbooks for any reference to the material the professor had covered in his lecture, but there was nothing. It was hopeless. I knew nothing. I could have raised my hand in class and asked a question, but then everyone in the lecture hall would have been witness to my ignorance. It was bad enough that I had to witness it myself.

For all my difficulties that first semester, it was the distance from my mother that troubled me the most. I knew she'd come to depend upon my frequent visits, and the times I took her out of the hospital for an afternoon or a weekend. To compensate I wrote her more often, and she responded in kind. Something about the miles between us fueled my determination that somehow, someday, I'd obtain her release. But I didn't know how. I was paralyzed with indecision. I knew her being at Central State Hospital was wrong, and had been wrong since the beginning, but for the time being, I accepted my impotence to do anything about it. I told myself there was nothing I could do from Ithaca, and I didn't know what I could have done had I stayed in Oklahoma. I tried, not very successfully, not to think about it.

That first semester I received two Ds: one in Economics (whatever economics is), and one in Government. It was a devastating blow to my star-powered ego, which had become habituated to success in Oklahoma. I returned to the Pahlkas' home for Christmas, feeling unsure of myself and my place at Cornell. I seriously considered alternatives. I considered... enlisting.

Harlan and Esther would have none of it. They weren't interested in my whining or excuses. They kicked me in the butt and sent me back to Ithaca. With their encouragement, I struggled on. In the spring I applied to, and was accepted into, the prestigious Cornell Summer Intern Program, and over spring break I took a bus to Washington, D.C., for interviews. I stayed at the YMCA near the White House because I could afford it (barely). I went to the Smithsonian and the Library of

Congress. I crisscrossed the National Mall, and from the steps of the Lincoln Memorial I tried to imagine where my mother might have walked and stood in August of 1963. I interviewed with staff from the offices of Oklahoma senators and congressman. Before I left D.C. that weekend, I'd secured a summer job interning with Senator Fred Harris. It was a plum job. I was on my way. This is what I wanted.

For a month, anyway. Then I changed my mind.

The more I thought about the job, and the trajectory it might place me on, the less alluring it was. The fact was I was struggling in government and economics, but at the same time, I was excelling in theatre. I was acing my theatre classes, had made good friends in the department among the students and the faculty, and had found a place in student productions. I learned of an opening for a box office job with the Cornell Summer Repertory and I applied for it. When I was hired, I notified Senator Harris he'd have to get another intern.

Was I an idiot? Who knows? Although I was handed a ticket to the greatest show on earth, the grand circus of Washington, D.C., I settled for a summer gig counting change in an obscure box office in upstate New York. I can't say I've ever regretted the decision, though I've wondered often about what might have happened differently if I'd taken that internship with the senator?

While my two semesters at Cornell were hell, my first summer in Ithaca was a paradise. I ran a good box office, which I found oddly satisfying, and I assisted the rep in countless ways with every available minute of my time: painting sets, making props, hanging lights. Sixteen hours a day weren't enough for me.

The theatre crew—actors, techies, et al.—was a fun, hard-working crew, and every night we played together. Late at night, down at Johnny's Big Red, we ate meatball sandwiches or heaping plates of lasagna, which we downed with tumblers of cheap Chianti and even cheaper Canadian beer. And many nights after work we'd feel our way along the narrow trail down into the gorge, where we'd skinny-dip below the waterfall under the twinkling stars and, if we were lucky, in the glow of a little moonlight.

Something else happened that summer that had a lasting impression on me. A program called Upward Bound had brought a group of high school students from Harlem to Cornell for a few weeks, and I was invited to teach an acting class for these kids. They were only two or three years younger than me, but honestly many of them seemed much older. I wasn't that good of a teacher, not having taught before, but I nonetheless connected with a few of them.

None of them would be going to college. They had neither the credentials nor the resources. This summer trip would likely be the sum of their college experience. None of them would ever be entitled to student deferments. They knew and I knew that most of them—the boys, anyway—would be bound for Vietnam. We talked about that. And it bothered me. It bothered me that I had something denied to them.

I knew what it was like to be poor. I never felt superior to any of these kids, who were more than my equal in intellect. Sure we were different, but the biggest difference was I had opportunity, and they didn't. And I had a student deferment.

I started my sophomore year still a virgin.

By October I was a bit more experienced. I had a girlfriend, Gretchen, a Chicagoan and a fellow traveler in the undergraduate theatre program. And I had a boyfriend, Steve, a student from Long Island in the architecture school, who introduced me to marijuana in his fairy book cottage on the edge of Cornell's famous Sapsucker Woods, the home of the Cornell Ornithological Laboratory.

The three of us fell into a pattern that year. On Friday nights Steve spent the night at Gretchen's Collegetown apartment. On Saturday night I stayed at Gretchen's. On Sunday night I spent the night with Steve in his cottage, falling asleep to the hooting of owls and awakening to the screams of peacocks. Ours was a very 1960s kind of arrangement, I suppose, but it satisfied the three of us. Everybody at Cornell was experimenting with something, and our experiment was not so unusual or noticeable.

Life was very good (even if, perhaps, a bit confusing). The cultural alienation of my freshman year was being replaced with something altogether different. I'd grown a new skin, and I was feeling comfortable in it.

That fall I maintained a full class schedule while working two jobs. I could have gotten by with one, thanks to the generosity of my Cornell grant, but my brother Jim was having a hard time paying for school, and I took the second job to help Jim.

If I hadn't received a full scholarship to Cornell, it's likely that our father would never have agreed to provide any support for Jim in college. He'd contributed nothing to Gordon's education, and he'd made it clear to Jim and me, when we were both still living at home, that he didn't believe in a college education and wasn't going to contribute a dime. I think my success shamed him into begrudgingly supporting Jim during his freshman year at OSU, but at the beginning of Jim's second year, Dad laid down an ultimatum. Jim was majoring in Speech and Communications, which my dad thought was ridiculous. He insisted that Jim major in business with a goal of becoming an insurance salesman like himself, otherwise he'd cut Jim off. Jim had no interest in business, and even less interest in insurance, so he decided to go it alone. I suspected at the time that Dad knew how Jim would respond, and that his ultimatum was a convenient way to stop funding Jim while laying the blame on him.

It'd been four years since I'd taken so much as a nickel from our father, and even then, it'd always been money I'd earned in the first place. I'd had nothing to do with my father since I left home, and in the intervening years he'd made no gesture to reconcile with me. Now it seemed he was about to lose the one remaining son with whom he still maintained a relationship.

I sent Jim some of my grant money, and made up the difference by working the second job. But there was another reason I needed extra cash: I wanted to do something special for my mother. I wasn't sure whether I could pull it off, but the first step was to save some money.

I worked as a projectionist for Cornell University Cinema, a cherry job with good pay, great benefits, and not a lot of sweat. On Friday and Saturday nights, I'd arrive an hour before the screening at Alice Statler Hall and rack up the film. Being a projectionist was easy work for me. After all, I worked as a projectionist in Warr Acres when I was eleven. I'd start the movie and then have nothing to do for the next twenty minutes until it was time to change reels. I'd watch the movie or do homework. Statler had a small private viewing room next to the projection booth, and often I'd invite friends as my guests. I could party as I worked and I often did. CU Cinema showed a lot of European flicks like Godard and Bergman, as well as spaghetti westerns and American classics, ranging from early silent movies to Casablanca. There were frequent showings of *Yellow Submarine*. When we showed the French classic *Jules and Jim*, I watched it with Steve and Gretchen. It affirmed the tenderness of our own affection for each other. It validated what we were doing with each other. It even made us feel a bit, well, Continental.

My second job was at CURW—Cornell United Religious Works—on a work-study grant, which meant it paid well. CURW inhabited a sprawling gothic building called Anabel Taylor Hall, a complex of offices, meeting rooms, an exquisite and intimate chapel, and a popular coffee house. It was my job to sort through various opportunities for students to volunteer in struggling parts of the world, for example, Appalachia, sub-Saharan Africa or Central America. I maintained information on placement opportunities and I advised interested students on completing applications. In one of the more absurdist moments of my life, I provided job counseling to the son of Dean Rusk. Rusk was LBJ's secretary of state and one of the several architects of the Vietnam War. His son understandably kept an low profile on campus. His visit to my office signaled to me that he perhaps didn't share his father's politics.

In January of my sophomore year, following a lengthy correspondence with doctors at Central State Hospital, I was able to obtain a two-week furlough for my mom. Using the money I'd carefully saved, I brought her to Ithaca, and I treated her to a side trip to Manhattan.

She stayed in my Collegetown apartment. She slept in my room while I slept on a mattress in my closet. She met my friends, toured the campus, attended lectures, and browsed the library. I was proud of my mother, and I was proud of my life at Cornell. It was a great pleasure to bring them together.

I've lived an extremely happy and fortunate life. Truly, it seems as if I've gone from one terrific set of circumstances to another, from one great adventure to another. Of all my good memories, my recollection of those two weeks rises above the rest. It was as if all the bad stuff that had happened to my family, to my mother and to me, fell away, and we were left with only the good. During her time at Cornell, she was treated royally by everyone she met, and she made good friends. We didn't know then that she'd need these friendships in later years.

In the middle of her visit, we boarded a bus to Manhattan, where we stayed with the family of one of my roommates. We walked for miles and miles, from one end of Manhattan to the other. We ate salted pretzels, visited the Empire State Building, took the Staten Island Ferry, rode the subway, explored the Village, saw two Broadway plays, strolled Fifth Avenue, lunched at the Plaza, and ambled our way through museums.

My mother had never tried to place the burden of her hospitalization on me. As we walked the streets of New York, I gave her the opportunity to do just that. I asked her questions. I gently prodded. I wanted to know from her point of view what had happened, how she came to be in Central State Hospital, what life was like there for her, how she survived it, and what hopes she had for someday getting out. I was no clearer about how I might obtain her release, but I was gaining a better understanding of her situation.

Rosalyn Gilchrist in Ithaca, January 1968

Still, I never asked the one question that remained unresolved. The fire. Was it an accident? Having never spoken directly about it, we didn't speak about it then or any time after. It was a forbidden conversation, forbidden not by edict but by the assent of everyone connected to it. It's hard to judge who or what was being protected by this assent. Perhaps initially it'd been Jim and me, not quite eleven years old, too young to hear that our mother may have tried to kill herself by horrible means. Or perhaps it was always our father, not willing or able to bear the shame of being married to a woman who hated her life so much she'd do such a thing. Or was it my mother whose feelings were being spared? Or was there really nothing to talk about? Was it really just an accident?

Would she have welcomed the chance to talk about it? Or would it have been impossible? And what about my brothers? Why haven't we had this conversation?

My relationship with my mother changed during this visit. Before, I'd been a son. I still was, but now I was also a friend, an equal. Without knowing it, perhaps I'd grown up.

But here's what I remember most about that trip: My mom and I are walking down a Manhattan street. My arm is around her, my hand on her shoulder. That's what I remember. My hand. Her shoulder. My mom.

In my peculiar childhood, I'd developed a habit of sticking my head into the sand and not paying close attention to things going on in the world around me, but in my sophomore year of college, there was no ignoring the rest of the planet. The entire world, it seemed, was wrenched with violence, protest, and change. There was no avoiding it. 1968 changed everyone and everything. It changed me.

On October 22, 1967, tens of thousands of protesters marched on the Pentagon, placing daisies in the rifle barrels of the soldiers who surrounded the defiant building. The protest included a sizeable Cornell delegation, although I'm sorry to say I wasn't among them. There had been national protest marches against the war before, but this one set in motion a cascade of marches.

Only one week later, a much smaller group of just four men and women garnered almost as much attention as the earlier gathering of thousands. These four war resisters upped the ante. In a nonviolent act infused with multiple layers of symbolism, they strolled into a draft board of-

Daniel Berrigan
Courtesy: Cornell University Library
Rare Books Manuscript Collection

fice in Baltimore in the middle of the workday, passing the curious stares of the bureaucrats who work there. They opened a file cabinet filled with the Selective Service files of potential draftees. Then they poured their own blood over these files and waited patiently, while praying, to be arrested.

One of the four was a Josephite priest, Father Phillip Berrigan. His brother Dan, a Jesuit, had an office directly across from mine at CURW.

Father Dan's office was a place of great intrigue to me. It was closet-sized—barely large enough for two small desks, two chairs, and one crammed bookcase. Nonetheless it was filled most days with visitors standing or sitting on the floor and spilling out into the hallway, visitors from all over the United States and the world. It also attracted a steady stream of Cornell students, but not—at least not yet—me. I remained firmly planted across the hall.

Dan was a priest, a poet, a philosopher, and a self-proclaimed radical. The walls of his office resembled the conversations that took place within them: a pastiche of color and slogan, a cornucopia of art and artifact that constantly morphed as visitors bestowed new items and walked away with old. In order to accommodate the new, it was necessary for Dan to dispense some of the old, and he did so cheerfully, granting this poster or that sketch to whoever admired it.

Dan was small and came and went with a battered leather backpack always slung over his shoulder and a wine-red beret perched on the side of his head. He listened more than he talked, but when he talked, in his quiet and measured tone, those around him listened closely. Although he scared the bejezus out of me, I observed him and the many comings and goings in and out of his office from a short distance.

After Phil Berrigan's arrest in Baltimore, the frenzy in Father Dan's office accelerated. Though he himself was not involved in the Baltimore action, Dan was cast in a new light among those who came to see him. Dan's normally open door was now occasionally closed as he engaged in quiet talks with some of his visitors.

One of the many who spent time in Dan's office was a Cornell student named Bruce Dancis, who burned his draft card that fall in a campus demonstration. Bruce wasn't the first in the nation to burn a draft card, but he was the first student from Cornell to do so. He also was the head of the nascent Cornell chapter of SDS—Students for a Democratic Society. Bruce's action took on a life of its own, spawning a series of demonstrations, rallies, and pamphleteering. Before long a few other Cornell students joined him in defying the draft.

1967 ended and 1968 began, bringing about more protests coast to coast. In January the famous baby physician Dr. Spock was indicted in New Haven for counseling young men to resist the draft, while across the Pacific the Viet Cong launched the Tet Offensive: a massive surprise attack against U.S. and South Vietnamese troops. Seventy thousand Viet Cong attacked over a hundred South Vietnam cities in what many later described as the turnaround moment of the war, not because it marked the defeat of American forces, but because it marked the moment when a majority of Americans started to oppose the war.

In February draft deferments for graduate students and most occupational deferments were eliminated, ratcheting up the stakes for tens of thousands of students and draft-age men. In March Robert F. Kennedy, anticipating his presidential run, spoke out with a powerful voice against the war, as American planes bombed Hue to rubble in twenty-five days of horror. Hundreds of villagers were massacred in a hamlet named My Lai. At Cornell the drumbeat call for action grew louder. Demonstrations and rallies went from monthly, to weekly, to daily.

On March 31, 1968, Lyndon Johnson announced he would neither seek nor accept the nomination of his party for a second term as president. The war, meanwhile, raged on.

April 4, 1968—one of the darkest days in American history. While in Memphis to march with striking sanitation workers, Martin Luther King was assassinated.

All hell broke loose as, frankly, it should have. Riots erupted in more than a hundred cities across the nation. In Ithaca classes were disrupted hourly by bomb threats, and at night firebombs destroyed several buildings on campus, including a small Gothic chapel just down the hall from my office at Anabel Taylor Hall. Everyone with authority pleaded for calm, while many people without did what they felt they had to.

Off in my own world of theatre, I was preparing for the annual spring concert of the Cornell Dance Company, for which I was both stage manager and lighting designer. A special guest was going to perform his original compositions for the dances—a little known maker of electronic instruments named Robert Moog, a musical hermit who lived in rural Trumansburg, not far from campus. He called them synthesizers (later known as Moog Synthesizers). No one had ever heard music quite like it. As I readied the University Theatre for the concert, it was temporarily in my charge.

On Saturday, April 6, my roommates woke me egregiously early because I had a phone call. I was needed at the theatre. Joan Baez, who happened to be on campus for a previously scheduled concert at Bailey Hall, had announced she was going to have an open discussion with students about the war and the draft that afternoon. For inexplicable reasons, the small three-hundred-seat theatre in the basement of the student union was announced as the venue. The theatre department wanted me to manage the arrangements.

After enlisting help from my roommates—Michael, Phillip, and Ric—I arrived at the union, Willard Straight Hall, in late morning to find everything already in chaos. Several hundred anxious students were assembled below the lower entrance to the Straight, word of the rally having been broadcast on the local radio station all morning. It quickly became clear that the small theatre would be insufficient for the crowd. Shortly after I gained entrance, staff from the radio station informed me that they planned on piping the rally to other rooms higher up in the Straight for overflow audiences.

After securing and cleaning the theatre, we waited for Joan Baez, who arrived unceremoniously around one p.m., wearing jeans, a blouse, and a denim jacket. She told me she didn't plan on using microphones (and I'm sure she didn't need to), but when I explained the plan to pipe the rally to the overflow rooms, she agreed to their use. She introduced me to her fiancé, a pleasant and strikingly handsome man named David Harris. I knew who he was.

While a graduate student at Stanford, David Harris had started something called the Resistance: an alliance of draft-age men united in their opposition to the draft. The Resistance was a different kind of organization—almost a non-organization. There was no leadership, no by-laws, no structure. There was no application form; membership was attained when one had resisted the draft by refusing induction. David himself had refused induction and was awaiting trial. Meanwhile, Joan was a member of a growing phalanx of women that had adopted the slogan: *Girls say 'yes' to boys who say 'no'!*

I signaled for Michael, Phillip, and Ric to open the doors, and the seats and the aisles were quickly filled, as well as every inch of space. Joan invited people to join her on stage, and when we knew we couldn't pack anyone else in, we closed the doors.

As rallies go, it was quiet. Very quiet. You'd have thought it was a church service. Joan Baez talked about the loss we all felt over the assassination of Dr. King. She talked about the war, racism, and King's position against the war and the draft. David talked about the Resistance. Why to resist. How to resist. What to expect if you do resist. He talked about prison.

In the front rows there was a small group of Cornell Resisters: Bruce Dancis, Jeff Dowd, Chip Marshall, and Tom Byers. It was the first time I'd paid attention to them. There was something about these Resisters and their friends: a tranquility, a certainty, a resolve. Draft resisters were portrayed in the mainstream media as rabid fanatics, but there seemed nothing fanatical about these four at all. They were placid, peaceful, content, and assured.

I was mesmerized by Tom Byers in particular. He was beatific in his bearing. Tom was small, with a short mane of blond curls and a smooth face that looked as if it'd never felt a razor. He sat next to a girl, whom I assumed was his girlfriend. They held hands, embraced, leaned against each other. Tom was the very image of a cherub, hardly the image of a fiery radical.

These students, these resisters, were at peace in their conflict. Whatever happened to them, they were okay with it. In the midst of the horror of the war, the assassination, and the riots, perhaps there was reason to hope.

After ninety minutes or so, the rally ended as quietly as it'd begun.

A number of people crowded around Joan and David, seeking an autograph or a moment of private conversation. They were gathered on the front of the stage, which was in actuality a twenty-foot wide elevator that could either descend to become an orchestra pit, or rise to stage level where it was then. I was sitting on the edge of the stage listening to the ongoing conversations when the stage suddenly started to descend with everyone on it—not a good situation. I jumped off the stage, and, in attempting to run backstage to stop whatever lame-brained offender had hit the switch, I tripped over a microphone cord. Something snapped in my foot. Whatever it was, it hurt like hell. I hobbled backstage to find a radio engineer firing the lift buttons. He wanted to retrieve his microphones and cables, and he thought raising and lowering the stage would be the best way to encourage people to get out of his way.

I turned the theatre keys over to my roommates. Joan and David gave me a ride to the hospital. At the emergency room David offered me an orange, which he pulled from the pocket of his surplus army jacket. I don't know why he offered me an orange. Perhaps he thought I looked like I need one. I took it most gratefully. I had no inkling that this simple act of generosity would impact me many times in the coming years. Oranges would become a lifeline in hard times to come.

I knew then what I was going to do. Perhaps I'd known it for a while. It'd been only a question of when. My mother's visit, the assassination of King, the riots, my encounter with Joan and David—these were the things that answered the question of when.

On Tuesday, April 10, I trudged on wooden crutches from my Collegetown Apartment to campus. I crossed the Collegetown Bridge and passed the Engineering Quad, the law school, CURW, and the Straight. I paused on the Arts Quad, between the facing statues of Ezra Cornell and Andrew Dickson White, to enjoy for a moment the promise of spring. I moved on to Lincoln Hall. I found myself alone in the Theatre Department library—nothing more than a small meeting room really, with a few books lining one wall. There, on a borrowed typewriter, I composed a letter to my draft board. A secretary in the adjoining office provided me with an envelope upon my request. I folded the letter and put it in the envelope. I enclosed my draft card. I sealed the envelope. I hobbled back across campus to the Straight, where I purchased a stamp. I mailed the letter.

I'd ignored the itch of conscience at the back of my skull until the weight of all the events of that winter and spring (culminating in King's assassination and Joan Baez's visit) forced me to take notice. Finally I felt compelled to do something, to add my small voice to all the others who were speaking out in various ways against the war and the draft.

For months I'd done nothing. There had been no cost involved, other than the cost of living with that itch. I'd liked the life I was living and I wanted more of it. I'd found my place at Cornell, academically and socially, and I'd fought against any reason to mess it up. I had a student deferment. I was safe, personally, at least for the time being. The war and the draft didn't really touch me. And yet they did. Hour by hour, day by day, month by month, they'd eaten away at me until I could bear them no longer.

And then there was that other thing: How could I be my mother's son and ignore the war and the draft? If her example had any meaning at all, didn't it mean that there may come a time for comfortable people to shed their comfort, to speak out, to take action, to seek change? If 1963 was her time, was this mine?

I had no appetite for grandstanding. I was no Bruce Dancis and had no wish to be. There was something about the burning of a draft card on the stage of a rally, symbolic though it was, that disturbed me. From a distance of many decades, I know it was disingenuous of me to think that what I did was any different, but at the time it felt different.

What I did was quiet. It was private. It was personal. I simply couldn't bear to carry that draft card around in my wallet anymore. A lot of students had stopped carrying their draft card—in itself an illegal act—but so long as they didn't boast about it there was no consequence. I could have thrown my draft card away and not said anything to anyone. But that wouldn't have solved the problem of my itch. I had to return the card to my Oklahoma draft board. I might be quiet, but I wouldn't be silent.

This is the text of the letter:

April 10, 1968

Selective Service System
Local Board No. 119
1010 Leonhardt Building
Oklahoma City, Oklahoma 73102

Gentlemen:

After long and careful consideration, I have found the carrying of a draft card on my person to be inconsistent with my religious, ethical and moral beliefs. For this reason, I am returning to you my draft card and my classification card.

I do this fully aware of the possible consequences and I do it in the hope that someday the war in Viet Nam and the process of conscription will no longer exist. I do this with a freeing of my conscience, satisfied that I can now, at one and the same time, be honest with myself and with this country that I love. I do this with a deep feeling of concern for the thousands of young men who are now facing the question of whether to support the draft or rebuke it; but more than this, with a concern for the young men who, having received a deferment, refuse to step outside of the comfort of accepted society; to discuss, inquire and finally to decide, whatever that decision may be. I submit that my act is one of love for humanity and not one of treason; a call for a better method for settling human affairs – non-violence – and not a call of cowardice; that my act is sincere.

I invoke the words of Henry David Thoreau, "If a man does not keep step with his companions, perhaps it is because he hears a different drummer. Let him step to the music which he hears, however measured or far away."

I regret that my country has given me no other choice. I cannot in good conscience serve or support the present military conscription. I can only choose to voice my opinion and return my draft card.

Sincerely,
Joe Gilchrist
34-119-48-391

There were different levels of classification for draft registrants, which at the time included every U.S. male citizen over the age of eighteen. Full-time students were classified II-S and were not eligible for the draft. IV-F meant you had a physical or mental deficiency that made you ineligible. I-A meant you were at the top of the list, and your number was about to be called. There were other classifications: for people too old to be drafted, for doctors or teachers, for men who were married with dependents, and others.

General Hershey, head of the Selective Service, made no secret of his hate for draft resisters. He railed against protesters of all stripes, but he especially hated draft resisters. In his mind we were all communists and pinkos and traitors. I imagine Hershey lying awake one night with a bad case of indigestion, watching some late night news footage of one anti-war demonstration or another, when he gets a brainstorm that results in a new classification of his own making.

Whatever his inspiration, he personally created the classification "I-A-

D" (the D stood for "Delinquent"), a punishment for anyone whose political views or behavior he didn't like, and especially for anyone who'd
burned or returned his draft card. In General Hershey's world, which
was the world of the draft, I-A-Ds were drafted first, even before the rest
of the I-A's.

In May I was reclassified I-A-D by my Oklahoma draft board, and I went
to the very top of the list. Now I had another decision to make.

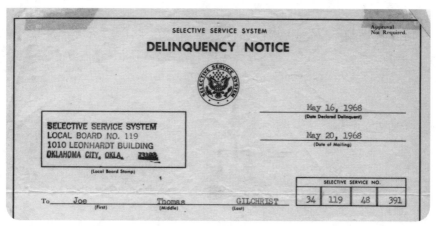

So far as I could learn, in discussions with Cornell draft counselors who
studied this sort of thing, the only draft resisters to date in Oklahoma
had been a handful of Quakers and Mennonites who'd applied for alternative service as conscientious objectors but had been denied. Their
arrests, trials, and imprisonment had gone unnoticed, perhaps because
they were considered too marginal by the mainstream press, or perhaps
because the young men themselves did not seek any publicity.

The law about conscientious objectors and the draft was clear. It granted
to members of the so-called "Peace Churches"—Mennonites, Church of
the Brethren, and Society of Friends (Quakers)—the option of performing alternative service instead of serving in the military. Unlike military
service, alternative service involved no pay and no benefits, and it usually meant working in some menial capacity in a hospital, most often a
mental hospital.

Oklahoma draft boards tended to ignore the law. They didn't believe in
it. Nor, apparently, did the judges who dispensed maximum five-year

sentences to these religious conscientious objectors without blinking an eye. If the federal bench in Oklahoma disliked religious COs this much, I imagined they'd like me even less. I had no doubt that if I went to trial in Oklahoma, I'd receive a five-year prison sentence, and that scared me half to death.

Cornell draft counselors advised me to have my induction transferred to either Syracuse or Rochester. This was *pro forma*. It happened all the time. Draftees were routinely inducted where they happened to be living at the time they were inducted, and not where they originally registered for the draft, and that made Upstate New York the likely induction venue for me. Besides, the Oklahoma draft board would probably be glad to pawn me off on another jurisdiction.

As an added benefit, I was nearly guaranteed a more lenient sentence in Rochester or Syracuse than I'd surely get in Oklahoma. Federal judges in Upstate New York had reputations for going easy in draft cases. A resister in Syracuse had recently received a two-year sentence, and one in Rochester had received probation with no jail time. If I transferred my induction to Upstate New York, in all likelihood I'd get similar treatment.

But it wasn't that simple. The Upstate New York region had already seen a fair number of draft resisters, and there was robust anti-war activity throughout the area, from Buffalo to Albany to Manhattan. All of the campuses were alive with anti-war protests, as were many churches and high schools.

But in Oklahoma, nothing was happening. Absolutely, positively, nothing. My twin brother, Jim, reported to me from Oklahoma State University in Stillwater that on his campus there were neither groups nor individuals speaking out against the war. The same seemed to be true for Oklahoma University in Norman and for Oklahoma City University. The rancor about the war and the draft that was present on both coasts and in the upper Midwest was totally missing in the central plains. Oklahoma boys were dying in Vietnam at the same rate as boys from other states, but to Oklahomans that was simply their patriotic duty. It was occasion for pride, not protest.

As ridiculous as it sounds, in high school I'd been something of a minor celebrity in Oklahoma. I was especially well known in our suburb, but also in greater Oklahoma City, and even in some more remote parts of the state, mostly due to my American Legion Oratory eminence. Oklahoma took its American Legion Oratory contest very seriously. Perhaps not as seriously as its Miss Oklahoma Pageant, but you get the idea. Football, patriotism, and beauty queens were the three legs of the dust-bowl stool that was Oklahoma.

Oklahoma was one of the newest states, barely fifty years old. Oklahoma City, its largest town and capitol, boasted a population of only three hundred thousand in the entire metropolitan area at the time. I knew if I went back to Oklahoma, if I refused induction there and went to trial, it'd make a lot of noise. I could perhaps encourage the formation of an Oklahoma anti-war movement, small though it might ultimately become. I could give voice to people who were looking for a voice.

I'd also confuse the good people of Oklahoma. I had no doubt their image of draft resisters was profane, long-haired, pot-smoking, pinko commies—the same image that gave General Hershey indigestion.

Okay, I smoked a little pot, but I had short hair, I wasn't a communist, and I was otherwise respectable. I was comfortable in a suit and tie, and reasonably well spoken. I was an Oklahoma golden boy, full of apple pie, Jesus, and sunshine. In Oklahoma, it might be a bit harder to dismiss me than to dismiss someone else who spoke out against the war. Of course, there was that other thing. If I stood trial in Oklahoma, I'd most certainly be put away for five years.

Now perhaps would be a good time to step back from the narrative of events to share with you my personal philosophy and the reasoning that informed my actions.

That winter and spring of 1968, when I began to pull my head out of the sand, I thought long and hard about war and its justness or lack thereof. I was drawn to pacifists who objected to all wars, any war, in any form for any reason. But I couldn't get past the argument that some wars might be necessary.

In my understanding of history, World War II was such a war. I believed I'd have fought in World War II (as much as anyone can know what he might have done in a hypothetical situation). But Vietnam was different. It was my belief that in WWII the Nazis were the aggressors and the Americans the defenders, and that the atrocities committed by the Nazis were so extreme that an armed response was morally justified, even morally mandated. I wasn't comfortable with what I considered American overkill—the firebombing of Dresden, the annihilation of Hiroshima and Nagasaki. But the invasion of Normandy made sense to me, as did the liberation of Europe and the freeing of the concentration camps.

Vietnam was different. In Vietnam we were the invaders, the aggressors, inserting ourselves into what was essentially a civil war between the North and South Vietnamese. In the spring of 1968 I read a history of Vietnam written by two Cornell professors, and I attended their lectures on the history of the war. Vietnam had been torn apart for centuries by invading countries: China, Japan, France, and now the United States. We were the bad guys, I now thought, and my country wanted me to be one of the bad guys.

As a good Oklahoman who'd grown up saying the Pledge of Allegiance at the start of every school day, who knew by heart the preambles to the Constitution and the Declaration of Independence, and most of the Bill of Rights, this blew my mind. I felt betrayed. I could see clearly that the emperor wore no clothes, and it pained me so many people really didn't notice, especially in conservative states like Oklahoma. Maybe my voice was needed to open their eyes. Maybe that would be all that was needed.

I was informed by the example of Dietrich Bonhoeffer and other Germans who didn't march in step with their fellow countrymen but instead worked to stop the Nazi atrocities. I hoped that had I been alive then, and German, I'd have had the courage to be a Bonhoeffer, that I wouldn't have followed orders.

Often I've been asked why I didn't apply for CO status, and in part it's because I couldn't. I wasn't a CO by any definition the Selective Service would acknowledge. The Selective Service Act provided for conscientious objectors, but it reserved the status for pacifists who objected to all wars. There was no acknowledgement or recognition of *selective* conscientious objection.

Even if I'd been a true pacifist, I don't think I'd have applied for CO status. After all, I already had a II-S status as a student and I threw it away of my own volition. At Cornell, I'd been diagnosed with a heart murmur, which could have exempted me from the draft had I chosen to call attention to it. And I could have played, as many did, the homosexual card. But in the end, accepting any draft status that continued my deferment meant a level of cooperation with the Selective Service, which had become untenable to me. Any deferment was just a way of hiding from the problem, and the problem was the bureaucracy that was systematically recruiting and killing tens of thousands of my fellow young Americans in the service of an unjust war.

To meet its quotas the Selective Service targeted those young men who were vulnerable and less fortunate. Anyone with money and smarts could stay in school until he was too old for the draft (like Bill Clinton). Anyone from a family with connections could parlay those connections into a safe stint in the National Guard (like George W. Bush). Anyone out of options could feign a disability, or claim to be a homosexual. But the poor kids, the inner city kids, the disenfranchised—kids like the ones I'd taught in the Cornell Upward Bound program—those kids had no options. They were fodder for war. And they were dying. The cynical disregard for human life embodied in the very structure of the Selective Service made it unpalatable to me. There was no way I could have continued to cooperate with it.

That winter and spring, I immersed myself in writings on civil disobedience, starting with Thoreau's "On the Duty of Civil Disobedience," and King's "Letter from Birmingham Jail." A series of essays by Albert Camus, *Neither Victim Nor Executioner*, mysteriously resonated the most with me. Perhaps it was because I'd been reading this tract the week of King's assassination. Forty years later, I still have the original, dog-eared copy that instructed me then—one of only a handful of items I still possess from that time.

And so it was. In April I returned my draft card. In May I was reclassified as delinquent. In June I was ordered to report for induction in Oklahoma and given a date in July for my appearance. Caught on a train that had left the station, I was fast losing any hope of effecting my mother's release from Central State Hospital. I certainly wouldn't be able to do anything from a jail cell, and I sure as hell was going to jail.

Holy Shit. What had I gotten myself into?

I needed help. And help arrived in the form of many people.

It arrived in the form of Suzanne Shipe and Ron Filewich, two Cornell undergraduates who befriended me and helped me plan a campaign of sorts to launch a peace effort in Oklahoma. In a ramshackle, off-campus space on Stewart Avenue founded by a graduate student, Jack Goldman, and shared by various peace constituencies, loaded with used equipment and pilfered supplies, and aptly named "The Office," they conducted research, drafted press releases, stuffed envelopes, raised money, and calmed my fears.

Help arrived in the form of Joan Sullivan, another Cornell student who was a senior in the theatre department. Later she'd disclose an unfortunate crush on me, but at the time she provided resources and an open heart, both of which I needed. None of these three—Suzanne, Ron or Joan—had previously been involved in anti-war activities of any kind. They were simply friends who offered a helping hand.

Help also arrived in the form of Daniel Berrigan, S.J., poet, priest, and soon-to-be fellow traveler in civil disobedience.

On May 9 Dan, his brother Phil, and seven others walked into a draft board in Catonsville, Maryland. Under the alarmed eyes of the disbelieving clerks, they emptied draft records from a file cabinet and dumped them into metal wastebaskets. These they carried to the parking lot, where they doused them with homemade napalm, concocted from a recipe in an Army manual. As the press snapped photos, they joined hands around the burning draft files, a gesture intended to contrast with the burning of children by American napalm in Vietnam. The action of this group, who called themselves the Catonsville Nine, made big news. The Berrigan brothers, as they were now referred to in the media, were becoming an annoying thorn in the side of the American war effort.

That spring Dan became my confidant, my counselor, and my friend. On April 11, the day after I put my draft card in the mail and a month before Dan's Catonsville action, I stopped by Dan's office for a chat. I hadn't told anyone yet what I'd done, and I was anxious to get it off my chest. Dan's office was crowded as usual with other visitors, and I sat quietly on the floor, lost in my own thoughts. Dan must have noticed my need, for as he closed up his office he asked me if I'd like to join him for dinner. He was making a simple pasta, he said. His apartment, a single room with a very modest kitchen, was just across the gorge.

It was the first of many meals I ate with Dan. We talked at first of other things: his family, mine, his brother Jerry in Syracuse, his mother, his nephews, his poetry, and eventually the war. When we talked about my coming resistance, he listened as I voiced my hopes and my fears. To my hopes he offered caution; to my fears, solace and understanding. He too had hopes, but they were tempered with a mature understanding that change would not be easy, ending the war would not be easy, changing minds would not be easy, and dismantling the war machine would not be easy. He too had fears.

On my behalf he wrote three letters that helped pave the way for my up-coming Oklahoma odyssey. One was to Bishop Reed, head of the Okla-homa Diocese. Dan was acquainted, though not well, with Bishop Reed, and knew him to be a man of peace and a forward thinker in the church. He asked Bishop Reed to welcome me to Oklahoma and to assist me in my work there. The second letter was to Father Bill Nerin, who headed a renegade Catholic church called the Community of John XXIII. This small church community in Oklahoma City had no church building, opting to spend their money on social causes rather than mortar. They hadn't to date been vocal or active against the war. The third was to a

Father William Kelly, a priest serving at St. John's Student Center on the campus of Oklahoma State University. I didn't know it then, but Bill Kelly was to become my rock.

Douglas Dowd, an economics professor at Cornell, also became my friend. Doug had trained at Tinker Air Force Base in Oklahoma City before flying a bomber in the Pacific theatre in World War II. He and I shared the philosophy of just and unjust wars, although his philosophy came from first-hand experience and mine did not. Doug's son, Jeff (who would later be tried in Seattle as one of the Seattle Seven before going on to become a Hollywood producer and the inspiration for the movie *The Big Lebowski* starring Jeff Bridges), was also a Cornell draft resister. Jeff Dowd and I never struck up a close relationship, probably because Jeff was a leader of Cornell's SDS, whose rhetoric I found off-putting. But Doug and I became close. As I prepared for my trip to Oklahoma, I dined with Doug and his wife at his modest home on Cayuga Lake several times a week.

Later there would be those (including the publisher of the *Daily Oklahoman*) who claimed I was brainwashed by "communist mentors in the east"(meaning, I suppose, Doug and Dan, neither of whom were communist), but that wasn't the case. Before I returned my draft card, I'd not even had a conversation with Doug, Dan, or any of the Cornell resisters. My resistance was based not on brainwashing but on my family history, my core set of beliefs, my own research into the war in Vietnam, and my long-held affinity for the philosophy of civil disobedience. If I had mentors, it was after, not before, I'd made up my mind to resist, and their mentoring took the form of advising me how to maximize the effectiveness of a course I'd already chosen.

There was one other person who helped, someone who was in a remarkable position to provide assistance. I didn't know Paul Rahe well. He was in the prestigious "fud" program, the six-year Ph.D. program that accepted only a score or so elite students a year. I'd met him through another fud, who was a theatre major and a friend of mine. Paul's interest was journalism, and he'd taken a summer job writing for, of all things, an Oklahoma City newspaper, *The Oklahoma Journal*. The Journal was a new publication, a rival to E.K. Gaylord's staunchly conservative *Daily*

Oklahoman and *Oklahoma City Times*, which had enjoyed a decades-long monopoly. Gaylord also owned the state's most popular radio and television stations.

In some of his writing, Paul put words in my mouth—words I never spoke. But I didn't mind. They were always good words. I had the impression Paul was living out his own resistance vicariously through me. Unable or unwilling to do it himself, he channeled me in his writing. Whatever he was doing, I appreciated it. He was a huge help.

Paul said he wanted to break the story of my resistance. And boy, did he ever. A week before I was scheduled to return to Oklahoma, the *Journal's* Sunday headlines blasted the news.

Paul nailed it. He understood everything I was trying to do. A native of Oklahoma, he also understood the culture of the state and knew how to write articles that would get under the thick patriotic skin of its denizens. He wrote honestly, he backed up his articles with facts and more facts, and he churned out a copious amount of newsprint. Surprisingly, he convinced his editors to give him the front page, again and again.

A week after his first story broke, Paul wrote that Cornell Economics Professor Douglas Dowd was going to join me in Oklahoma in a series of speeches surrounding my act of resistance. He highlighted Doug's Oklahoma connection—his bomber pilot training at Tinker Air

Force Base in Oklahoma City—and he wrote that not only was Doug a decorated WWII veteran, but that he was currently a candidate for vice president of the United States on the Peace & Freedom Party ticket. His running mate was Eldridge Cleaver, author of *Soul On Ice*, former Soledad inmate, and outspoken Black Panther.

Paul's reporting was so in-your-face that the *Daily Oklahoman* had no choice but to respond with its own spin regarding my resistance. The *Daily Oklahoman* article was a far cry from the reasoned and supportive articles written by Paul. Paul had highlighted my background, my credentials as a student and a scholar, and as an American Legion orator. Paul had quoted my letter to my draft board. Paul had enumerated my arguments against the war and the draft. Paul had emphasized Doug's robust credentials as a war veteran.

E.K. Gaylord's paper took a very different tack. They weren't interested in any statement or quote from me, in any justification I might have given for my resistance. They certainly weren't going to provide ink for any arguments against the war or the draft, from me or anyone. Gaylord's papers had one aim in their reporting, and that was to discredit me, to turn me into a monster.

They knew just where to go to find someone to speak ill of me: the American Legion.

At least the *Daily Oklahoman* called me a draft "resister" in-

stead of a draft "evader." The term "draft evader" was in wide use then by anyone who wanted to disparage young men who were avoiding the draft by any means: falsifying a disability to obtain a IV-F, by pretending to be a conscientious objector, by leaving the country for Canada or Sweden, or by taking a stint in the National Guard expressly to avoid service in the Army. Those few hundreds of us, soon to become thousands, who were staying home and facing the music, who were refusing induction and going to prison, preferred another term altogether. We weren't "evading" anything, but we sure as hell were "resisting" it. We weren't running for cover. We were standing in front of a speeding train.

Throughout my Oklahoma ordeal, all of the print and broadcast media continued to refer to me as a draft "resister," and I'm confident that wouldn't have happened had Paul not set the ball rolling. Perhaps it was a small thing. Just one simple word instead of another. But words have meaning, and mine was a war of words.

On Monday, July 22, 1968, Doug Dowd and I touched down at Will Rogers Airport. We proceeded immediately to a press conference that was convening in an airport meeting room and was arranged by *Oklahoma Journal* reporter Paul Rahe. I stood for the first time under the glare of TV lights and photographers' flash bulbs. Doug and I each read short prepared statements, and then we took a few questions. The attending newsmen were all courteous. The *Daily Oklahoman* hadn't sent anyone, of course. Like I said, they had no interest in what I had to say.

Nonetheless, television and radio stations across Oklahoma ran the story, and they broadcasted notices of our scheduled appearances that afternoon at the Unitarian Church in Oklahoma City and that night in the student union at Oklahoma University.

On the morning of Tuesday, July 23, Doug flew back to Ithaca and I continued on my own. My first stop was the Army Induction Center. The day I'd been simultaneously anticipating and dreading with all my heart had arrived.

A few supporters with handmade signs circled slowly in front of the induction center after I went inside. Among them was my twin brother, Jim, a student at OSU. I hadn't been sure whether he'd show up or not. I'd written to him and talked to him a couple of times by phone, but he'd been hesitant and noncommittal. He'd been battling it out with himself what he should do. He wasn't sure of his own feelings about the war; at the same time he was reasonably certain what our father's reaction would be if Jim showed me any support. The decision to lend his presence and his support couldn't have been easy for Jim.

By this time in her incarceration at Central State Hospital, my mother could sign herself out for brief furloughs, and she'd done so that morning so she could be with me and demonstrate her support for my act of resistance.

Until I saw her there that morning, I hadn't realized how important her support was to me. Unspoken was the understanding that by doing this, we were foregoing any immediate possibility of my assisting her with her own quest for release. She had never once, in all these years, specifically entreated me to help secure her freedom, and I had never explicitly offered to do so; but like the elephant in the room, the compulsion and the need to do so were always present when we were together.

Rather than dwell on her own needs, she was there for me, her son. And I knew she was there for a second reason: After her own period of study she now also opposed the war and the draft, and her presence was her own way of making a stand. In a way this was her chance to continue the work she'd started with the sit-ins and demonstrations with the NAACP. Her opposition to the war and the draft was a part of the same impulse. My actions had given her voice new life. In the coming months, she'd have many opportunities to stand beside me and occasionally speak out, and she never wavered.

I was so proud of her. And so grateful.

I suppose that when I'd first made my decision to resist, on that fateful morning in April when I mailed my draft card back to my draft board, I'd taken my mom's eventual support for granted. I'd been confident that if I provided her with sufficient information about the war, the draft, and my own feelings about both, then she'd come to share my conclusions, and perhaps even a bit of my fervor. It could have turned out differently. She might have disagreed with me, or she might have agreed with my dissent against the war but opposed what I was doing for fear of how it'd affect my future. My impulse to resist could have created a rift between us. Of the other resisters I'd met, very few had any kind of support from their families. Yet here she was, willing to make her own stand alongside me.

Back in April I'd initiated a steady correspondence with my mother. I wanted her to understand what I was doing and why. She initially reacted with some dismay (and a substantial fear for her son's welfare), but eventually I won her unwavering support. I sent her the full text of the speech in which Martin Luther King proclaimed his opposition to the war and the draft, a speech he'd made only a few months before I returned my draft card. King's speech was the tipping point in my mother's examination of the war. Her faith in King convinced her. If he'd taken this unpopular stand at the risk of harming everything else he fought for, she felt there had to be something to it.

She was a dedicated student. She read every book, every tract, and every newspaper clipping I sent her about the war and the draft, and she sent me various articles and clippings she'd discovered herself. By the time I appeared at the induction station, she was quite knowledgeable about the war, and she was vehemently anti-war and anti-draft.

She'd awakened early and walked to the Norman bus station, where she took a bus to downtown Oklahoma City. From there it was only a few blocks to the induction station. Her picture in the paper that day is one of only three I possess of her taken after the fire. It's a grainy and aged clipping now, but her scars are clearly visible.

In the photo she's wearing men's sunglasses. Dr. Anderson hadn't been able to completely reconstruct her eyelids, so her eyes never entirely closed. Because of this, her eyes had become extremely sensitive to light and dust, and she wore oversized sunglasses almost everywhere she went, indoors and out. She frequently moistened her eyes with drops and constantly dabbed at them beneath the sunglasses with tissues, which she always kept handy.

The scars around her neck were tight and hard and acted like a neck brace. In order to turn her head, she had to turn her whole body. Her arms were heavily scarred, as is also evident in the photo. Her left hand was permanently fixed in an open position, and her right hand in a position half closed. She had only the remnants of thumbs on either hand. Still, with these broken and crippled hands, she'd learned how to do almost anything people do with normal hands.

Perhaps what made me the most proud of her was her fearlessness. I don't know where it came from, how she attained

Mrs. Rosalyn Gilchrist, mother of draft resister Joe Thomas Gilchrist, waits outside induction station with his twin brother, Jim. (Times Staff Photo by George Tapscott.)

it, or how she maintained it for so long. But she'd become comfortable going out in public, comfortable with the unavoidable stares, the questioning looks, the mothers pulling their children back and quieting them when they asked questions or cried. At some point my mother had decided not to hide. "I am who I am," she seemed to proclaim to the world—a message that would have greater and greater importance to me in later years. "I don't apologize for it. I don't even have to explain it. I am who I am."

Her comfort ultimately made other people comfortable with her disfigurement as well. After a while it wasn't what one noticed about my mother. Instead, one noticed her wit, her laughter, and her energy. She liked to stay busy. She was a voracious reader. She had opinions. She valued friendship. She liked to be helpful. That's what people noticed.

Having her with me on the morning of my resistance was fantastic.

While the support of my mother and my brother meant a great deal to me, it also meant something to my father, who by this time had retired and moved with our stepmother to a new subdivision in rural Enid, about ninety miles northwest of Oklahoma City. Dad took Jim's support of me as an excuse to disown him one more time, which also meant stopping the trickle of money he sent Jim to support his college educa-tion. He was especially angry about Jim's photo in the paper standing next to our mother. This pattern of Dad disowning and reconciling with his one remaining faithful son, Jim, is one that would continue for many years.

Upon arrival at the induction station, I went through all the preliminary steps of induction. I stood in lines, I filled out forms, I stood in more lines. I waited. A doctor asked me if I was homosexual and I said no, more or less truthfully. I'd experimented my sophomore year with a man and a woman and quite liked both. I assumed I'd eventually settle down to just one woman. I very much wanted to have a family of my own someday, with kids of my own. At any rate, I thought the question irrelevant. I wasn't about to let my answer to this question interfere with my act of civil disobedience.

I suppose it'd have been easy for me to say yes to the doctor's question, and that would have been the end of it. I knew kids at Cornell who had done this—some honestly, some not. Like them I could have gotten a medical deferment and consequently I'd never have been bothered by the draft again. But I didn't want to hide behind a medical deferment any more than I wanted to hide behind a student deferment, or flee to Canada. At the root of my being, I thought the draft itself was morally abhorrent. Playing the queer card to get out of it was not an option for me.

When the time came, I stripped down to my skivvies and was cursorily checked for a hernia by a bored-out-of-his-mind physician, who'd seen way too many boys with pimply faces. I was asked about inoculations and diseases, sexually transmitted and otherwise. I was asked if I were a member of the communist party, to which I replied, "No."

Just before the final step, the induction itself, I was handed what they said was a loyalty oath. I read it over, and knew immediately I'd be un-able to sign it. The wording of the oath demanded exactly the kind of blind, unquestioning obedience to authority I was rebelling against. I found myself in a quandary. I was anxious to get through this business of refusing induction. I wasn't interested in any kind of delay. No one would know if I signed this piece of paper or not, except me, so the easiest thing would have been just to sign it and move along. But I couldn't.

It hadn't been that long since America had participated in the Nuremburg Trials, where the world held good German soldiers accountable for "just following orders." The lesson of Nuremburg was that military orders don't discharge the individual from the duty to perform according to his own conscience. This oath in front of me said the opposite. It said that by signing, I agreed to forfeit my own conscience and follow whatever orders I was given. I couldn't sign it.

My refusal to sign the oath totally confused the staff at the induction center. This had never happened before, at least not at this Oklahoma induction station. They didn't know what do. They didn't know whether they could pass me on to the next step, the induction itself. So they sent me away.

The reporters, who'd been poised to write the story of my refusing induction, had to write a different story that night. Oddly, the official word out of the induction center was simply that my processing was delayed for "administrative reasons." That was good enough for me. I knew it'd do me no good in the eyes of my fellow Oklahomans if they learned the "administrative reason" was my failure to sign something labeled a loyalty oath. That would be more fodder for Gaylord, just another reason to round up some Legionnaires for a good bout of Joe Gilchrist bashing. So I kept my mouth shut and hoped it never made it into the press. It never did.

After I left the induction station, I had lunch with Jim and my mom and a few supporters. Then Jim went back to OSU. Mom went back to Norman. That evening I led an informal discussion on the war at the En Rapport coffeehouse in Oklahoma City. There I met an attractive firebrand named Mary Ann Hodges. Mary Ann was a few years older than me, tall and blond, a recent OU graduate who worked as a secretary in a state office and had an apartment on the northeast side of town with a roommate, who was another young professional woman. She offered help: her car, a place to stay, but most of all, her shoulder to lean on. The immediate problem of a place to sleep was solved.

The next day, July 24, I was scheduled to speak at the OSU campus in Stillwater. Thanks to the paranoia of the Oklahoma State Board of Regents, the Stillwater event was the most successful of the four events scheduled these first two days. The week before my announced visit to OSU, the Regents voted to ban me from the campus. Not only was I not allowed to speak in a classroom, I wasn't even allowed to walk on OSU sidewalks and streets. I was told I'd be arrested on sight. My photo was distributed to campus police. This ban on my speaking was most certainly not constitutional, but fighting it was not a skirmish I was equipped to undertake. I had enough legal battles to juggle.

So the rally was moved to St. John's. St. John's wasn't on campus; it was on private property just blocks from the main quadrangle of OSU and within easy walking distance of student housing. The Regents had no authority there.

The Board of Regents actually did me a favor. By marginalizing me, they publicized me and made me bigger than life. Without the Regents' action, it's entirely possible the crowd that first night would have been much smaller. The Regents' action prompted a backlash, and St. John's was packed to the gills. The curious filled the pews, choked the aisles, and spilled out the doors. Stillwater, it seemed, was hungry for someone to speak out against the war.

Out of that first meeting came a new organization of students, faculty, and townspeople opposing the Vietnam War and the draft. They called themselves simply "The Coalition for Peace." They started a newsletter. They organized events and rallies and marches. Some Oklahomans, it seemed, found their voices.

Father Kelly (the priest to whom Daniel Berrigan had written on my behalf) was not at that first Stillwater rally. He was traveling in Europe and would be back the following week. Instead I was welcomed at St. John's by Ray Repp.

Ray was a well-known composer of religious folk music, which had begun to insert itself into Catholic Masses in America. It would ultimately
modernize the music performed and sung in the majority of Catholic
and Protestant churches. The Pope had only recently allowed Mass to be
said in English instead of Latin, and now Ray and a few others like him
had gone a step further by introducing contemporary folk music into
the ritual of the Mass. Many older Catholics couldn't stand the changes—either the English-language Mass or the jarring folk music. A lot of
younger Catholics loved it. Not too surprisingly, Ray had run into difficulty from the clergy in his conservative home diocese in St. Louis, and
had subsequently been offered a place to live and work for the church by
Oklahoma's Bishop Reed, who was more in tune, so to speak, with the
changes Ray was introducing.

I arranged with Ray that I'd come back to St. John's the following week
after Bill Kelly had returned from Europe.

Before my arrival in Oklahoma that summer in 1968, there had been no
organized anti-war movement anywhere in the state. With astonishing
speed, soon there was clearly the beginning of a movement. As I continued my work through the summer and into the fall, mostly in Stillwater
and Oklahoma City, I found myself surrounded by a growing allegiance
of new friends. And yet something was missing.

I'd grown up in a suburb of Oklahoma City, where I'd lived for twelve
years and made many good friends. Perhaps I shouldn't have been surprised that those friends were absent from all of the rallies or organizing
events, but I was nonetheless disappointed. I'd hoped that of the more
than six hundred who were in my graduating class, many of whom I
called friend, there might be a few people who felt as I did about the
war, or were fond enough of me personally to show up, or were at least
curious enough to listen to what I had to say. If not a classmate, maybe
someone else: one teacher, one person from my church, one neighbor—
anyone from my past.

As it happened, there was one. Just one. In my junior year in high school, Tim Kline had played my dying brother in *Look Homeward, Angel*, the play that led to my father raising his belt one last time and my walking out his door forever. Tim had also been a debater, and he and I had briefly been teammates. Tim was a year younger than me, and was now a sophomore at Oklahoma University. In my first and second appearances speaking out against the war in Oklahoma—at the Unitarian Church and at the OU Student Union—Tim's was the only familiar face, and it was good, very good, to see him there. He told me he was against the war, but he wasn't sure how he felt about what I was doing. He also told me his father was David Kline, the U.S. Attorney whom I'd soon face in court as my prosecutor. As odd as it must sound, there was something comforting to me about knowing this. I didn't expect any less aggressive a prosecution, but knowing Tim made me confident that buried somewhere in the prosecution might reside a morsel of sympathy. While this eased my way, it made for a very rough time for Tim.

I had a number of things on my to-do list that week. At the top of the list was my need for a defense attorney. My search didn't go well.

Since I had no money, I needed volunteer legal counsel. It's not likely the search would have gone any better had I been able to pay. Before leaving Ithaca, I'd contacted the Oklahoma ACLU and summarily was turned down by them. They wouldn't even schedule an appointment for me to discuss my case. Draft resisters weren't on their radar. I got the same rebuff from the Oklahoma branch of the National Lawyers Guild.

In desperation I contacted the New York ACLU. One of their attorneys, Melvin Wulf, agreed to represent me if I couldn't find anyone local, but he pointed out something I already knew: that a New York ACLU lawyer arguing on my behalf in an Oklahoma federal court might not be well received by the court, by the press, or by anyone. They sent me a list of potential lawyers in Oklahoma who might be sympathetic, based on pro bono cases they'd taken in the past, and one by one they also turned me down.

Being against the war in Oklahoma wasn't only a novelty, it was anathema. No attorney wanted to touch my case. No one was willing to associate themselves with me. The refusal of any lawyer in Oklahoma to represent me was a problem that would haunt me for months.

Only a couple of days had passed since I'd been turned away from the induction center when the notice arrived for me to report again. It was sent to me by registered mail delivered to Mary Ann Hodge's apartment. The notice was delivered by hand at first light, and I had to be at the induction center later that same morning.

By this time I'd garnered enough support that even on short notice a large group of supporters—twenty or so—marched outside while I did my business inside. Mary Ann and her roommate were there. Some clergy were there, including Bill Byerly, of the Oklahoma City Society of Friends, and Father Nerin from the Community of John XXIII.

Finally, inside the induction center, the moment came. I stood in a line with about thirty other boys to my side, all of us facing the inducting officer. All my fellow inductees were black or Native American, except for a couple of farm kids. Most were a couple of years younger than me, freshly eighteen, and none of them had been blessed with the opportunity to go to college. I was sorely aware of my privilege. One by one our names were read. We were told to step forward to accept induction into the United States Army. Everyone stepped forward. Except me. I stayed where I was.

I don't know what my fellow inductees felt about what I did. Surely they saw it. They had to have known that one among them had refused to step forward. But none of them reacted in any way. They neither looked at me or said anything.

The induction staff were similarly mute. I suspected the staff shared the same opinion of me as the now oft-quoted Legionnaires who'd appeared on Gaylord's television stations and in his newspapers. But, professionally, they kept their mouths shut and their eyes averted, and they focused on the business at hand.

I don't think I ever felt stronger in my life than I felt at that moment—the moment I simply stood still, the moment I didn't step forward. I've never felt more at peace, more confident, more assured. I was facing a certain prison sentence, and soon. But I'd made the decision that I wasn't going to be a "good soldier." I wasn't going to simply follow orders. And that knowledge gave me great joy.

This war was horribly wrong. This draft, which targeted the most vulnerable young men and exempted the favored, was wrong. The living proof of that was the assembly of young men standing beside me in the induction line. And to all of it I said, "No."

I wasn't arrested immediately. I was told to go home, and that the U.S. Attorney would be in touch when my indictment was handed down.

On Sunday, July 28, my business in Oklahoma being completed, I returned to Ithaca. I spent the next week moving out of my apartment, disposing of almost everything I owned (most of which, except for my vaunted Bob Dylan collection, I didn't value), and saying goodbye to friends. I also spent precious hours idling on the Arts Quad, swimming off Doug Dowd's pier on Lake Cayuga, and hiking the Ithaca gorges.

Ron Filewich, who'd helped me plan my Oklahoma appearances, introduced me to a friend of his named Burton Weiss. Burton and Ron were both friends with the popular author Paul Goodman, best known for the book *Growing Up Absurd*. The *New York Review of Books* had asked Goodman to write a review of contemporary Cuban literature. Goodman had found it impossible to lay his hands on any Cuban literature inside the United States, but he knew of a bookseller in Montreal who could provide the material he needed.

There was one book in particular he required: *Contes Cubain*, a collection of contemporary Cuban short stories translated into French. Burton had offered to drive to Montreal from Ithaca on Paul's behalf and at Paul's expense. Burton invited Ron, and Ron invited Suzanne Shipe and me. This was to be my last weekend before returning to the hard work ahead in Oklahoma. I'd never been to Canada, and a weekend jaunt to Montreal with friends sounded like great fun.

And it was. It was a beautiful late summer weekend and the countryside in northern New York and southern Ontario was in full glory. I shared the driving with Burton, trading off every hour or so. We'd had an early start, so we arrived in Montreal in full daylight. First we sought out the downtown bookstore and retrieved the one hardbound book and several magazines and leaflets. Then we toured Montreal, including the site of Expo, Montreal's World's Fair, that had recently closed. We dined that night *al fresco* at a French bistro and retired to a hotel room, which Paul Goodman had arranged for us. In the morning we headed back home.

Our reentry into the United States at Alexandria Bay on the afternoon of August 3 didn't go well. Our car was pulled over for a thorough search, and *quelle horreur*, the customs officers discovered contraband in the form of actual literature in our vehicle—Cuban short stories and poetry, some of it in Spanish and some in French. Our car was impounded and we were detained while the officers discussed what to do with us.

One hour faded into two, and the longer we were detained the more certain we were of our imminent arrest. I imagined fresh headlines in Gaylord's Oklahoma newspaper: "Gilchrist Nabbed at Border—Smuggling Communist Propaganda." I felt trapped inside a Ken Kesey novel and unable to get out.

Finally the customs officers made another determination. They'd release the car and us if we signed a form—a form agreeing to the destruction of the literature.

I suppose it would have been simple to sign it, but we couldn't. As Burton later wrote in a letter to the Commissioner of Customs at the U.S. Treasury Department, "In the first place, we would have relinquished our personal property rights, and we would have become accomplices in an act of book-burning to which the historical parallels are uniformly grim." Nonetheless, the material was seized and we were released with the caveat that customs officials from Washington would be in touch with us regarding the disposition of our case.

The case dragged on through the fall. The Treasury Department ultimately determined we should be fined for our transgression, and a fine of five dollars was levied. By this time the literature had long since been destroyed and Paul Goodman had secured from another source the material he needed to compose his review.

Today, somewhere deep in the bowels of the Treasury Department, on a forgotten ledger coated with layers of dust, is a five-dollar balance still unpaid by this recalcitrant smuggler of poetry.

On August 4, I returned to Oklahoma. I borrowed Mary Ann's car and drove back to the St. John's Student Center in Stillwater.

St. John's was a modern and rambling facility, covering half of a city block, with a small, attractive chapel, a number of offices and meeting rooms, a parish hall for dinners and special events, and four spacious and furnished apartments for the resident clergy.

Ray Repp introduced me to Father Bill Kelly, still red-eyed from his return from Europe, and we sat in Bill's office and talked. They told me there were many people in Stillwater who were against the war and the draft, though to date there had been no organized movement. They both appeared genuinely happy that I'd arrived to stir things up, and especially that I'd come to OSU. Bill said one of the four apartments at the center was empty and I was welcome to it while I was awaiting trial and trying to get things going on campus. I gratefully accepted.

Thanks to their generosity, I had the use of a two-bedroom apartment and more. The priests at the center had a housekeeper, who not only cleaned our rooms, but also cooked our meals, and once or twice a day,

I took my meals with them. At last I had secured a roof over my head and food to eat while I awaited trial.

Bill Kelly and I became instant friends. Had he been working in a different church in a different diocese under a conservative bishop, it's likely he wouldn't have been allowed to roll out the welcome mat for me, and our friendship wouldn't have had an opportunity to take root.

Bill was in his early thirties, stocky, and prematurely balding. He was dark Irish with piercing blue eyes, a hearty laugh, and a strong grip. Bill was a popular priest—popular with the students, the townspeople, the nuns, and with the ladies. He faced every day with abundant humor and energy. He was a tonic for the journey I'd set myself on. Before my trial took place later that fall, I'd fallen in love with Bill Kelly.

Over the next few months, I was so immersed in Bill's church and my work in Stillwater that I almost felt like a Catholic. We held frequent meetings and anti-war rallies at St. John's, and during the Sunday services Bill often asked me to speak or do readings from the pulpit. I became friends with others at the church, including a small group of nuns and a number of parishioners, and one in particular: Vince Uhl.

Vince was a graduate student in engineering who'd recently returned from serving in the Peace Corps in India, where he worked on projects to bring clean water to rural towns. In another show of generosity, Vince gave me the use of his little red Kharman Ghia convertible. That summer and fall, while I was confined by the terms of my bail to ten counties in Oklahoma, I put hundreds of miles on Vince's car, driving back and forth between Stillwater and Oklahoma City, with occasional trips to Norman. The car afforded me an indulgence that helped keep me sane.

Occasionally I got in Vince's car and just drove. I'd head east, north, or west; out into the red Oklahoma plains; or along dusty country roads. I drove through crossroad towns that were so small they didn't even have a name. I stopped at out-of-the-way taverns and have a burger and a coke. I stopped by the side of a barren field and watched the hawks making lazy circles in the sky.

I knew that after the trial, I wouldn't have the opportunity to be alone again for a long time. Prisoners serve their sentences in crowded cell-blocks or in open dorms packed with scores and scores of raucous inmates. Even solitary confinement provides only an illusion of privacy since an inmate in solitary is always under observation by guards. In some prisons that observation is constant, around the clock. In others it's intermittent and you never know when you're being watched. In either case, there's no privacy in prison. Someone—either a guard or another inmate—always knows where you are and what you're doing.

There was another reason I took these drives. In Stillwater and Oklahoma City my face was known. I'd been on television and in the newspaper so much that everywhere I went people recognized me. Increasingly I was rebuffed, reviled, and rejected by waitresses, gas station attendants, movie ushers, and store clerks—good patriots all, who felt it was their personal duty to castigate me for the unpatriotic sin of speaking out against this war. In my organizing work I found myself surrounded by people who shared my beliefs and ideals, but once I set foot outside St. John's, I entered a different world. To most of the people of Oklahoma, I was the face of the enemy. I was the Viet Cong come to the Sooner State, and they made it their personal business to abuse me.

In Oklahoma that summer and fall, I was spat upon. Doors were closed in my face. I was refused service at restaurants. I was given the finger at stoplights and cursed walking down the street. The newspapers and airways were filled with letters and editorials denouncing me as a traitor, a coward, and a communist. I began to restrict my own freedom, venturing out only when necessary, choosing the shortest path between two safe havens.

During my solo drives in the country, I was blissfully anonymous. The country rednecks I encountered didn't read newspapers or watch the news on television. They didn't know who I was. They left me alone.

And so I treasured these pastoral drives. Alone, under Oklahoma's broad sky, cruising through a blinding thunderstorm or suffering the searing heat of a cloudless August day, I didn't think about the war, about my trial, about prison, or about anything. I just drove. I caught the sunset. I felt the breeze. I rode the back roads of my boyhood state.

August brought more appearances, more rallies, more meetings. I received invitations to appear in churches and classrooms, and to engage small groups in individuals' homes. There were more interviews, more articles, more flashbulbs. Kids facing the draft sought me out for counseling. I never told anyone what they should or shouldn't do. I simply laid out the alternatives, and told them to examine their own hearts. I was not a recruiter for the Resistance. As much as I believed in it for myself, I couldn't push it on anyone else.

Bill Kelly made an appointment for us to meet with Bishop Reed. The Bishop himself hadn't spoken up on my behalf or provided any direct support (at least not yet), but he approved of the support I was receiving from Bill and from the student center in Stillwater. I like to think that I helped Bishop Reed advance in his opposition to the war. It'd soon appear I might have done just that.

I was invited by John Olsen, the President of Oklahoma City University, to speak on his campus. He was upset over the action of the OSU Board of Regents to ban me from their campus, and his invitation was a direct response to that ban. OCU is a private college, and wasn't cowed by public support for the war. In the heart of their campus, OCU had just opened a beautiful new chapel, which was filled with students and faculty on the afternoon of my appearance.

Although I continued to spend most of my time at OSU, I tried to spend some time every week at OCU. OSU students had quickly grown fond of sit-ins and demonstrations, of marching with signs. At OCU, however, the students favored cerebral discussions about the history of American involvement in Vietnam and of the conscription of young men. At OSU there were dozens of newly minted activists vying for leadership in the struggle against the war, but at OCU my work was centered round one student, a mercurial philosophy undergraduate named Gary Seay. At OSU the anti-war students wanted action, while at OCU they sought study and reflection. I'd come to Oklahoma to encourage the former, but it was the latter I found more nourishing.

I also enjoyed frequent visits to OCU because it was easier to visit my mom from the city than from Stillwater. Sometimes I drove to see her, and sometimes she came to see me.

In September I decided to seek an apartment in the vicinity of OCU. I'd been staying at Mary Ann Hodge's apartment, but lately Mary Ann had become more than a bit amorous, and I wasn't in an amorous frame of mind. Staying in her apartment had become uncomfortable. Increasingly I craved whatever privacy I could find, and a place of my own fit the bill. I found the perfect place: a two-room basement apartment on 23rd Street, directly across from the OCU chapel.

To pay for the apartment I needed income, so I looked for a part-time job. I still had a bit of money Cornell friends had contributed, but I didn't want to go back to them for more. Working a job would also afford me a modicum of normalcy. I'd been spending all of my time speaking and organizing about the war and the draft, and I desperately wanted to spend some time not doing any of those things.

I'd been well-liked and respected when I worked at the Pizza Hut in high school, so I applied at a new Pizza Hut that had opened up on Classen Boulevard, a short distance from OCU. Fortunately I knew the manager. He'd been a manager-trainee at that first Oklahoma Pizza Hut, the one where I'd worked in high school. He hired me, with the proviso, which suited us both, that I'd stay in the kitchen, away from the public. For the next few months, relatively anonymously, I flipped pizza dough and sprinkled it with mozzarella and pepperoni two or three nights a week. The work was mindless and heaven-sent.

One Sunday I decided to go to a morning service at my old church. I still hadn't encountered anyone from my childhood past other than Tim Kline. If people from my past weren't going to come to me, I was going to go to them. I showered, shaved, and combed my hair, and dressed in dark slacks, a freshly ironed white shirt, and striped tie. I drove Vince's Kharman Ghia to Warr Acres and parked in the lot of the Putnam City Christian Church, just blocks from the house where I'd been raised.

As I got out of the car, I recognized many of the faces of others who were entering the church. No one acknowledged me. I approached the entrance to the church. Reverend Dunn was standing there, as he always did on Sunday mornings, Bible in hand. I greeted him, and started through the door. He blocked my entrance. Fumbling for words, his face in a rigid grimace, he held out his Bible to me and said, "You're not welcome here. But take this. You take this. It's my family Bible. You need it more than I do. It might do you some good. Now get out of here."

I didn't take the Bible in his outstretched hand. I simply left. I wasn't going to arm wrestle the man to worship in his church. And I didn't want his damn Bible.

I wasn't surprised by Garrell Dunn's actions, but once again I was disappointed. Perhaps naively, I had hopes there would be someone, anyone, just one person who'd known me as a child, who'd stand beside me, who'd welcome me home.

What made it all the worse for me was the insanity of it all. For twelve years I'd attended Sunday School and church services at Putnam City Christian Church. I even had a pin celebrating my perfect attendance for ten years; it was a small enameled white shield with a little red *fleur-de-lis* and a gold banner at the bottom which said "Ten Years." I'd worn it proudly to church as a junior and a senior.

On numerous occasions, when Reverend Dunn was on vacation or away on a church-related trip, I delivered the sermon in his place. I'd been a "junior deacon," passing the communion trays and collecting the offering at Sunday services once a month. I played the piano and the organ, and I sang in the choir. For twelve years I was at every event—every ice-cream social, every potluck dinner, every CYF teen dance. I'd taught

Sunday School for the younger kids and helped out with Vacation Bible School in the summers. I'd taken piano lessons from Reverend Dunn's wife. I was baptized there in 1958 by Reverend Dunn. I knew everyone in the church and they knew me and now, on this summer day in 1968, I was turned away.

Had I shown up in uniform, fresh from the killing fields of Vietnam, I'd have been showered with affection. Had I devastated entire villages of women and children with napalm and cluster bombs, I'd have been welcomed as a hero. But when I showed up having repudiated these things, I was reviled.

Religion. It'd turned its back on my mother in her time of need; now it turned its back on me. Even the kindness of the good folks at St. John's Student Center in Stillwater wasn't sufficient to reconcile me to religion. I was done with it. I still am.

In September, shortly after I moved into my Oklahoma City apartment, I received a phone call informing me a Federal Grand Jury had returned an indictment charging me with refusing induction. The U.S. Attorney—David Kline, my classmate Tim Kline's father—kindly afforded me the opportunity to turn myself in.

I called Esther Pahlka at work to give her the news that I was about to be arrested. I told her I wanted her to hear it from me, before she heard it on the news.

My relationship with the Pahlkas had not been good ever since I returned my draft card in April. Harlan Pahlka was a retired Lt. Commander in the Navy, a decorated WWII veteran who'd seen battle on the *U.S.S. Drew* in the Pacific. In correspondence and by phone, Harlan and Esther had argued, cajoled, and even threatened me regarding my plan to refuse induction. In one phone call and in a follow-up letter, Harlan told me if I went through with it, he had some information of his own which he'd release to the press. I never knew what that meant. I had no idea what he might possibly have on me that would be of interest to the press. I'd never given him or Esther any reason to distrust or dislike me when I'd been living with them, and they'd been phenomenally generous to me. I wrote his threat off as anger. He simply didn't want me to do it.

Harlan also had made it clear to Esther she was to have nothing to do with me. Esther was not a woman who took orders from anyone, even her husband, but Harlan's edict was one she accepted, and most likely completely agreed with. Since early June I'd had no contact with them, at their request.

I remained in touch with both of their sons. Bill had graduated from Yale, and having been in ROTC, he joined the Navy. He'd married his high school sweetheart and was now on board a ship out of Norfolk, Virginia, serving as a communications officer. Bill was personally supportive of me, but he was in no position to make that support public or to demonstrate it in anyway. Bill would later be visited by the FBI and by Navy Intelligence and questioned about our relationship and about his knowledge of my activities. He answered the questions honestly. He considered me his brother, he told them. But he could shed no light on what I was doing.

Bob was a student at Kansas University. Bob ignored his parents' insistence he disassociate himself from me, but he also pretty much ignored me and what I was doing. Politics wasn't Bob's thing. In that respect, he was apparently smarter than me.

Perhaps I should have continued to honor Harlan and Esther's request to leave them alone. Perhaps I shouldn't have called Esther about my impending arrest, but I was emotionally compelled to. Somehow I felt she'd want me to. And apparently I was right. She asked how I was going to get to the Federal Building to turn myself in, and I told her I didn't know. She told me to stay where I was; she'd come to get me.

That day Esther drove me to my arrest. She cried most of the way there. She told me not to let Harlan know that she'd seen me, and I promised. Ten years would pass before I'd see Esther Pahlka again.

The act of resistance was a lonely act. I took comfort in fellow resisters, in supporters, and in friends. I took comfort in my mother and my twin brother's support. But it was Esther's compassionate offer to drive me to my arrest that I'll always remember as the single most supportive moment of my journey. Esther wasn't there because of what I was doing. She hated what I was doing. She was simply there for me. The emotion she showed on that drive showed me just how much she cared. Of course I wanted her to agree with me, to support my opposition to the war. But lacking that, I wanted her love.

Because of her, I was able to walk into the Federal Building calm and oddly confident. Alone, I took the elevator to the U.S. Attorney's office and announced myself to the receptionist. I was politely arrested, fingerprinted, and escorted to a holding cell, where I waited for Bill Kelly to arrive with bail, which had been set at a thousand dollars. The money had been wired to Bill by Daniel Berrigan. My friends at Cornell were still taking care of me.

Among her many fine attributes, Mary Ann Hodges moved freely between the white and black communities of Oklahoma City. She and her roommate lived in a section of northeast Oklahoma City, which was predominantly black. She and her roommate were the only white residents of their apartment building. Mary Ann and her roommate socialized with, and occasionally dated, black men, which was recklessly audacious in Oklahoma in 1968.

Among her best friends was a woman, Maxine, who ran a Soul Food Kitchen, not far from the Lincoln Park Zoo. Mary Ann and I ate a lot of meals there that summer and fall. We were always the only white faces in the restaurant every time we dropped in. I swear it was the best damn restaurant in the state. All the food was local and fresh—turnip greens and cornbread, tomato salad and brown beans, raw onions and fried okra, and breaded catfish and smoky barbecue ribs.

Maxine never let us pay for a meal. She hated the draft and the war. She knew too many black boys who'd been killed, and too many others who were likely to be. When we arrived at the Soul Food Kitchen, we were always greeted with hoots and yells and complimentary plates full of steaming food. Her kitchen was our kitchen, she told us, and we were welcome any time.

Mary Ann was also a friend of one of Oklahoma's youngest state senators, and its first and only black state senator, E. Melvin Porter. She introduced me to him one night, after I'd spoken about the war at an east side church in Oklahoma City. As he shook my hand, he looked into my eyes and said, "Gilchrist. Gilchrist." He was thinking about something, and I didn't know what it could be.

"Gilchrist… I used to know a Rosie Gilchrist," he said. "I sat next to her on a bus to Washington, D.C., in 1963. You wouldn't be related to her, would you?"

I told him I was, that Rosie Gilchrist was my mother.

"Whatever happened to her?" he asked. "She just seemed to drop off the face of the earth."

I told him it was a long story, but that I'd like to share it with him if I could. And we arranged to meet the next day at his office.

E. Melvin Porter had been born and raised in rural Okmulgee, Oklahoma. Not many kids from Okmulgee went to college in those days, and even fewer black kids, but Porter went on to graduate from Tennessee State University. Next he became the first African-American accepted to the Vanderbilt University Law School. He was bright, ambitious, and motivated.

Upon graduation he planned on working for a prestigious East Coast law firm, until Clara Luper convinced him he was needed back home. He gave up a lucrative career, hung his shingle outside of a shabby office, and went about the business of defending the hundreds of individuals who were arrested in the Oklahoma City sit-ins in the late 1950s and early 1960s. In 1961 he was elected head of the Oklahoma NAACP. He made a name for himself as an astute attorney, an eloquent speaker, and a level headed seeker of justice. In 1964, when the Oklahoma legislative district boundaries were redrawn in such a manner to provide, for the first time, the opportunity for a non-white person to win an election, he ran and he won. He was a state senator for twenty-two years.

The Oklahoma State Capitol stands in a unique setting, smack dab in one of the richest oil fields in the country and surrounded by a forest of pumping oil derricks. With the chug-chug of the derricks drumming in my ears, and the fragrance of the oil field filling my nostrils, I ascended the steps of the stately edifice and found my way to Senator Porter's office.

I told him what I knew. I told him about how my mother had been burned; about her hospitalization and her friendship with Mrs. Fulbright; how that led her to Clara Luper and the NAACP Youth Council; and the sit-ins and demonstrations at Wedgewood Amusement Park, Bishops Restaurant, and Anna Maude Cafeteria. He remembered my mom at these events and others, but mostly he recalled talking with her on the bus to Washington. He hadn't known about her plans to sell her house to a black doctor.

Then I told him about the Warr Acres posse: Garrell Dunn, Eldon Lawson, Chief Beckett, and my father. How they arrested her and took her before Judge Theus. How they took away everything she owned and locked her up in Central State Hospital. I told him about how she'd tried and failed to effect her own release, and that she'd been confined for five years.

In my presence Senator Porter was not a demonstrative man. He was youthful, handsome, and serious. He wrote everything down. He thanked me for my time. Then, to my surprise and great delight, he told me he'd look into my mother's situation further and get back to me.

And he did.

A few days after our first meeting, he called me back to his office. He said he found no trace of a legal record of her commitment, and even if there had been such a record, the proceedings themselves were highly suspect if not illegal. He offered to go with me to the hospital to demand her immediate release, and if the hospital refused, he offered to represent my mother in court to obtain her release.

I told him about my relationship with Paul Rahe, the reporter for the *Oklahoma Journal*, and suggested we let Paul in on this. We called Paul, and over the phone Paul agreed to join us on our trip to Norman.

My objective was her immediate release. But if the hospital authorities faltered, then Porter was prepared to file a writ of *habeas corpus*, followed by a law suit naming the hospital, Judge Theus, Garrell Dunn, Chief Beckett, and Eldon Lawson and asking for damages; and Paul was prepared to publish the story of my mother's lengthy incarceration.

The story was never published.

Senator Porter made an appointment with the head of Central State Hospital. As a state senator, he possessed the clout to demand one and get it immediately. Paul and I met Senator Porter at his office, and together we drove to Norman. Quietly and directly, Senator Porter told the hospital's administrator that he came seeking the immediate release of Rosalyn Gilchrist, and that if she wasn't released, he'd file suit that afternoon in Oklahoma County, and Paul Rahe would print the story of her illegal incarceration in the *Oklahoma Journal*. Half an hour later we left the hospital. My mother, with all of her belongings in a single tattered suitcase, rode back with us.

Her nightmare was finally over.

I sat in the back seat with my arm around my mother's shoulders as we drove away, with Senator Porter behind the wheel and Paul Rahe riding shotgun. It was a bittersweet drive. She was trying to process what had just happened, and so was I. Porter dropped us off at my apartment across from OCU.

"Welcome home, Mom," I said.

When I started my resistance, when I returned my draft card to my draft board, I despaired of being able to do anything to help my mother. As it turned out, my act of resistance led me to Senator Porter, who'd briefly known my mother, and who now championed her release.

Never let it be said there is no hope. There is always hope.

Book Two:
The Fracture of Good Order

OUR APOLOGIES,
good friends
FOR THE FRACTURE OF GOOD ORDER,
the burning of paper
INSTEAD OF CHILDREN.

DANIEL BERRIGAN

New York City — July, 1971

I slept well, having long since mastered the art of falling asleep under the worst conditions. The federal halfway house had been quiet enough. I'd been given my own room, securely locked from the outside, which seemed to settle any question of my (or anyone else's) safety. As dawn broke I awoke, showered, and shaved, but skipped the institutional breakfast. At the appointed minute of the appointed hour, I was allowed to leave. My friends were waiting for me on the sidewalk.

Prison shuts down one's senses, even when one tries to keep them open. The monotony of confinement, coupled with the dangers lurking in every shadow, forces a constriction of perception, emotion, and will. In Milan I'd invented small ways to stay human, and I treasured every trick of those inventions. But here, in the sun and on the streets with my friends, I realized how much I'd been denied. And I breathed, tasted, and soaked it in with abandon.

Each footstep I chose could take me in any direction I wanted. For the next few hours, I could decide what to do next, and what to do after that. Even the very act of breathing seemed infused with a new power, a privilege I hadn't realized was missing.

Had the sun ever shined so bright? Had the air ever been so filled with smells and sounds and sights as it was that mild July morning in New York? And what's more, now I could *touch* my friends. Hold hands with

Susan and I at the Woodstock Jesuit Seminary the afternoon of my mother's funeral

them. Wrap my arms around them. Kiss them. No Plexiglas barrier separated us. No fence, no wall, no razor wire. No guard kept us apart. No rifle was aimed at my back.

But there was business at hand. I had my mother's funeral to attend.

Susan had arranged for the service to be held at the Woodstock Jesuit Seminary in uptown Manhattan. Through Daniel

Berrigan, we'd become friends with a few of the priests who were living there. Leaving the halfway house, we approached a subway for the journey north, but I held back. "No," I said. "Let's walk." And we did. We had time. The funeral was not scheduled till that afternoon.

But first we enjoyed a quick breakfast at a convenient diner. Omelets, bagels, lox, hot coffee, fresh orange juice. Then, sated and fortified, we took off on foot. We hiked the New York City canyons of concrete, steel, and glass for hours—four maybe, perhaps five. We were in no hurry. One block made way for the next as we crossed the grid and crossed it again, and all the time my hands were held, my shoulders embraced, my arms entwined by my friends. My skin awakened from a long, long sleep.

We scared up flocks of pigeons in Washington Square, ambled our way north on Broadway, dodged sightseeing throngs in Times Square, body-blocked shoppers on Fifth Avenue, paid our respects to Rockefeller Center, and navigated a path through Central Park. We ogled beggars, runners, peddlers, and horse-drawn carriages; we passed business-men hailing cabs, mothers pushing strollers, kids racing to school, and caretakers tending the elderly. I marveled at the breadth and depth of humanity—the shapes, the colors, the velocity, the attitudes. We took in the art and the architecture and the ambience, and we took in each other. If my friends were any less thrilled than I with the miracle of it all, they gave no evidence. Arriving at the Jesuit House was almost a disappointment because it meant the end of our walk and the start of something else—the business we'd come for.

Everything was in readiness. There would be a small group, no more than a score. My mother hadn't been in New York long enough to make a lot of friends. The staff at the Jesuit House had set out a modest buffet to feed those gathered before and after the service. They provided a lounge area where we could visit that afternoon until the service began. And for Susan and me, they offered a private room.

Love is sweetest when it has been long denied.

This might be a good time to inform you, the reader, about sex in prison. Sex in prison is not romantic. It is not loving. It is exploitive and ugly, and usually one or both of the parties involved are harmed in ways physical and otherwise..

As a young man who was attracted to both men and women, I readily admit there were times in lockup that my hormones wanted to get the best of me. I was tempted, and there was plenty of temptation around. Now, some forty years later, I can close my eyes and recall in vivid detail specific features of specific inmates, features I found frighteningly tempting.

As lacking in privacy as prison is, someone in need of sex can always find it. But I wisely refrained. I neither made nor accepted advances. I was a paragon of restraint, and for good reason. I didn't have to look far to find evidence of sex and sexual violence all around me. There was never anything pretty about it. In prison, sex isn't about affection. It's about dominance. It's about fear. It's about conquest.

Nonetheless, in the shower my eyes would insist on a fleeting glance at a particularly attractive specimen, and I'd have to force myself to locate an interesting tile on the shower floor instead. There was one inmate with the most remarkable posterior curvature; another with the dreamiest of lips and liquid pools for eyes. A particular glint of sunlight on a cheek, or a shadow on a muscled thigh, would torment me. And sometimes it wasn't just other inmates who ignited my twenty-three-year-old libido. There was one young guard who caught my interest: tall and lean, easy-going and damned good-looking. I'm pretty sure he was as interested in me as I was in him. I didn't mistake his intent. So I avoided him like the plague.

An inmate once branded for having sex with other inmates, willingly or otherwise, can never lose the brand. It follows him, even into another prison. He becomes a favored target. The best he can hope for is a lengthy confinement in solitary. The worst? Well, let's not talk about the worst. When I was a prisoner, I did what I had to. I neutered my body and mind.

And so, following long months of imposed denial, I came to this unlikely time and place, to this fleeting hour in a Manhattan seminary, alone with Susan in the moments before my mother's funeral.

I'd requested a Quaker-style service, one with no minister or priest presiding, no predetermined and rigid format, no overblown reading of scripture, singing of hymns, or prayers for the dead. My mother wouldn't have wanted any of those things and I didn't either.

My brother Gordon arrived just before the service. He'd flown in the night before, arriving after I'd gone to the halfway house. While I'd been hiking the streets of New York with my friends, he'd spent this day managing the myriad details of funeral preparation with the folks at the Catholic Worker and at the mortuary. He'd arranged for my mother's cremation, and was planning to take her ashes back to Vernon, Texas, where she was born. He'd have them interred in the cemetery with her parents, her older brother Floyd, her twin J. Marvin, and the infant twins she'd lost in 1935.

In the past year Beverly had divorced Gordon, and for a good reason. When they'd first married, it'd seemed that his life was in ascension. He worked hard to put himself through college, with Beverly's ample support. Early every morning she drove Gordon the fifty miles to the campus of Central State College in Edmond, before returning to Warr Acres where she worked a full-time job. After work she picked up their daughter from the babysitter, and then make the round-trip again to retrieve Gordon from campus before cooking dinner for her family.

Upon graduation Gordon got a good job that just kept getting better. Starting off in sales with Johnson & Johnson, he quickly was promoted to sales manager. Seeing himself for the first time in his life in the fast lane, he succumbed to a pleasure he'd already tasted in high school: copious amounts of beer and whiskey. And to that pleasure he added a second: obscene portions of food. Gordon gained a lot of weight in a very short time. But food and whiskey weren't enough.

One day he came home in a shiny new Corvette, which nearly drove Beverly nuts. As successful as they were, they were still a struggling young family, and Beverly was pregnant again. To her mind, they needed that car like a hole in the head.

Their relationship became unsettled, argumentative, unpleasant. Gordon, who'd gone for years without even his own bed to sleep in when he was a boy, could now buy himself anything he wanted. When his baby needed diapers, he splurged for a new set of golf clubs for himself. When Beverly needed his help at home, he stayed out late with his admiring buddies who appreciated his undeniable wit and charm. Gordon was the life of the party—a party that left his pregnant wife and two children behind.

He was promoted again, and the family moved to Shreveport. There Gordon quickly took up with a new company of drinking and fishing buddies. His relationship with Beverly faltered. He had less and less to do with his own children. His work suffered.

I can only surmise what drove Gordon to soil his own bed. His wife, Beverly, was everything a man could want: smart, generous, beautiful, articulate, loving, caring, a great cook, a wonderful mother. And he treated her like shit. His children would have made any father proud. And he ignored them.

I know in the very depth of my soul that my brother Gordon was a very kind and loving man, yet he treated those he loved most unkindly. How is one to explain this? In part it could have been the demon alcohol itself, but that doesn't entirely explain it, and it certainly doesn't excuse it. I think it was something else.

Gordon lived his life in pain. He suffered pain from a loveless father. He suffered pain from being the caretaker of his own mother when he himself was still a child. He suffered pain from the horror of extinguishing the fire, which burned her, and of sitting up with her night after grueling night tending to her wounds. He never escaped the pain, and as much as he sought something to replace it, what he found was never enough. Inside that bubble of pain, he did the best he could to forge a life, and he often didn't succeed.

I make him sound horrible, and to his family he was. But he was still my charming, intelligent, and quick-witted brother. He had a way with words that still makes me jealous. And when Gordon was in the room, he was always the center of attention—not because he placed himself there, but because everyone else did.

Several people from the Catholic Worker arrived: Barbara Hawkins, Dale Alley, and Dale's on-again, off-again girlfriend Bonnie Barnes. I'd met them at OSU and we'd become friends at St. John's in the months before my Oklahoma trial. They'd helped fuel the OSU Coalition of Conscience, and they'd all been great support to me. In 1969 Dale and I had hitchhiked together from Oklahoma to New York, enduring heat and rain and one suspicious state trooper. Bonnie had trailed Dale to New York, continuing her custom of defining herself by mimicking Dale. The previous year Barbara and I had collaborated on starting up a free-school called Cuando in the Bowery. Barbara did all the work, really; my part was just helping raise some funds at Cornell for the school.

They now performed various jobs at the Catholic Worker. Dale and Bonnie helped with the soup kitchen every morning, and Dale assisted with the newspaper the Worker put out monthly. In addition to Cuando, Barbara was running a used-clothing store across the street, an adjunct to the soup kitchen and a place where people in need could get clean clothes, warm coats, and good shoes. My mother had helped out there too, assisting Barbara.

At the service there were two others from the Worker whom I hadn't met before, but who'd become friends with my mother: Jan Adams and Kathy Schmidt. They seemed to have been her closest friends in her final weeks.

Filling out the rest of the seats were my friends from Cornell, my brothers, and several priests from the Jesuit House. Three clergy from Cornell United Religious Work attended, including Jack Lewis, David Connors, and Paul Gibbons.

I began. I welcomed everyone and thanked them for coming. I explained how the service would work: Nothing was planned, and everyone was welcome to contribute in any way they wished. I began with a poem I wrote in prison the night I learned of her death:

L'etranger non plus.
Aujord'hui, maman est morte.

News of her death reached me in prison.
It was raining. The end of a long dry season.

Where is the woman who gave me life?
Where shall I seek the woman
Who gave me the courage and the reason
To become free
As free as the changing seasons
As free as the passing of the hours
As free as the moisture in the morning air

Where shall I reach
For the shoulder my hand rested on
As we walked the many streets together?

Where shall I be able to drink her strength?
To taste her unyielding love?
To glimpse her tenderness?

Where has she gone? Who is she now?

I look over my shoulder
Expecting feelings I do not find
There is no grief or sorrow
For those she never gave me
Only joy and hope

I stretch my neck to the stars
And discover no anguish in their silence

My hand bathes in the evening breeze
And I know
I am at peace
She is free
She is one with the universe
Her voyage here has ended

Once again
She is the window through which I look

Because she dared, too late, too alone
I may start now
Because she began to see
I will learn to see
Because she began to hope
I will learn to hope
Because she lived and died
I will live, and she in me
She is free

Wife, brothers, good friends
Gather now close round her grave
And you with ears to hear
Will recognize her eternal whisper
For it is also yours and mine and ours

My mother lived
I loved her
And she loved me.

The service continued in leaps and starts—typical to any Quaker service. There would be gaps where no one spoke for several minutes, and then several people would all try to speak at once. Gordon spoke at length about Mom coaching his golf team when he was in high school, even though she didn't know a damn thing about golf. He told everyone how Mom took care of his friends who needed a little help.

Dale talked about how strong my mother had been at my Oklahoma trial, how everyone worried how she would deal with it, but the reality was that as my trial drew closer, she took care of everyone else instead of the other way around.

One nice thing after another was said about my mother, until Carolyn Micklen spoke up. Carolyn had driven in from Rochester. My mother had stayed at Carolyn's home during my Rochester trial, and they hadn't gotten along well. I never knew why. I'd been too preoccupied with my own problems at the time to pay attention to their unease with each other.

Carolyn had listened quietly while everyone else spoke. When others had laughed, she remained quiet. When others had smiled, her face remained pensive. Finally, during a quiet moment, she stood and said, after a deep breath, "Frankly, I didn't always understand Rosie. She made me mad as hell and I know I made her mad." We all laughed at Carolyn's remark. We'd all been inhaling for an uncomfortably long time and could finally let go and exhale.

Carolyn disregarded our laughter and continued. She described how my mother set such high standards for herself and often for others, standards that weren't always realistic. She wanted people to be better. "Still," she said, "Rosie got under my skin. When I heard she had passed, I knew I had to be here to say how much I loved her, and how much I'll miss her. She challenged me to be better."

Jan and Kathy talked of my mother's final weeks and months at the Catholic Worker: how she was always the first to care for the sick, how she always took on the dirtiest jobs in the kitchen, how excited she'd been when she arrived and how unhappy she'd seemed at the end. They said she'd been trying to get them to help her realize a dream to use her scars somehow to help the lepers on Molokai in the Hawaiian Islands. They weren't sure just how this scheme was supposed to work. It never made a lot of sense to them. But they said my mom believed her scars were very similar to those of a leper, and she felt she might find a way to advocate for the lepers. It frustrated her that her dream could find no traction.

Story begat story, and one hour turned to two. Using a guitar borrowed from one of the Jesuits, I closed with a song I'd written in prison, inspired by a Robinson Jeffers poem, which went in part:

> *A little too rich, a little too wise*
> *It's time to kiss the earth again*
> *Let the leaves rain to the ground*
> *Let the rich life run to the earth again*

After the service, we ate and talked and visited. Our numbers thinned. Finally, it was just Susan and me and it was time for us to leave. We hopped in a taxi for the journey downtown. The city streaked by outside the windows of the cab, disappearing building by building, block by block. Susan kissed me at the door of the halfway house. We tried not to make a big deal out of it—this forced separation after such a short reunion. She stood alone on the sidewalk as I left her behind and transformed into a prisoner again.

The next morning I had an early flight. I'd told my friends and family not to see me off, that they should enjoy a nice evening together, stay up late, and sleep in. The truth was I didn't think I could handle having to say any more goodbyes.

I had to go back to prison, and I wanted to get it over with. Truthfully, in the eight months I'd spent in Milan, I'd gotten used to being locked up. Prison had become who I was, what I did, how I lived, and I'd convinced myself I was happy in confinement. I'd found a way to go to bed without sorrow and wake up without pain. This trip to my mother's funeral had opened wounds I'd worked hard to close. Getting back to Milan was just the tourniquet I needed to staunch the flow of feelings.

Of course, if I'd had a choice, I wouldn't have gone back. But there was no choice.

I used the money Trudy had given me to pay for a cab to the airport. I presented my ticket and got on a plane. In Detroit Trudy was waiting at the gate to escort me back to prison. She was cheerful as ever, but recognizing my unease, she refrained from pressing me with questions about my trip. After the short drive we arrived at the front gate. She pulled up and dropped me off, and more or less voluntarily, I placed myself back into custody. I passed though the prison sallyport, entered A&D, and disrobed for the peremptory cavity search.

I couldn't believe my mother was gone. I still can't.

Oklahoma City — October, 1968

My diminutive Oklahoma City apartment had not been intended for two people. It was in a cinderblock basement, entered from the rear parking lot, with windows on the back and one side. The outside door opened into a small, low-ceilinged living area with a kitchenette, a well-used sofa, and a wobbly coffee table. An inner door led to the lone small bedroom through which one traveled to the closet-sized bathroom. There was a built-in, three-drawer dresser and one closet, barely large enough to hang a week's worth of clothes. The floor throughout was a dingy tan linoleum. There was a lingering hint of mold in the air.

Fortunately, neither my mother nor I had much by way of possessions; everything we owned could be packed into our respective suitcases with room left over. In recent years we'd each become used to living in small spaces inhabited by too many people—her crowded and noisy hospital open dorm, and my shabby Collegetown apartment. For me, a college student, our new humble abode was *de rigueur*. For her it was a luxury and a respite from the cooped-up, cacophonous dorm she'd daily endured. She took the bedroom. I took the sofa. And we set about making this hovel our home.

In the scant weeks that I lived there before she joined me, I'd made no effort to soften the place. For me it was simply a place to be alone. I didn't care what it looked like so long as it was private. The space itself meant nothing to me, but to my mother, it meant the world. She immediately took up the task of making it livable, comfortable, and, as much as possible (and this is a stretch), attractive.

Because she'd saved some cash from her job at the hospital canteen, she had more money on hand than I did. She filled the cabinets and refrigerator with Jell-O and canned goods, with ground beef and green beans. She acquired a few needed utensils and towels, and purloined from one of the OCU gardens a bouquet of fresh flowers. She had an unquenchable need for fresh flowers, and for the two months we lived together, she kept the vases full.

She learned to cook again. You don't know what joy there can be in a can of tomato soup and a grilled cheese sandwich until you have the opportunity to make these for yourself after being denied the pleasure for five years. One fried egg. A bowl of hot oatmeal. A steak. A potato. Ice-cream. Now she could eat whatever she wanted to eat, whenever she wanted to eat it.

She bought an alarm clock and a radio; toothpaste, soap, and lotion; a nightgown, robe, and soft slippers. She got her hair done. She bought a new dress, new shoes, a purse, and wallet.

The President of OCU, who'd already been so kind to me, offered my mother a housekeeping job in one of the campus dorms less than a five-minute walk from our apartment. Both of us breathed a sigh of relief when she started working. She needed to work—for the money of course, but also because she needed something to do and a means of meeting new people. Me? I needed the assurance she'd be taken care of after I'd gone to prison; assurance that she'd be able to pay the bills, to have a roof over her head and food to eat.

In all the times I'd imagined her freed from the hospital, I hadn't thought about how and where she'd live when she was finally released. She was an aged, handicapped, scarred, lonely woman, who'd spent five years locked up in the state mental hospital. Freeing her might have been viewed by some as cruel, as subjecting her to a future she wasn't equipped to handle.

In those first days and weeks of her freedom, I finally realized the magnitude of the change in her life and the challenges she'd face. What's more, she'd have to face them without me since I was soon to be imprisoned.

My trial was set for Friday, November 22. As October faded into November, I still hadn't obtained the services of an attorney, and the New York ACLU, which had earlier promised assistance, informed me that due to a heavy docket of cases they had no one available to travel to Oklahoma around the time of my trial. I had no idea what I was going to do.

And then one day the phone rang.

"Hello," I said.

"Is this Joe Gilchrist?" a pleasant voice asked.

"Yes," I answered. I was wary. I had an unpublished number, I didn't get many phone calls to begin with, and I invariably recognized the voices of people who called me or my mother.

"My name is Eugene Matthews," the caller informed me. "Are you still looking for an attorney?" he asked.

"Yes," I said.

"Can you meet me in half an hour?" he proposed. I said yes, and we arranged to meet in a coffee shop not far from my apartment.

"How will I know you?" I asked.

"I'll know you," he said.

Eugene Matthews, it turned out, was a successful corporate lawyer and senior partner in the firm which bore his name. He was in his late thirties, tall and lean and possessed with Kennedy good looks. Later I'd meet his beautiful wife, and his three more beautiful young daughters.

He said he'd heard me speak a couple of months earlier at Father Nerin's church, the Community of John XXIII. He'd just returned from the Democratic Party Convention in Chicago, where he'd been the lone Oklahoma delegate for Eugene McCarthy. From his room at the Hilton on Michigan Avenue, he'd watched the police strike the anti-war protesters with nightsticks, and the tear-gas clouding Grant Park wafted through the cracks of the window into his room. He'd arrived at the Convention hopeful for a McCarthy win, but he departed despondent and dismayed by what he witnessed both inside and outside the Chicago Coliseum.

He told me he was not a criminal attorney. He'd never defended a criminal case, and he'd been using that as an excuse for not calling me earlier. He said he'd been thinking about offering his services since the first time he read about my resistance, and when he heard me speak, he was more convinced than ever it was the right thing to do. But he was worried about how defending me might impact his corporate law business, a reasonable worry since he had a family to feed and a partnership to maintain. He was worried about how defending me might affect his relationship with the judges he routinely appeared before, including Luther Bohanon, the federal judge who'd preside over my trial. But, he said, if I was still without an attorney, he was willing to represent me if I'd have him.

I was ecstatic.

Eugene Matthews may have been an untried defense attorney, but his offer was so generous and so courageous I could hardly say no. Of course, there was that other thing that encouraged me to accept his offer: I didn't have lawyers lining up asking to take my case for free. Not only was Gene Matthews a good choice for a defense attorney; he was my only choice.

I gave him the contact information of the New York ACLU, which had offered long-distance consulting on the case if I could come up with my own local attorney. And this proved to be of help in the months and years to come. Gene had less than two weeks to prepare to defend me in court.

Then the phone rang again.

My brother Jim had given my phone number to Ted Coonfield. Ted had been a classmate and a fellow 1966 graduate of Putnam City High School. We'd known each other since grade school, and Ted had been as active in our church as I'd been. Ted's father, *Major* Coonfield, had been my little league baseball coach and our senior year high school counselor. (Major Coonfield preferred to be addressed with his former rank.)

Ted was one of the half a dozen 1966 PCHS graduates who, like me, had fled the state after high school. Ted had defected to TCU in Fort Worth, greatly disappointing his father who was a staunch OSU man himself.

Ted told me he'd been following my case from Texas, where he spent the summer and where he was now in school. He said because of me he'd argued non-stop with his mom and dad, who believed me to be the devil incarnate. Ted said he was active in a peace group on the TCU campus and had helped organize some rallies and demonstrations there. "I just want you to know," he said, "I support what you're doing."

I'd been hoping there would be just one person from my past who'd understand, who'd be supportive, who'd stand up for me. And at last, in the final weeks before my trial, there was. If I'd laid a bet on who that person would be, I wouldn't have bet on Ted Coonfield. But why not Ted? In many ways, Ted and I were cut from the same cloth. Sons of the plains, former junior deacons, both honored with ten-year-perfect-attendance pins. We'd never been best friends, perhaps, but we'd always been good friends. While I warmed the bench on his father's little league team, the Starfighters, Ted had been the pinch-hitter and first-baseman. A lefty, he drove the pitchers mad. In junior high I'd even attended a couple of sleepovers at his house, camping in his backyard under the watchful eyes of Major Coonfield. On more than one occasion during high school we'd double-dated. The year I'd been Student Council President, Ted had been elected Student Chaplain.

When I told Gene Matthews about Ted, he asked if Ted might be willing to testify at my trial as a character witness. Ted immediately said yes. His relationship with his father would never be the same.

As the date of the trial grew closer, anti-war activity on the campuses increased, especially at OSU but also at OCU and OU. The OSU group—

the Coalition for Conscience—planned three events around my trial. They announced a dinner to be held at Maxine's Soul Food Kitchen, followed by an all-night vigil the night before the trial. For the vigil they secured the permission of Bishop Reed to use the chapel at a sprawling Catholic Pastoral Retreat on the far northwest side of Oklahoma City. For the day of the trial they planned an all-day sit-in on the OSU campus and a demonstration at the Stillwater draft board.

Other groups joined in organizing the all-night vigil, including the OCU and OU anti-war groups. They were aided by individuals from a number of religious organizations that had become supportive, including the Community of John XXIII and members of Mennonite, Unitarian, and Quaker congregations. Still more support came from PIPE, "People Involved in Peace and Equality," a recently formed federation of Oklahoma professionals—lawyers, teachers, and ministers—that networked together to advocate against the war. Together these groups programmed a full night of song, poetry, dance, and speeches, interspersed with time for reflection and prayer.

As the trial approached, I was spending as much time as I could in two separate and sometimes conflicting pursuits. I continued to seek opportunities to be alone. Each week I put more miles, and more Oklahoma dust, on Vince Uhl's red Kharman Ghia. My disappearances caused some consternation for my mother and my friends. It seemed everybody wanted a piece of me, and I felt like I had fewer and fewer pieces to give. I'd like to say these solitary excursions to nowhere made me feel better, that they strengthened me, but that's not the case. They merely allowed me to forget, for a short while, what was about to happen.

The other pursuit was simply hanging out with my mom: shopping for groceries, cooking meals, going for walks, watching sitcoms on our TV from the thrift shop. She herself was approaching my trial with surprising equanimity. She knew as well as I the certain outcome, but she offered no pushback and demonstrated no distress. Her demeanor gave me strength, and I began to be convinced I needn't have worried about her continuing welfare. She was not only taking care of herself, but was also, in many ways, taking care of me. She was working. She was providing meals. She was giving me strength. She was showing me through her example that life goes on. It did for her, and it would for me.

I wish I were as calm as she appeared to be, but I wasn't. I wasn't worried about the trial. What would happen in Judge Bohanon's courtroom was a foregone conclusion, and I was more or less prepared for it; but I remained terrified of prison. I was not at all convinced I could handle it, that I'd survive it. I kept these thoughts mostly, but not entirely, to myself.

On the evening of November 21, I joined a core group of supporters, about forty people in all, at Maxine's Soul Food Kitchen. Maxine had graciously offered to cook a last supper as a going-away gift to me and my friends. It was a raucous affair. We gorged on her delicious food, raised our voices and our glasses in cheer, and charged ahead into what everyone believed would be my last night of freedom for a very long while.

Later we gathered with over two hundred supporters at the pastoral retreat center. This event was held in the center's chapel, which automatically lent a more subdued and respectful atmosphere. This intimate but soaring modern chapel boasted thirty blessed saints peering down from angular stained-glass windows, and a wide marble platform in the apse, which provided an ample stage for the entertainment. As the night progressed I moved among my friends; I sat and listened to their songs, their poems, and their remarks; I held their hands and graciously accepted their hugs and good wishes. Finally, as night turned to morning, I slipped away to a room that had been provided for me. While the group was planning for the vigil to last all night, I knew I needed to get some sleep to face the day ahead.

But first, at Bill Kelly's suggestion, I placed a call to Ithaca—to Daniel Berrigan. I told him of my fears, the same fears I'd disclosed half a year earlier when he invited me to his apartment to dinner. I confessed a big part of me simply wanted to run away.

Dan reminded me I was only human. Of course I wanted to flee. Then he told me arrangements had already been made to take care of me. There were people who'd get me out of the country, into Canada. And there were people in Canada, at McGill University, who'd been alerted to my potential need for a place to start over—to live, to work, to go to school. He said all I had to do to activate this network of support, this underground route to Canada, was to say the word.

Without my knowledge, friends known and unknown had already prepared a way out for me. God, how I wanted to take them up on it.

Dan also told me what I already knew. He said there was no disgrace in leaving the country. He said thousands of young men had already done so, and more would in the coming months and years, for the same reasons that were prompting me. He said the act of leaving the country was not an act of cowardice but took a kind of bravery all its own.

But, he said, if I felt I could withstand it all—the trial, imprisonment, becoming a felon—the country was in need of people who'd stay behind and make their stand here, at home, in America.

Dan didn't elaborate on this point. He stated it simply. He didn't try to talk me into making one decision or the other. He concluded the conversation by saying that whatever I decided to do would be the right thing, and that I had his full support.

Bill Kelly had joined me in my room for the conversation with Dan. He and Dan had spoken earlier, and Bill was prepared to secret me out of the retreat center, to put me into the hands of people who'd keep me safe.

This offer astonished me. I imagined myself underground, passed from hand to hand until deposited safely in Canada. I imagined a new life as a Canadian, with new friends, a new home, a new country, a new citizenship. The thought of it scared me, but was it more frightening than the certain prospect of prison?

"Two roads diverged in a yellow wood," I thought. And I?

Ultimately there was nothing to decide. I'd made my decision months before, and every time I'd made a speech, every time I'd written a letter, every time I'd met privately with an individual or publicly with a group about my opposition to the war and the draft, I'd affirmed my choice.

I said no. I was staying.

That night, Bill held me. We didn't sleep. In the morning I went to trial.

Gene Matthews had suggested I wear a suit, and Gordon loaned me one. I hadn't seen a lot of Gordon in the months leading up to the trial. He was occupied providing for his young family, having recently taken a job as a traveling salesman for Proctor & Gamble, which put him on the road a lot. Gordon was taller than me, but otherwise about the same size. The sleeves and legs of his suit were a bit long, but if I held my arms with my elbows bent and cinched my belt a little higher than normal, no one would notice.

Our defense strategy was minimal. There was no denying I'd committed the offense with which I'd been charged. I did, after all, refuse induction. How judges across the country were treating draft resisters varied greatly, however, and it was this that Gene hoped to exploit. If Judge Bohanon could be persuaded that I wasn't a fiery radical, a profane communist hippie freak, but rather a thoughtful and patriotic young American whose conscience had brought him to this time and place, perhaps Bohanon would move somewhat in the direction of those judges who'd found cause for leniency.

Bohanon was not without his good points: he'd been the federal judge who ended segregation in Oklahoma schools only a few years earlier, which had been an unpopular decision that brought him statewide disapproval and more than a few death threats. He was considered by many to be a "liberal" judge.

It was a pipe dream, but it was all we had. Unfortunately it was a dream that denied the reality of the Oklahoma City Federal Court. For half a century OKC judges hadn't relented in their zeal to punish anyone who defied the draft. While I'd been awaiting my own trial, an Oklahoma court had sentenced a young Quaker, Pat Vaughn, to a five-year prison sentence. And on the very same morning as my trial, Pete Washek, an eighteen-year-old Mennonite, would be standing trial in the courtroom next door. I'd had an opportunity to get to know both Pat and Pete—along with their families and members of their churches—and they'd all been warmly supportive of me.

The "conscientious objector" classification was established by Congress in the early part of the twentieth century and was designed expressly to accommodate people like Pat and Pete—young men who'd grown up in the "Peace Churches." So why were they denied CO status by their Oklahoma draft boards?

Simply because that's the way business was done in Oklahoma. Oklahoma draft boards had a long history of ignoring the law regarding conscientious objection, and Oklahoma courts had a long history of letting them get away with it. During the First World War, things were far worse than they were during the Vietnam War. During the run-up to WWI, thirty-five Oklahoma Mennonites were sentenced to *life* imprisonment for refusing to serve in the military. I guess you could say Oklahoma's COs had made a lot of progress since then.

There had been no publicity surrounding Pat Vaughn's trial. His picture hadn't appeared in the paper or on television. No reporter attended his trial. The Oklahoma press wasn't interested in what happened to members of fringe religions, especially when they offended the patriotic sensibilities of the citizenry. Pete Washek's trial wouldn't get any ink either. Religious objectors, in Oklahoma, just weren't good press. The ink was saved for me.

As I journeyed downtown for the start of my trial, I wondered: If Oklahoma federal judges had thrown the book at Pat Vaughn and were surely going to do the same thing to Pete Washek, what hope did I possibly have?

Every seat in the wood-paneled courtroom on the third floor was taken, and spectators spilled into the marble-lined hall and out onto the street. I sat with Eugene Matthews at the polished defense table, my mother and twin brother on the hard pews behind me.

Gene had recommended against a jury trial, which made sense. In other parts of the country, it might be possible to obtain a jury with one or more sympathetic jury members, but in Oklahoma City it wasn't likely a jury would be any less vehement than the judge. If we had any hope of fair treatment, it'd be at the hands of Bohanon alone.

Bohanon entered and took his seat behind his high desk. The trial began.

It seemed to end before it started.

The prosecution called two witnesses. Comet Johns, the head clerk of my Oklahoma draft board, was asked the details of my classification and of my order to report for induction. She answered precisely and efficiently, and there being no questions from the defense, she was excused.

The inducting officer was asked about my first and second appearances at the induction station. The issue with the loyalty oath was not raised. He testified that I'd been deemed by the examiners as qualified for induction, but when ordered to step forward, I did not. Again, there being no questions from the defense, he was excused.

The prosecution rested its case.

Gene opened the defense with a short statement extolling the founding principles of America, reminding the judge that our country was brought into existence by dissent, by people who followed their own conscience. He told the judge he aimed to prove in testimony that the young man on trial was following this American tradition, that he was not a criminal in the normal sense of the word, but was a patriot attempting to serve his country in the best way he knew how.

The judge suffered these remarks without comment. Gene called his first witness, Father Bill Kelly. As Gene asked his first question, the prosecution objected, citing relevancy. The judge sustained the objection. There was to be no testimony from Father Kelly.

Gene persisted. He called Father Bill Nerin. The prosecution objected. The witness was excused. Gene called Ted Coonfield to the stand. The prosecution objected. This witness was also excused.

Finally Gene called me. The judge allowed me to answer a handful of questions about the circumstances of my returning my draft card, and why I hadn't applied for status as a conscientious objector. When Gene started asking me why I opposed the war in Vietnam, the prosecutor again objected and the objection was summarily sustained. Evidently what I thought about the war or the draft wasn't relevant. The war itself wasn't relevant.

The defense rested. Closing statements were short. The prosecutor—my friend Tim Kline's dad—tersely restated the facts of my resistance. Gene made a final plea for compassion and leniency. Judge Bohanon needed no time to consider his verdict.

The whole trial lasted just over an hour.

The courtroom was silent following the verdict. I turned around to face my mother and brothers and noticed Tim Kline, the prosecutor's son and my friend, seated behind them, tears running down his cheeks. No one cried out, no one uttered a word, no one moved. Except the marshals, who expertly handcuffed me and removed me from the chambers, whisking me through a door at the side of the judge's bench.

I was taken to a holding cell in the federal building to await transfer to the county jail. I was there only a few minutes when a door opened,

'He Wants to be a Hero and a Martyr'

Draft Resister Found Guilty

By Bob McMillin

Declaring that Joe Thomas Gilchrist, 20-year old draft resister, "wants to be a hero," U. S. District Judge Luther Bohanon Friday found the youth guilty of refusing to be inducted into the armed services.

Following a 2-hour, non-jury trial, Judge Bohanon said that in his opinion "this defendant has asked for this prosecution because he wants to be a hero and a martyr."

"This is his right, but this court has a duty to follow the law and there can be no question but what he is guilty as charged," Judge Bohanon said.

Gilchrist, a former Cornell University student and American Legion oratorical contest winner, was charged with violation of the selective service act after refusing to be inducted.

Gilchrist said he objected to the war in Vietnam because "it is immoral and unjust."

He had earlier stated that he would fight in something like World War II, but not in Vietnam because he feels it is immoral.

During the brief trial Friday, in which the government called only two witnesses and the defense four, Gilchrist testified he had never applied for deferment as a conscientious objector although he does have religious

(See JUDGE—Page 2)

and my mother entered the hall outside my cell. I burst into tears. I was shaking uncontrollably and racked with fear and pain.

She looked at me, and put out her hand, pointing at me with her crippled fingers. "Don't," she said. "Don't."

That's all she said. And I stopped. I regained control. Only one person could have calmed me at that moment, and it was my mother. She'd been there. Whatever I was about to experience, she'd experienced worse. With a single word, she'd told me to bear it. And I knew that somehow I must.

Throughout her entire life, my mother had been stalwart to a fault—throughout her childhood as a quasi-orphan, throughout the struggling years of the Depression and the War, throughout her difficult and loveless marriage with my father, and even throughout her lengthy recovery from the fire. But all of that paled in comparison to her remarkable stoicism during the five years of her incarceration.

Years later my brother Gordon wrote to me about my mother's implacable strength:

> Before moving to Shreveport in the summer of '68 we would go to Norman and check Rosie out for a weekend. [Beverly and] I would pick her up on Friday, promising to have her back by Monday night. We did this about every 2 months during that time. She never once complained to me about the unfairness of it all and how she had to endure that hospital/jail she was in. I knew she had been railroaded into that horrible place, yet I couldn't see where I could help her.

My experience was the same. My mother had never once complained to me. Rosie was never one for aphorisms, but there was one she repeated a lot: "When life hands you lemons, make lemonade." I don't know how she made lemonade out of the sour fruit of Central State Hospital, but she did.

I'd embraced draft resistance knowing full well that it'd likely end in a prison sentence, but my mother's long confinement had come as a complete surprise to her. It'd never have occurred to my mother that her vengeful ex-husband and his soulless Warr Acres pals would be vile enough to have her declared insane in order to prevent her from selling our home to a black couple. After a time it probably made a kind of sadistic sense to her. In all of their minds this scarred, crippled woman was expendable, while the racially pure sanctity of their community was not.

Throughout the worst kinds of deprivation and humiliation she'd kept her sense of worth and value and even her sense of humor. She kept her humanity. I'd seen it myself, month after month, year after year, during all of my visits with her inside and outside the hospital. I'd witnessed the way she treated other patients, the way they respected and loved and trusted her. I'd experienced her amazing ability to squelch the impulse to bellyache on her own behalf. I'd read countless letters from her in which she always found positive news to share while never complaining. She persevered. Often without any reason to hope, she lived life as if there were reason to hope anyway. She had made lemonade.

"Don't," she said. Just the one word. In my darkest moments in the years ahead, that was what I remembered, what I turned to. My mother. One word. "Don't." A single word, containing all the heartache, hope, and wisdom in the world.

From that moment on I never complained about my own situation. I'd chosen this path and it led where I'd predicted it would. She was right. Bellyaching was for sissies. And besides, it did no good. The only way I was going to be able to make my life any better was to buck up and to look for the silver lining. And if I couldn't find a silver lining, then it'd be up to me to make one. To make lemonade.

She sat for a while outside my cell, not speaking, just being with me, until it was time for my transfer and she was asked to leave.

Normally prisoners are transferred from the Federal Courthouse to the county jail by car, but the marshals had something else in mind for me. It was the lunch hour on a Friday in downtown Oklahoma City. They cuffed my hands and secured me with leg irons. They wrapped a chain about my waist and connected it to my handcuffs and leg irons. They guided me down the elevators and out onto the street. There, in the scalding sunshine, past the throng of supporters and onlookers who'd gathered that day, they paraded me the half a dozen blocks to the county jail along the crowded sidewalk. "Federal prisoner!" they called out, in case anyone should mistake the spectacle for anything else. "Make way!" As office workers and shoppers hurried out of my path to safety, my humiliation was complete.

At County I was fingerprinted once more, and my mug shot was taken. I was deprived of my suit, and examined from orifice to orifice before being handed a pair of flip-flops and a prison jumpsuit. Then I was taken to my cell.

Before I got to the cell I was assaulted by a smell I will not—cannot—ever forget. It was a stench brewed from years of unwashed human flesh, of perspiration and refuse, of bad plumbing and no ventilation, and it was suffused with a heavy cloud of astringent ammonia. During the ensuing years I'd have occasion to be housed in three federal prisons and ten county jails. In none of them did I experience anything remotely like the foul, painful odor of the Oklahoma County Jail. It burned my eyes and nostrils. It violated my skin. To this day I cannot tolerate any hint of ammonia.

I was thankfully not housed with the general population, but was taken to a more remote cell, which I shared with only one other inmate. This cell was surprisingly large. It had four sets of metal bunk beds and an open space with a small metal table and metal benches. The table and benches were bolted to the floor. A toilet without a seat or lid displayed itself in one corner. I was admitted to the cell. The doors clanged shut. And my lone cellmate introduced himself.

I hid my reaction when he told me his name. If he recognized mine, he gave no indication. He might not have known who I was, but I sure as hell knew who he was.

In high school my girlfriend for a time had been Jolene Hudson. Jolene's older cousin had been a nursing student at Oklahoma City University.

One weekend during my senior year, Jolene learned her cousin had been brutally murdered in her dorm bed. She'd been raped and repeatedly stabbed to death, and then her corpse had been set on fire. The murder had gone unsolved for years, until recently. I'd followed the news of this monster's capture over the summer, and I knew he was awaiting trial.

My new cellmate was the accused rapist and murderer of my ex-girlfriend's cousin! Life, as they say, is full of strange and surprising twists.

As cellmates go, he was ideal. He was quiet, private, and polite. He turned his back when I used the toilet and I did the same for him. We talked a little, but very little, and said nothing about our respective offenses. Well, I said to myself, I guess this must be my first opportunity to look for the silver lining.

That's when I recalled a James Kirkwood novel that included a story about two twin boys. Worried that the boys had developed extreme personalities—one was a total pessimist, the other a total optimist—their parents took them to a psychiatrist.

First the psychiatrist treated the pessimist and took him to a room filled with brand new toys. Instead of yelping with joy, the little boy burst into tears. "What's the matter?" the psychiatrist asked, baffled. "Don't you want to play with any of the toys?" "Yes," the little boy bawled, "but if I did, I'd break them."

Next the psychiatrist treated the optimist. He took him to a room filled with a pile of horse manure. But instead of wrinkling his nose in disgust, the boy yelled in delight. Then he climbed to the top of the pile, dropped to his knees, and began gleefully digging out scoop after scoop with his hands. "What are you doing?" asked the psychiatrist, as baffled with the optimist as he'd been with the pessimist. "With all this manure," the little boy replied, "there must be a pony."

There must be a pony. So I set about looking for it.

My cellmate introduced me to the routine. I spent twenty-four hours a day in the cell, unless I got a visit from my lawyer, at which time I was taken to a small windowless room. Once a week I was escorted to the shower, where I was also allowed to shave under the watchful eyes of the guards. The lights were turned out at ten p.m. They came back on at six a.m. Each morning we got a pail filled with coffee and a biscuit wrapped in a brown paper towel. That was breakfast. After breakfast we dumped out the pail in the toilet, and through the bars it was filled with an ammonia solution. Then we were handed a sponge, which we used to mop the floor and clean the toilet. This had to be done each day. At noon we each received a plateful of cold beans and a single slice of raw onion. Some days we got brown beans, some days white. For dinner, we got a slab of bologna on two pieces of white bread.

That was it. The whole routine. There was nothing to read. Nothing to do. Nothing. Just four steel walls with no windows and one bare light bulb hanging in the corridor outside our cell. My cellmate had already been there for four months. I was his first roommate. He didn't get any visitors.

On Saturday I was escorted out of my cell to a small, airless room for a visit with my attorney. Gene told me I'd be sentenced on Monday, which was good and bad. Normally there was a longer delay before sentencing. Bohanon was proceeding immediately, which indicated he'd made up his mind, and that didn't bode well in our favor. But it was also good because I'd be transferred after sentencing to a federal prison, which should be more comfortable than the county jail. There's that pony again.

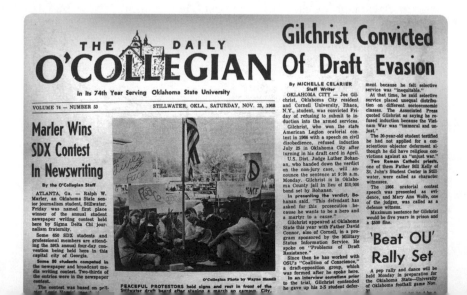

Gene said he'd already had conversations with the New York ACLU about drafting an appeal, which he hoped to file in the next few days. Once the appeal was filed, he could ask for appeal bond. He said there was no reason Bohanon shouldn't grant it, and I could be out of prison before Christmas.

Gene said the sit-in at OSU had drawn a good crowd and a lot of attention. He brought greetings and best wishes from my mom and my friends.

Neither Gene nor I had any illusions about actually winning an appeal. Delaying the start of my sentence didn't seem like a good idea, but given my fright and my state of mind, I'd accept any excuse to get out of prison for a while.

On Sunday Bill Kelly visited as my pastor, which wasn't completely dishonest; he looked nonetheless unnatural in his black shirt and priestly collar—a garb I'd never seen him wear before. We sat across from each other in a stifling room, our hands clasped atop a small metal table. Neither of us knew what to say, so we said very little. It was enough to be together.

Bill brought with him a letter from my mother:

November 24, 1968

Joe,

I know with your courage and faith you aren't worried about your-self. And do not worry about me. Work is the best and most effective therapy. I shall work. I shall stay busy. I shall not lose faith.

Your friends have been constantly with me. Bless them.

Make the best use of your time where you are. Honey, I learned so much while serving my five years at Central State Hospital. You will also grow and learn and serve.

Be staunch. I'd do the same again for civil rights. Be true to yourself and your cause.

I love you,
Mom

When I read that letter today, half a century later, it still has lessons for me. "Be staunch," she said. Be staunch.

Bill told me that Bishop Reed and other clergy were going to hold a press conference and make an appeal to the judge for leniency. No one thought it'd work, but it mattered that they were doing it. If clergy in positions of power were willing to speak out in my behalf, well, that was a pretty good-sized pony.

On Monday, November 25, I was escorted from my cell. Under the disapproving eyes of two guards, I showered, shaved, and dressed in Gordon's suit and tie. I was cuffed and shackled, but this time there was no parade through the streets. I was driven by the marshals to the courthouse.

Before announcing my sentence, the judge was obliged to offer me a chance to make a statement. Over the weekend I'd managed to scribble a few sentences on a scrap of paper with a pencil stub my cellmate had provided. I knew I wouldn't be able to take anything with me from my cell to the courtroom, so I'd smuggled the notes to Bill Kelly when he'd visited me on Sunday. In the courtroom, he returned them to me, passing them to me via my attorney.

This statement at sentencing was important to me. It was these words, I thought, that I'd be remembered by. They anchored me as I stood before the judge. Now, of course, I'm the only one who remembers them. I still have this pathetic document—this distressed and almost unreadable fragment, filled with desperate words most floridly written—some forty years later. When I read them now I recognize the ravings of an earnest young man on the threshold of a long prison sentence. While I was undoubtedly florid, at least I was, as my mother proscribed, "staunch."

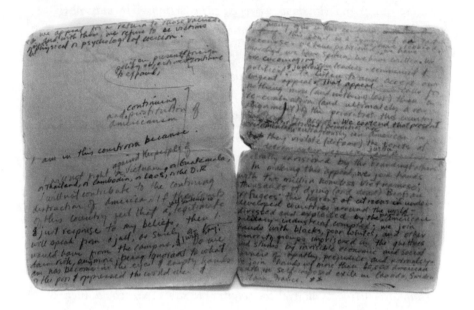

For many of us, this courtroom is a symbol of a last recourse. We have petitioned, we have lobbied, we have marched, we have spoken, we have written. We are encouraging our leaders to listen to and accept our urgent appeal. That appeal calls for nothing more (and nothing less) than a re-evaluation (and ultimately a re-alignment) of the priorities this country has come to accept. We contend that present governmental and institutional priorities are outrageously un-American, in that they violate the tenets of self-determination, equality, justice and freedom initially envisioned by our Founding Fathers.

We appeal for a return to those values. In making this appeal, we join hands with two million homeless Vietnamese; thousands of dying (and dead) Biafran refugees; the legion of citizens in underdeveloped countries around the world—divested and exploited by the mammoth American military-industrial complex. We join hands with blacks, poor whites and other minority groups imprisoned in the ghettoes and slums by invisible economic and social barriers of apathy, prejudice and normalcy. We join hands with the more than 60,000 American youth now living in self-imposed exile in Canada, Sweden, Britain and France. And with them, we refuse to be victimized by mass physical and psychological coercion. We seek change.

We recognize that we are, in the initial and final analyses, Americans—and Americans who desire and advocate only the highest moral, ethical and political standards for our homeland. We stand with pride beside our country's unequaled technical and scientific innovations, but we shudder at their misuse.

We have witnessed the assassination of some of our greatest men, and we carry their reflections and their concerns with us. We heed the April 1967 warning in Dr. Martin Luther King's Declaration of Independence from the War in Vietnam, that: "A nation which continues year after year to spend more money on programs of physical destruction than programs of social uplift is approaching spiritual death." In response to that warning, we are assembled in this courtroom (and in similar courtrooms all over the country) to say, "Yea, behold, there is yet a hope for spiritual rebirth—in and through our witness."

I thus should amend my opening remark. This courtroom is not the last recourse, for the last recourse is also the first—the conduct of our daily lives. (Such is the content of our "kingdom not of this earth"—a "land of freedom… where all men are as brothers.")

I am in this courtroom because I will not fight against the people of Vietnam, (or, if our foreign policy objectives continue to expand, the people of Guatemala, Laos, Thailand, Cambodia or the Dominican Republic). I will not contribute to what I consider to be the continuing destruction of America and the continuing prostitution of Americanism. If the courts of this country feel that a jail sentence is a legitimate and just response to my beliefs, then I will speak from a jail as surely as I would from a campus and I will say:

"Do we dare risk any longer being ignorant to what America has become in the eyes and empty hands of the poor and oppressed the world over, and having overcome our ignorance, do we risk not breaking silence? For more is at stake than our comfort."

From the moment the sentencing hearing had started, Judge Bohanon displayed his anger. Steam was spouting from his ears. He was livid that clergy would dare attempt to discourage him from throwing the whole weight of the law at me. They should stick to the business of saving souls, he said, and he'd attend to the business of dispensing justice on earth. He disparaged the clergy from the bench, and he made it clear his contempt that morning was as much for them as it was for me. He blustered. He railed. He vented. He pontificated. But first, he had one more nail to drive in this felon's coffin.

He hoped after spending a weekend in the county jail I might be terrified enough to change my mind. He said he'd spoken to the commanding officer of the induction center, and if I were willing to join the Army that morning, he'd rescind my conviction.

I was speechless. Had the man heard nothing I said?

Bohanon exhaled. Shook his head. Bit the inside of his cheek. If Judge Bohanon was a mystery to me, I was more of a mystery to him. In pronouncing the verdict, Bohanon peered at me and said, "The court finds that you have been a disservice to your family, a disservice to yourself, and a disservice to your school." My brothers and my mother sitting in

the courtroom might have disagreed with him about the disservice to family, whatever that meant. As to the alleged disservice to myself, that made even less sense to me. Who was he to decide what was and was not a service or disservice to myself? And disservice to my school? What was that all about? What did my school have to do with any of it?

He sentenced me to five years in prison. He banged his gavel. The hearing was adjourned.

For five more days I ate brown beans and onions, breathed foul air, and occasionally engaged my murderous cellmate in inconsequential conversation. I wore out my body with sit-ups and push-ups. I learned the fine art of pacing. I lay on my back on my bunk, gazing at a ceiling imprinted with the graffiti scratches of hundreds of prisoners before me. I slept day and night. I waited.

At midnight during my fifth night back in County, I was awakened and hustled from my cell. I was handcuffed and chained and handed over to two federal marshals. It seemed odd to me they chose midnight on a Friday to execute my transfer. At any rate, I was glad to be leaving, to be getting on with whatever came next.

We left the lights of the city for the inky night of the short drive through the country. For the first time in a week, I could see stars again and breathe fresh air. Too quickly the prison was visible across the flat plains—the bright perimeter lights and razor-wired fence defining it for what it was. We arrived at the high gates of the El Reno Federal Reformatory, as it was called then, a little before two a.m. A guard lowered a bucket from the main gun tower, and after the marshals placed their guns within the bucket, he raised it to the turret again. I was removed from the car and hustled inside.

In the lobby I passed through the front sallyport and was guided to A&D, the Arrival and Discharge unit. I was stripped and searched again, to make sure I hadn't magically acquired contraband while shackled in the back seat of the government car. I was handed a set of used army khakis, underwear, socks, and a pair of well-worn black shoes. I was told my new identity was 34633-118. The 118 meant I was in El Reno. The 34633, that was me. Then I was locked in a holding cell, to wait while an inmate was awakened and brought to A&D to complete my intake.

In most prisons, prisoners have jobs, and at El Reno the task of taking mug shots had been assigned to an inmate. I don't know why the officer on duty couldn't have snapped a picture, but apparently he couldn't, and so we waited for the inmate photographer. Finally he arrived.

I watched in disbelief from inside my cell. This young, handsome man, perhaps a year or two older than I, was ebulliently happy. That was the first thing that was wrong. The second was that he didn't look like he'd just been hauled from his bunk. His hair was tidy, his khakis were crisply pressed, his shoes were brightly shined. The third thing wrong was that he not only knew the officer, but they seemed to like each other. There was a warm greeting, with patting on the backs, as if these two were friends.

The cell was unlocked and I stepped up to the white X taped on the floor. I looked in the direction of the mysteriously contented inmate, Phil Shuman, who stood behind the camera. "Smile!" he said.

Smile? Was he insane? What the hell was there to smile about? It was two in the morning, I was tired and hadn't showered or shaved in a week. Oh, and in case no one had noticed, I was in fucking prison.

I didn't smile.

The next morning I awoke in the orientation dorm to the amplified clanging of a toy xylophone over the prison loudspeaker. I watched the other inmates to see what I should do, and as they crawled out of their bunks and started to dress, I did the same. Before long I was noticed, and not long after that, I observed that items of value were being passed from hand to hand—cartons of cigarettes, candy bars, bars of soap. These items wound up in the hands of an inmate across from my bunk who'd won a bet. He'd correctly chosen the date I'd arrive in El Reno.

In El Reno prisoners watched a lot of television, which meant that lately they'd seen a lot of me. There wasn't an inmate or a guard who didn't know who I was and why I'd been convicted. And they'd been waiting for me, betting on the date of my arrival.

It may be illogical, but prisoners are, by and large, ultra-patriotic. What's more, their patriotism competes with that of the federal prison guards who were mostly ex-military, hoping to squeeze the most out of their federal pensions by extending their service in a civilian capacity. Draft resisters were therefore not well-liked. We ranked somewhere below child molesters and snitches. I sensed this during my first few waking moments in federal prison. I'm not by nature a paranoid person. But it was clear that everyone—inmates and guards alike—had their eyes on me. I was in for a rough haul.

I did my best to keep to myself. If anyone in the prison felt friendly toward me, they gave me no indication. But I had plenty of indication otherwise. When we were free to move around in the dorm, I stayed on my bunk. When we were free to walk in the inside yard, I stayed on my bunk. At chow, I ate by myself, head down. I didn't know when the first blow would come, but I expected one any moment. I expected it in the morning in the showers, at noon in line for chow, and at night in my bunk. I was a marked man. This wasn't just my imagination. This was what I was told, by inmates and guards alike. Watch out, they said; it'd happen when I least expected it.

All this time I kept my eye on Phil. He was a mystery to me. He was like the misplaced object in the puzzles I'd loved as a kid, the puzzles where one is supposed to pick out the item in the picture that didn't belong. Phil didn't belong.

He didn't belong in this picture because he was so damn happy. Every time I saw him, he was happy. Inmates in the orientation dorm were mostly segregated from the general population, except during chow, so

I'd see him when he was standing in line across the mess or hanging out in the yard when I was on my way to some appointment. Phil was never alone. I was always alone. Phil was always laughing. I felt as though I'd forgotten how to laugh. There was something clearly wrong with him. Someone, I thought, needed to tell him he was in prison because he obviously didn't realize it.

Days passed. Nights passed. I didn't know how I'd be able to stand five years of this. I longed to be back with my murderous cellmate at County. There, at least, I felt safe.

December rolled around. To me it felt as if I'd been in prison a year, but it'd only been a week. Then suddenly I was released.

Daniel Berrigan and Doug Dowd had convinced eight other Cornell faculty, most of whom I'd never met, to empty their wallets for my release. Their ten thousand dollars in cash was deposited with the U.S. Attorney, where it'd remain until my appeal was decided. Should I decide to flee from the judgment of the court, the money would be forfeited.

My first taste of prison scared the shit out of me. I was vulnerable and freaked. I was convinced the only reason I got out alive was that my bail had been posted just in time. Another day, another week, and I'd have been toast. The judge agreed to lift my travel restriction during the appeal, and gratefully I put my tail between my legs and returned to Cornell. I wanted to get as far away from Oklahoma as I could.

Once I was back on the Ithaca campus, I wanted nothing to do with the war, the draft, or with dissent or protests of any kind. In spite of the example of my mother, I'd failed in this first round of imprisonment. I'd been roundly terrified and desperately unhappy. There was no pony to be found. All I wanted now was to escape the mess I was in, and to try to resume a normal life for as long as I could.

I found a room in an apartment shared by two hotel administration undergrads and one engineering senior, who was a button-downed, spit-shined standout in the Naval ROTC program at Cornell. I don't know what they thought about my status as a convicted felon because it was something we never talked about. I never talked about it with anyone. I stayed in the shadows.

I immersed myself in my classes and in theatre. I was the lead in a main-stage production of Harold Pinter's *The Homecoming*. It was presented in April, the one-year anniversary of the assassination of Martin Luther King. Just as King's death a year earlier had unleashed a series of unsettling incidents on campus, so it had again. False fire alarms emptied classes during the day and dorms during the night.

In the middle of the second performance of *The Homecoming* a fire alarm stopped the show. I stepped from the stage as the asbestos fire-curtain automatically lowered. I stood at the side of the house exit, ushering audience members out while I remained in character. Everyone thought it was just another false alarm—and it was—and a few minutes later I ushered the audience back in, climbed back on the stage, and resumed the performance.

The rest of our run was cancelled when, the next day, armed African-American students occupied the student union, Willard Straight Hall. Student occupations of buildings as a means of protest were nothing new, but no such occupation anywhere in the country had previously involved guns. The National Guard was called to campus to supplement the unarmed campus police, and a tense standoff ensued while negotiations slowly began.

For years black students at Cornell had been peacefully fighting for parity—in accommodations, in funding, in academic programs—but they sensed little progress and their desperation had led them to this.

Desperation I understood; guns I did not. Fortunately the takeover ended with no one killed or injured, and with the university's promise to embark upon a lengthy and complete reexamination of its policies toward, and its treatment of, minorities.

I watched all this from the sidelines. Later that spring I acted in another Pinter production, *The Collection*. When I wasn't onstage I was offstage, helping with the lighting or the sets, or printing up posters in the theatre shop. I tried, rather successfully, not to think about my appeal.

That summer I stayed at Cornell, employed once more with the Cornell Summer Repertory, performing minor roles and assisting with lighting and sets. I worked hard. I partied hard. I drank cheap wine and smoked cheaper marijuana. I went skinny dipping in the reservoir and the gorge. I discovered an Ithaca townie bar that, while not being specifically a gay bar, nonetheless provided opportunities to acquire short-term companions. I ignored whatever was happening in Vietnam, and I was grateful that appeals in federal courts move slowly. I wasn't ready to go back to prison. I didn't think I'd ever be.

My twin brother Jim came to visit and stayed for most of the summer. We bought two used, cheap Raleigh three-speeds, and we biked up and down hills to Enfield, a sprawling and magnificent state park that started at the top with a tame creek which became a raging torrent through a ragged slate gorge as it wound and dipped for miles below.

On the night that man first walked on the moon, I was on the Cornell stage, playing a soldier wearing a nun's habit in Brendan Behan's *The Hostage*. When the assembled cast sang, "Don't muck about, don't muck about, don't muck about with the moon," the audience broke into howls. In the greenroom between scenes, in our costumes and makeup, we crowded around a small portable black and white television and saw grainy images of the earth as it looked from the moon.

The summer ended, as summers always do. In September I made a new friend, Greg Smith. I took to Greg instantly, with his swarthy good looks and his lovable dog, Jude. He invited me to his house to meet his new wife, Susan, and I found myself equally smitten with her. Greg was in his senior year in engineering. Susan had graduated from Wells College the previous year. Whatever it was that drew us together, we became a trio. We ate together, played together, laughed together. Greg was a serious doper and always had good shit. We listened to the Moody Blues on his expensive KLH stereo. We picnicked in the gorges with their good dog. I cast Greg in an abysmal anti-war play I'd written about the battle of Stalingrad. I paid frequent visits to a classroom of truant kids whom Susan was teaching in a free school in downtown Ithaca.

That fall Bill Kelly and Ray Repp visited Ithaca, and Daniel Berrigan arranged for the three of us to join him in a Sunday morning ecumenical service at Cornell's baroque Sage Chapel. Although they had corresponded and spoken on the phone, Bill and Ray had never met Dan, and after our peregrinations the previous year, this was something they badly wanted to do. They also wanted to see Ithaca and the Finger Lakes region, which I'd often told them was unquestionably the most beautiful place in the world. Not long after, Bill and Ray moved to Trumansburg, about twenty miles outside Ithaca. Ray continued to write his music, and Bill signed on as his partner in the music business, forever leaving the priesthood.

The Sage Chapel event drew an overflow crowd of several hundred participants. At Dan's request, I did the reading. Ray and Bill participated in the Celebration of the Eucharist, and Ray led the participants in song. Dan delivered the sermon.

On the surface it may have been just another Sunday church service, but any event with Dan Berrigan was always more than that. Dan never lost an opportunity to speak out eloquently for peace and against injustice, and most of those who'd come to hear him that morning expected nothing less. He didn't disappoint.

His sermon was elaborately titled "Of Ghosts, a German Lieutenant, and Filetto; Trustees and Cornell; and Finally of Jesus, Who Has Something to Say and Great Trouble Getting It Heard." Dan spoke first about Bishop Mathias DeFregger, a German Lieutenant in the 1940s who'd reached an unholy compromise sparing some and condemning others arbitrarily in the town of Filetto, Italy. DeFregger had been ordered to kill all the inhabitants of the town. He bargained to save the lives of twenty townspeople, then went about the business of killing the rest.

> *"What could I do?" is the spastic cry of this Christian, years later.*

> *What a man can do is to refuse to be the instrument of those powers which claim men for death.*

> *What a man can do is to recognize the three or four metaphors which contain and convey the power of death over life in his own lifetime. I mean militarism, racism, nationalism and war.*

> *What a man can do is to strip his heart of the lying presence of death that flourished there; in fear, egoism, laziness, lust, in squalid obedience and in betrayal of the mind and of its powers.*

Then Dan turned his attention to the release of the "Robertson Report"— a report from the Trustees of Cornell University on the turmoil on the Cornell campus in the spring of 1969, and in particular on the armed-takeover of the student union:

> *The power of the trustees (together with the power of the faculty) lie very nearly at the heart of our trouble. The trustees, from Harlem to South Africa, traffic in human misery, huckster our paramilitary ideology and build their fortunes upon the despair of the powerless. How, in the nature of things, could they have issued any report but this one; a compendium of mythology, clichés, and Bible-belt righteousness; neither imaginative nor generous of spirit, ignorant of nature of that community whose building is all our hope? The report arises out of no tradition; how can it urge us to return to it, to create or to embody it?*

This, then, was my reentry into the world of protest politics, and it didn't feel all bad.

In October I joined Greg and Susan on a road trip to Washington, D.C., to participate in a march. I wouldn't have gone if it hadn't been for the opportunity to spend more time with them; it was just another march on Washington, albeit the biggest one yet. Hundreds of thousands of peaceniks were on the mall. Handwritten banners and tie-dyed shirts. Hare Krishnas, hippies, and anti-war veterans. Angry orations and street-corner musicians. Mounted police and snipers on rooftops. It was a circus, a celebration, a grand party.

But for me it was no party at all. The suffocating cloud of imprisonment hung over my head, casting me in a dark mood on this sunny and happy day. The revelry of revolution only deepened my despair.

At the Lincoln Memorial I ran into Dale Alley. Finding an acquaintance from Oklahoma in this maelstrom of thousands was miraculous, and we embraced at the edge of the reflecting pool. Dale asked me if I'd be at my appeal hearing the next week.

"What appeal hearing?" I asked him.

Dale told me he'd encountered my lawyer a few days earlier at a peace rally in Stillwater, and that Gene had mentioned my case was coming before the Tenth Circuit Court of Appeals, which normally met in Denver but had scheduled some cases to be heard in Oklahoma City. I knew nothing about it. It wasn't Gene's fault. I hadn't been good about staying in touch with Gene lately. He probably didn't even know how to reach me since I'd changed apartments that fall.

I found a pay phone and called Gene at home. He confirmed the details of the hearing. There was no need for me to be there, he said. The defendant doesn't play a role in appeals. Briefs are filed and the prosecutor and defense attorney make arguments. The justices ask questions, and everyone goes home. The decision isn't handed down until sometime later—usually months later.

I told Gene I'd see him in court. I needed to be at this event, this spectacle in which the defendant has no part, which would lead to the decision either to send me back to prison (most likely) or free me (not likely at all). I said goodbye to Greg and Susan and boarded a bus with Dale back to Oklahoma.

I'd seen my mother only once in the last year, when I'd returned briefly to Oklahoma for spring break. We wrote each other once or twice a week, and phoned whenever our budgets would allow it. During my absence, she'd done well for herself, continuing to work as a housekeeper at OCU in the spring and summer, before being asked to move into one of the dorms as a housemother, where she was working now. My new Oklahoma friends hadn't forgotten her. Practically every week Bill Kelly, Ray Repp, or Vince Uhl would visit her from Stillwater, taking her out to lunch or dinner or bringing her a bag of groceries. Mary Ann Hodges remained a true friend, taking her to movies, rallies, readings, and dinner at Maxine's Soul Food Kitchen. Dr. Olsen, the OCU president, kept an eye on her as well.

My mother's apartment in the OCU dorm was modest and not ideal for hosting a visiting son, so I crashed, with of all people, Phil Shuman.

Phil had presented himself at our doorstep shortly after my release from El Reno a year before, preceding my return to Ithaca. His arrival at my door was a complete surprise. During my brief incarceration there had been no chance for us to become friends. True, I was fascinated by him—but from a distance; I had no inkling that he had taken any interest in me. I couldn't recall giving him my address, but perhaps I had.

While still an inmate, he'd been accepted as an undergraduate at Oklahoma City University, and had been granted special status as a federal prisoner on study-release. Each weekday morning an inmate designated as the "study-release driver" drove a prison van the forty miles or so from El Reno to OCU and dropped Phil off at campus. During the day Phil went to class, studied in the library, and hung out at the student union. At night and on weekends, he returned to prison.

After I had left Oklahoma, Phil had dropped in to see my mother once or twice a week, and he and I had kept in touch by letter. I still didn't know what made this unusual man tick, but he'd integrated himself into my life and I welcomed him.

Phil may have been an inmate, but he still had the best drugs I'd ever had the pleasure of ingesting. That didn't entirely explain his upbeat personality, but it helped. After being convicted for trafficking marijuana and hashish on the campus of Kansas University, he'd been sentenced to a zip-six, a weird hybrid sentence popular for young first-time federal offenders. Zip-Sixers could be released from prison after as few as sixty days, or they could remain behind bars for as long as six years—at the discretion of the prison authorities and the parole board. The good thing about a zip-six was that after six years the prisoner's record would be expunged—leaving no permanent felony to stain a future career. The bad thing about a zip-six was the uncertainty associated with it.

But Phil didn't seem too bothered by any threat hanging over his head. He wasn't bothered by anything. He was just too damn happy. In plain view of the guards twice a day, he smuggled a small stash of hashish in and out of the prison in the base of a ChapStick tube. The cap of the tube had a hole poked in one side. He wrapped a small piece of adhesive tape around the cap to mask the hole. When he removed the tape, he could plunge the tip of a hollow Bic pen into the hole, giving him an effective hash pipe.

Phil had the best hashish. Lebanese gold. Peruvian black. It only took one good toke to evoke a lasting high, and if one held one's breath long enough, the smoke was wholly absorbed into the lungs, leaving little trace in the open air. Thus Phil was able to toke undetected at night in the private cell he was accorded as a student-release inmate. Phil seemed to have ignored whatever lessons he was supposed to be learning from his imprisonment.

As an inmate Phil wasn't allowed to have an apartment in the city, but that didn't stop Phil either. It was just one more rule to ignore. Attractive and cheerful, it hadn't taken him long to make friends with two undergraduate co-eds who had a small apartment off-campus and who subsequently invited Phil to make their casa his casa. Between classes, he was more often found in the apartment than in the library, listening to Santana, Joni Mitchell, or Led Zeppelin. Kicking back. Dropping dope. So when I said I stayed with Phil during this visit to Oklahoma, what I meant was that at night I crashed on the sofa at his friends' apartment, while Phil himself was safely ensconced in his prison bunk.

Gene Matthews had been right about there being no need for me to attend my own appeal hearing. Nothing that mattered to me was argued in the courtroom that day— other than my fate, but incredibly, my fate was never specifically referenced. At this elevation the law is little more than the parsing of words—this clause versus that clause, this interpretation versus that interpretation of a phrase or citation. The hearing had nothing to do with the war or the draft. It was about miniscule points of law. It felt as if I'd already lost. Whatever was happening in this courtroom didn't reflect why I'd resisted the draft in the first place. Although it was all about me, it wasn't about me at all.

I left the courtroom as anonymously as I'd arrived but considerably more dejected. As arranged, I met Phil for a matinee showing of a movie we both wanted to see. First we found an alley where we could get sufficiently stoned on his hashish. Then we entered a dark theater together to watch *Easy Rider*.

In the parlance of the day, going from my federal appeals court hearing to a screening of *Easy Rider* was a mind-fuck. I'd left the courtroom numb, feeling nothing at all. As the movie progressed, I got sucked into the story and the gory climax—the slaying of Peter Fonda and Dennis Hopper—exposed every nerve in my body. Every inch of my flesh was screaming with pain, as if I'd been filled with buckshot and flown off a motorcycle at high speed, the asphalt tearing my flesh. I nearly had to be carried out of the theatre. It was an hour before my voice found its way back into my throat.

The next morning I said goodbye to my mom and started back to Ithaca. Dale Alley said he'd had enough of college and wanted to do something real with his life. He was going to New York. He'd start out at the Catholic Worker, and then see what happened. Me? I was a mess. I was miserable. I was returning to Ithaca because I didn't know what else to do.

Neither of us had any money, so we did what kids did then. We hitchhiked. On a long rainy stretch around St. Louis where nobody seemed to want to give us a lift, a menacing State Trooper first threatened to jail us, and then transported us to the other side of town. Otherwise our trip was uneventful and pleasant. Dale was a good traveling buddy, content and taciturn. He left me to my own thoughts, confused as they were. And I had some figuring to do.

Winter came. At Christmas I stayed in Ithaca, house-sitting Greg and Sue's apartment and walking their dog Jude through chest high snowdrifts from a blizzard that had struck the Finger Lakes on Christmas week. Alone on a deserted campus, I felt as though I were a ghost. I went on long walks in the gorges. I sequestered myself in a high carrel in the undergraduate library, where I sat for hours watching snow settle on Lake Cayuga. I tried to write this story and failed.

At the end of December I surfaced from the depths of my despair and rejoined the community of resistance at Cornell. Daniel Berrigan had been working with a mutual friend, Doug Hostetter, to develop an electric mass, a *Missa Moratoria*, and on December 29 it was presented in the cavernous Memorial Room of Willard Straight Hall. I spoke that night to the crowd about the resistance. Perhaps I wasn't entirely coherent, since I hadn't yet figured out what it was I had to say following my year of silence. But I spoke.

That semester I shared a small Collegetown studio apartment with a classmate, Ric Lieberman, a better actor than I could ever hope to be. Only a low partition separated the lone bedroom from the small living area, and I offered Ric the use of the bedroom while I took the couch. On a January night, while a winter storm howled outside and flakes of snow flew through the cracks of our ancient windowsills, I was awakened by a loud knock on the door. I opened the door to find Sue standing there, her tattered vintage raccoon coat sheathed in snow and her face streaked with tears. I brought her inside, holding onto her tightly, oblivious to my nakedness or the melted snow from her coat pooling between us. I sat her down on the couch and, my arms wrapped around her, she told me she and Greg had been fighting. They fought often, she said, and lately about me. He'd accused her of sleeping with me and loving me more than him. He'd hit her.

This was absurd, I told her, and she knew that. What she didn't know was that if I could have slept with either of them I'd probably have preferred Greg. There was no reason to tell her this, since I had no intention to sleep with Greg, who was belligerently straight. If I ever made a pass at him, I'd be the one getting the beating.

I felt a shadow in the room and looked up to see Greg's silhouette in the doorway. Great, I thought. First he beats up his wife for allegedly sleeping with me, and then he finds her in my arms while I'm stark naked.

Greg entered. Sue and I stood. Tears were glistening on each of our faces. The three of us embraced in an awkward group hug. Greg frantically apologized to Sue. Eventually they left.

I sat back down on the couch, rather dazed. After a moment Ric came out of the bedroom. "What the fuck was that all about?" he asked, handing me a doobie.

A few weeks later our father stopped providing Jim with any funds for his living expenses at school. I gave up my apartment, breaking my lease, and sent my rent money to Jim to help him stay in school. I slept on couches and floors in friends' apartments the rest of that year. I didn't mind really; since I wasn't home much, I didn't need a home. I kept myself busy.

I kept myself busy with Sue.

Her reconciliation with Greg that night didn't last long. Within days I heard Sue had moved out, and was crashing at a friend's apartment. Honestly, I visited only to comfort her and see if she were all right. I had no idea that as soon as the door to the apartment opened we'd wind up in bed together. And I had no idea I'd love her so much. Perhaps Greg had been prescient.

That winter and spring, during the scant moments I disentwined myself from Sue's athletic loins, I started paying attention to the world again. I re-engaged.

The war ground on.

In February the Chicago Seven were convicted. In March three Weathermen blew themselves up in a townhouse in Greenwich Village, and twenty-five hundred students burned their draft cards in a single rally at Berkeley. At Cornell I attended rally after rally about the war, the draft, poverty, and racism. I resumed my visits to Daniel Berrigan's office. I felt a familiar itch.

I accepted an invitation from one of Dan's closest friends, James Matlock, to a farewell dinner for Dan on April 8. I was asked to bring my make-up kit, the one I used when on stage. It was a peculiar request, but if someone wanted to play with my make-up, that was okay with me. The dinner was to be held at Dan's small apartment, so I knew there wouldn't be more than a handful of people there. I felt like an intruder as I approached the apartment. I'd been closer to him two years earlier. And soon, Dan would be gone. The appeal for his conviction for burning draft records with homemade napalm with the Catonsville Nine had run its course, and he'd been ordered to report to prison. He'd had a few days to put his life in order, as they say, and those days had passed. Tomorrow he'd begin his sentence.

The conspiracy was in full swing before I arrived, and had been for some time. I was merely the newest conspirator, and my willingness to come along for the ride had never been in doubt. Dan wasn't going to turn himself in, but rather was going underground. He, his brother Phil, and two others of the Catonsville Nine had decided to defy the court order. They didn't concede the right of the government to imprison them any more than they conceded the right of the government to wage war in Vietnam. They were fully aware that becoming fugitives would likely result in additional charges and a longer confinement ultimately, but they were willing to take that risk. In prison their voices would be silenced; underground they could still speak out and agitate against the war.

We all assumed Dan was under constant surveillance. We'd grown familiar to the presence of unusual clicks and groans on his phone, and to the presence of certain shadowy figures at public events. After dinner Dan would quietly disappear. The trick was evading detection.

"How can I help?" I asked. They needed me to provide Dan with a disguise to help him elude any observers that night.

Unfortunately my experience using make-up didn't extend much past pancake and eyeliner. Disguises were way out of my league. Nonetheless I crafted a fake mustache for Dan (he often wore a goatee, but was beardless at the moment), and I darkened his hair, masking the gray. When I finished, he looked exactly like Dan Berrigan except with a blatantly fake mustache and badly colored hair. Wrapping himself in the coat and hat that one of his visitors had worn to the party, Dan left in the company of two of the conspirators while the rest of us remained behind, casting shadows on the curtains to confirm to any federal spook that the party was still in progress.

I joined an energetic group of Dan's many supporters to plan a massive three-day celebration to coincide with his going underground— a Woodstock-inspired love-in with music and speeches and theatre. We secured the use of Barton Hall, the cavernous arena at the north end of campus used for basketball games, phys-ed classes, and convocations.

The event itself was called "America is Hard to Find," after a poem Dan had written and which had been turned into a song by John Hostetter. It'd begin on Friday, April 17, and would include a "Freedom Seder"—a theatrical representation of the traditional Jewish religious observance performed by New York's Bread and Puppet Theatre. Other performers who signed on for the weekend included Phil Ochs, Judy Collins, Country Joe and the Fish, Jerry Jeff Walker, and a lot of local bands, writers, and poets.

On the day of the event I went to a farm outside Ithaca where Dan had been hiding since his disappearance. In spite of my earlier failing, I'd been asked to bring my make-up kit again, and once more I applied such masking to Dan's face as I dared. At the appointed hour a motorcycle drove up the lane to the farmhouse and the cyclist entered, carrying an extra helmet and leather jacket for Dan. Fully outfitted, Dan was unrecognizable, due entirely to the helmet and not at all to the make-up. I went ahead to Barton Hall to help prepare the way.

Not an inch of floor space was available, and hardly an atom of oxygen. The *Cornell Daily Sun* reported that more than fifteen thousand people attended. The party had started, and the echoes of voices, drums, guitars, and cymbals ricocheted and pulsed through the giant hall. At each entrance and several points near the stage, another presence was visible: unsmiling men in somber suits, obviously on the lookout for Daniel Berrigan.

Behind the stage was a door leading to the service alley where the Bread and Puppet Theatre truck was parked, and where the actors were climbing into their ten- and fifteen-foot tall puppets. A motorcycle pulled into the alley with a passenger on the back. Dan Berrigan dismounted, removed his leather jacket and helmet, and climbed into a puppet just in time for the actors to enter Barton Hall in a slow and dramatic procession accompanied by the banging of drums. Now disguised in one of the puppets, Dan ascended the stage. He removed his costume and the crowd went wild. Some hundred or so supporters, who were previously recruited, circled the stage and locked arms to protect Dan from the overwhelmed feds. Ever the poet, he shared a verse he'd written for the occasion. Then, profoundly at ease, he sat down on the stage and

enjoyed the performances.
He remained there for two
hours in full view. Then, as
suddenly as he'd arrived,
he was gone, his departure
shielded from view by gi-
ant puppets and a mob of
jubilant friends.

Back at the farm I climbed
into the driver's seat of
the borrowed getaway car
and I drove Dan to Long
Island. I dropped him at

The Bread and Puppet Theatre. Photo courtesy
of Cornell University Library Rare Books
Manuscript Collection

Coney Island, passing him into the hands of other friends there, people
I didn't know and whose names I didn't ask. The drive to Coney Island
was the longest time I'd ever spent alone with Dan. We talked about the
trivial and the personal: food and family and spring. We talked about
the war. We talked about resistance. He told me about a friend of his,
John Grady, and he invited me to John's home, a retreat at some place
they called "Iron Mountain" in the Bronx. There I could meet others
who wanted to stop the war and the draft.

I stopped in Manhattan on my way back, too tired to attempt the drive
back to Ithaca that night. By the time I arrived at the Catholic Worker,
where I hoped to crash with Dale, everything was locked up and all
the lights were out. I stopped for a beer at Julius, a Village bar on West
10th, and went home with a young composer named Richard. The next
morning, I drove home.

John Grady was a bear of a man, an Irish gorilla with a smile as broad
as Dublin and fists the size of a whole ham. He lived with his wife and
young children in a Bronx building, which had been a church but was
now his. He used the ample facility for his own purpose: recruiting and

organizing retreats that would result in "actions," which was code for raids on draft boards. John Grady was a protégé of Phillip Berrigan, his former roommate in college, and an acquaintance of Dan. John had made it his mission to keep the momentum strong while Dan and Phil were underground or in prison.

I didn't need any convincing. I was ready for action. The retreat I attended lasted for three days. The discussions were circular and bored me. "Why do you want to take action?" "What makes you think you're ready to commit?" "Why are you personally opposed to the war?" "Are you willing to go to prison?"

We broke only for meals, and even then the conversation continued. We slept in sleeping bags or on blankets on the floor, and there, too, murmurs were heard through the night. "Are you ready?" "Can we trust you?" "Can you trust other people?" I was anxious to get through all this talk and to get on with it, whatever *it* was.

During the month since Dan's disappearance, the entire anti-war scene had heated up. American troops invaded Cambodia to prop up the despot Lon Nol following the coup that had overthrown King Sihanouk. The Vietnam War was now also the Cambodian War. Back home in the states, thirty ROTC buildings were bombed or burned, and in response Nixon deployed the National Guard to twenty-one campuses in sixteen states. Twenty-thousand protesters marched in New Haven at the start of the trial of Black Panther Bobby Seale. And in what would become known as the Kent State Massacre, four students leaving a classroom building were killed by over-anxious guardsmen. Student strikes were called at five hundred universities, and seventy-five of them remained closed through the rest of the year. The country was sick of the war.

Quietly, two dozen peaceniks from varied backgrounds gathered at John Grady's Iron Mountain retreat to plan more draft board raids: nuns from Baltimore and Boston; professors, teachers, and students from Pennsylvania, New York, Rhode Island, and Connecticut; plumbers and nurses and veterans and housewives.

In May I was deployed to New Haven to apprentice the fine art of casing a draft board. I adopted a false name, Leslie Bright, stolen from a

Pinter play, and I entered a world of shadows. Lacking funds for shelter, I crashed in an empty Yale freshman dorm for two days, entering and exiting through an unlocked ground floor window, sleeping through most of the daylight hours before embarking on my nocturnal assignment. At night I was a bum in the alley behind the strip mall, which housed the New Haven draft board. With no ID on my person, and a bottle of cheap rum in a paper bag as my only possession, I crouched in bushes and watched the back door. I noted the time the last person left and the time the first person entered in the morning. I registered traffic on the streets, and clocked the absence of pedestrians. I kept an eye open for street-cleaners, garbage trucks, and dog-walkers.

On the third day I moved to an apartment made available through our network of supporters, and I set up a small portable darkroom in the bathroom. I dressed in clean clothes and presented myself as Leslie Bright to the New Haven draft board, pretending to seek information about obtaining a hardship classification. When no one was looking, I took photos of the doors, the windows, the file cabinets. I memorized the layout of the room and the location of the critical files.

In order to shut down the draft in a particular location it was necessary to destroy three separate sets of records. One was the individual files of the potential draftees, especially those who were classified I-A. Another was a set of index cards, which contained each registrant's name, address, contact information, and status. The third was a ledger in which each registrant's name was recorded as he became eligible for the draft. It wasn't enough to destroy only one or two of these sets of information. If any one of them was left, the registrants' information could be laboriously reconstructed. It was my job to find out where these three sets of records were stored, how difficult they were to access, and how they might best be destroyed.

I was only support staff then. I wasn't yet part of the inner circle, the "actors" as they were called, who'd perform the next "action"—the actual raid on the New Haven board. Before my face grew too familiar to anyone in or around the draft board, I boarded a bus to Baltimore, where I holed up in the crumbling brownstone that belonged to two inner-city priests, Joe Wenderoth and Neil McLaughlin. I was needed to help with the surveillance of fifteen draft boards that were housed in a single one-story building in Washington, D.C. I re-assumed the persona of a bum, and, bottle in hand, I returned to the gutters, to "sleeping" under the shrubs, to recording the street traffic in the dark of the night.

Then I was off again, this time to Chester, Pennsylvania. This would be the group in which I'd be an "actor." For the first two weeks we lived as squatters in an empty dorm of a religious-affiliated college. We slept in bunks, on cots, and on the floor. We ate communal meals, each of us taking turns cooking on hot plates, and we disposed our garbage in random trash bins and dumpsters. Our entire lives were lived in each other's company. There was nothing and no one outside the group.

Our target was each and every draft record in the state of Delaware. Delaware had only two draft board offices. I was part of the group assigned to concentrate on the office in Wilmington. A smaller contingent of our group was dispatched to engineer the job at the Georgetown office. In addition to the three sets of records stored at these local boards, there was a list of each registrant at the state headquarters in Dover, a short drive from Wilmington. The Wilmington group was also charged with removing or destroying the records in Dover. If we wiped out all of the draft records in Delaware in one night, that would be the end of the draft in the state.

Delaware was a poor state, with crowded ghettoes, high unemployment, and failing public schools. We hoped our "action" would put an end to the one-way street of conscription forced upon the unfortunate young men of Delaware's sprawling slums.

The Wilmington draft board was located downtown near the city center in what had once been a one-room schoolhouse. It stood on an isolated plot of land visible from all four sides, with a poorly secured front door and an even less-secured back door. I posed as Leslie Bright and "cased the joint"—again seeking information on what qualified as "hardship" status.

Because the building was on a main artery into the city, detailed surveillance was needed, and it was needed from every direction. The best vantage point was an under-occupied office building a block away. Five or six stories tall, it towered above the other buildings in the immediate vicinity, and an unlocked stairwell provided easy access to the roof.

I invited Sue to join me for a romantic night under the stars, and we dragged binoculars, sleeping bags, and wine to the roof for a night of surveillance and lovemaking. Elizabeth McAllister was ticked off that I invited Sue. Liz was a nun (soon to be ex-nun and wife of ex-priest Phillip Berrigan) and Liz had appointed herself the leader of the group. I argued that Sue was good cover should anyone notice my presence on the roof. Liz argued that people outside our group shouldn't be let in on the action. I replied that Sue was with me and that meant she wasn't "outside" the group.

Sue had already arrived and it was time for us to get in place. Liz didn't like it, but with the consent of the group Sue and I left the campground. The first night of surveillance on the roof went so well we decided to go for two.

Even with the rooftop as a surveillance point, we couldn't observe all sides of the Wilmington schoolhouse. One night, to learn what traffic we might expect from a certain direction on a certain street, we removed a taillight from a rusted car, and I climbed into the trunk with a notebook and a flashlight, prepared to spend all night looking through a small hole and jotting down notes. The car was driven to the lookout spot and left there, and then I was retrieved the next morning. We got the information we needed. The coast was clear for the Wilmington raid.

After our presence in the Chester dorm was detected, we took up residence in a Kampgrounds of America (KOA) in Dover. It rained every day and every night. The campground became a swamp, and our tents and sleeping bags got soggy and moldy. The frenzy of planning quickened. Every one of us was sick and crabby.

The state headquarters would be a tricky hit. The office was on the second floor of a small two-story building, located in the middle of a parking lot in front of a popular strip mall. It was accessed from a four-lane highway that connected with the Interstate. Nearby was the headquarters of the state highway patrol. All day and all night state troopers whizzed back and forth past our target, the Delaware State Selective Service headquarters.

On the other side of the four-lane highway was an unfinished fast-food joint where construction had been halted. It was a good place for surveillance, and for several nights I lurked behind cinderblocks and construction equipment, logging the comings and goings of police cars, trucks, and motorists. To observe the building from the other side, I spent a night in a drainage ditch. The next morning I awoke with a very bad case of poison ivy, which required a trip to the emergency room for treatment.

I accompanied a nun to interview the state director of Selective Service. She was posing as a reporter for UPI, and I was her photographer. My name was Leslie Bright again. Our fake credentials passed the cursory scrutiny of the Selective Service staff. While she asked the director how recent draft board raids across the country were affecting the ability of the Selective Service to meet its quotas, I was taking pictures of the doors, the file cabinets, and the desks. When the interview was over, we asked if we could use the restrooms. As we knew we would be, we were given keys to the restrooms in the hallway. In the hall we handed the keys to a co-conspirator, who then ran to the hardware store in the strip mall to make copies of the keys. He returned expeditiously, and we returned the originals to the receptionist. Then we left.

After we completed the surveillance and intelligence gathering at Wilmington and Dover, we came up with the action plan. We decided that the most effective way to dispose of the Wilmington draft records was to rifle them out of the building and destroy them somewhere offsite. The little schoolhouse building was too visible for our actors to linger long enough to destroy them onsite, and with the constant traffic on the streets around the schoolhouse, noise from inside would likely be heard if we tried. A car with a lone actor would pull up in the back, and he'd drill the lock on the backdoor. Once he was inside, other actors would be dropped off with large bags for transporting the files. Each actor would ransack whichever desks, file cabinets, and ledgers he or she had been assigned. When all the files, index cards, and ledgers were gathered, the group would leave.

In Dover visibility was even more of a problem: The building was in the middle of a brightly lit parking lot and only blocks away from the state highway patrol headquarters. Therefore the job had to be accomplished with as little movement outside the building as possible. We decided that on Friday morning a rented van would pull up to the building and two actors in white overalls would exit. They'd carry to the second floor certain materials—namely two four-foot by eight-foot sections of thick plywood, with ropes attached to each corner. Once upstairs they'd display a sign announcing the restrooms were closed for maintenance work on the air-conditioning system. They'd enter the restrooms with their copied keys, push back the ceiling tiles, and hang the plywood platforms from the steel beams above. Then they'd replace the ceiling tiles, remove their sign, and leave.

Throughout the rest of the day, one at a time, four men and four women would enter the building and climb to the second floor. Using their own copies of the bathroom keys, they'd admit themselves, remove a ceiling tile, and then climb up to perch on the plywood rafts. By the end of the day, all eight actors would be in place, their backpacks filled with the necessary equipment.

At five p.m. the offices would close and the cleaning staff would arrive. By seven p.m., eight at the latest, the cleaning staff would leave. By walkie-talkie, an observer positioned in the unfinished fast-food outlet across the highway would inform the actors on the rafts that the building was now clear. They'd descend from their lofty aeries and begin their work.

Two actors would inflate plastic swimming pools, while another rigged a garden hose from the restroom to the offices. The others would begin collecting files. When the pools were filled with water, chemicals would be added, and finally the draft board records would be dumped in the pools. The chemicals would turn the paper into mush but leave the plastic pools intact.

The actors would signal by walkie-talkie that they were ready to leave. The getaway van would pick everyone up and drive away. By sunup there would be nothing left of the draft files, and the draft in Delaware would cease to exist.

A few days or weeks later, the actors would "surface" at a press conference and announce that they "took responsibility" for the action.

That was how it was supposed to go, and to my knowledge that was how it went, although I wasn't there that night.

Liz McAllister's bad feeling about my involving Sue in the surveillance had continued to fester and sour my relationship with her. Then, a few days before the action, we had a surprise visitor: Dan Berrigan, who was still underground. It happened that Sue was visiting me at the time, and Sue had—on her own— brought my mother. This violation of our protocol of secrecy was too much for Liz.

By the time the appointed hour had arrived for action, I took myself out of the mix. I was angry and hurt and disappointed. I knew Liz's bad feelings were much ado about nothing, that both my mother and Sue were completely trustworthy. At the same time, I was determined a life of activism shouldn't prohibit every opportunity for, well, a life. I argued that if we let this war destroy who we were and who we loved, then we lost. Apparently, not everyone agreed with me.

At the end of June I returned to Ithaca. My participation in draft board raids was over.

Sue wasn't disappointed to have me back home. We rented a small apartment on State Street and started to plan our life. Sue would resume teaching at the free school, and I'd go back to school in the fall and finish my last remaining semester. I'd continue to support the draft board raiders, but from a distance. Working with funds supplied by John Grady, I'd open a bookstore selling textbooks to Cornell and Ithaca College students, and pass the profits to a defense fund managed by

Grady. Our business plan called for us to net fifty thousand dollars for the cause, a lofty but achievable goal.

That summer my mother moved to Ithaca. It wasn't that anything was wrong in Oklahoma; it just wasn't particularly right. Her life in Oklahoma wasn't as satisfying as she'd hoped. She'd thought that a job in the dorm might give her the opportunity to really connect to the students, but somehow it didn't, and in spite of the occasional visits from friends, she felt isolated and alone on the campus while surrounded by thousands of active students.

She'd heard about Dorothy Day and the Catholic Worker from me and Dale and Bonnie, and she wanted to see the place for herself. It appealed to her for several reasons: living one's life for others, foregoing the pursuit of wealth, fostering the community, and the simplicity of it all. I took her to the First Street House and she liked what she saw. But before joining the Catholic Worker she wanted to spend some time with me in Ithaca. She found a place to live in a co-op that was half graduate students and half townies. She started to look for work.

There's something special about an Ithaca summer, and that summer of 1970 was no exception. Time itself slowed down. The normally bustling campus was comparatively empty. Restaurants and bars and shops were tamer. There were more hours in the day, more stars in the night. Water beckoned one to play—the deep pools of Cayuga Lake and Beebe Lake, the rushing waters of the twin gorges that coursed through the campus, the cold streams of Enfield and Taughannock, and the hidden reservoir with its crystal clear pool that seemed made for swimming. Food was eaten outside. Love was made outside. Life was lived outside during an Ithaca summer. And that summer I fell deeply in love.

In early August I received a phone call from my Oklahoma attorney, Gene Matthews. The Tenth Circuit Court of Appeals had ruled in my favor and overturned my conviction. Citing a January Supreme Court decision (*Gutknecht v. United States*), they ruled the "delinquency" classification was a violation of free speech since it'd been administratively enacted by Selective Service chief General Hershey for the sole purpose of squelching political dissent against the war. Suddenly, I was free.

Sue and I hardly knew what to think. We'd always assumed I'd return to Oklahoma to serve my five-year sentence, though we tended not to talk about that eventuality. To say that we were ecstatic would be incorrect; more accurately, we were numb with relief. The sudden and unexpected absence of this agonizing fear left us bereft of any emotion at all. The earth had shifted in its orbit, and we were still finding our feet. What did this mean? Who was I now?

On August 11 we learned that Daniel Berrigan was captured by FBI agents posing as birdwatchers outside the home of poet William String-fellow on Block Island, Rhode Island. (Phillip had been captured in May, only days after he'd gone underground.) While underground, Dan had published extensively and popped up every now and then—usually in a pulpit—to continue his ongoing sermon against the war. Now, as a guest of the federal prison system for a while, Dan would be silent.

On the last day of August, as day was giving way to night, I answered a knock at our screen door. Standing there were two women I'd not met before, who introduced themselves as DeCourcy Squire and Suzi Williams. I'd heard of them, and they of me. I invited them in.

DeCourcy and Suzi were aspiring draft board raiders, operating outside the framework of the Berrigan/McAllister/Grady network. They told me that for three months they'd been planning a raid on six draft boards, which were all bunched together in one office in Rochester, and all had gone well until this week. Now that everything was planned, now that they were ready to make their move, two people had dropped out of their group. They'd already asked Ted Glick to join them, and he'd agreed. Ted had previously raided draft boards in Philadelphia with a group known by the name "East Coast Conspiracy to Save Lives," and I'd worked closely with Ted in Washington, D.C., and in Delaware. They needed one more person, and Ted had recommended me.

What would be the harm? I believed in the utility of the draft board raids no less than before, and I didn't want their three months of hard work to go down the drain. I liked these two young women—their chutzpah and their independence. And Ted had been one of my favorites among the people I'd worked with earlier that summer. Like me, Ted had a girlfriend, Sarah, and like me, he'd invited her to join him on weekends in Delaware. He and I seemed to share the belief that, as important as they were, there was more to life than draft board raids.

"Fill me in," I said. And that was how I joined what came to be known as the Flower City Conspiracy.

The raid was to take place the following weekend—Labor Day weekend—when activity around the Federal Building would be at its lowest. I arrived in Rochester on Friday night and met the other players, who ranged in age from a gaunt thirty-six-year-old Quaker missionary to an even thinner twenty-year-old high school dropout. I received my briefing, went over every detail of the proposed plan, and reviewed the surveillance records of the past three months. Compared to New Haven, D.C., and Dover, this job appeared to be a cakewalk.

The Federal Building in Rochester consumed a full city block and was hemmed in by office buildings and churches on all sides. The surveillance had been thorough and detailed. The plan had been well developed. Each of the eight actors was assigned his or her role. Another half a dozen or so people would assist in various positions outside the building that night.

On this Labor Day weekend, from the close of the workday on Friday until the beginning of the workday on Tuesday, the offices in the building should be empty, with the possible exception of the FBI office on the third floor, which had the potential to remain busy seven days a week. Of course it was possible that a few other workers might make their way to their various other offices in the building as well, tidying up bits of unfinished work, competing against whatever deadlines they were up against. There was no security. There were no alarms.

Late Saturday afternoon, on September 5, Ted Glick entered the building alone and proceeded to a corner stairwell. He climbed to the top landing, where we hoped he'd remain undetected until the last person left the building.

Hours passed.

Well after dark, Ted descended from his dark perch and inspected the building, traversing every hallway in every floor to confirm that the building was empty. Then he took his place in the foyer where he could see out the front doors onto the steps leading to the street.

At ten p.m. lookouts in two different directions gave the "all-clear" signal, and our two vehicles approached the building, stopping at the front just long enough for seven more actors, myself among them, to disembark. Backpacks and duffle bags in hand, we darted through the front doors parted open from the inside by Ted. No one had witnessed our arrival. The streets were empty. The surrounding buildings were vacant of activity. We all went to our assigned tasks and began what would be a long night of hard work.

The locks on the office doors were simple to break. Within minutes each team was at work. The six Rochester draft boards were located in an adjoining series of suites in the middle of the building's second floor. There we labored all night—prying open locked desks and file cabinets with crowbars, disgorging an avalanche of draft records, and then feeding them handful by handful into one of two paper shredders we'd brought with us. The shredders were noisy, but this didn't worry us. We were in the middle of the building on the second floor, and it was late night on a lazy holiday weekend. Downtown Rochester was a ghost town. There was nothing to worry about.

For four hours we shredded papers until the linoleum floor of the Rochester draft boards was a sea of confetti two or three feet deep. Twice during our furtive efforts, we were alerted by our lookouts on the outside that the Rochester Police were doing a perimeter check—something we were anticipating because it'd been observed during the three months of surveillance. At one a.m., and again at two a.m., we went silent inside the building while a cop car pulled up to the curb, and an officer came to the front doors to check that they remained securely locked. When the officer departed, we continued our work.

Finally, at a quarter to four in the morning, there was nothing left to shred; and six hours after we'd entered the building, we prepared to leave.

The Rochester Police didn't make their three a.m. check of the building. This was not unusual. Our surveillance had revealed that they made hourly perimeter checks, but it was common for them occasionally to skip one. We cowered out of sight in the darkness of the hallway, waiting for word that the police had completed the four a.m. check, but the word never came. Four o'clock. Four-o-five. Four-ten. No sign of the cops. Finally, at four-fifteen, Ted contacted our lookouts one last time. They reported no activity outside the building. All was clear. Confident that the police had decided to skip another check, we moved into place in the darkened vestibule and awaited the arrival of our getaway vehicles.

That's when it happened. A lone Rochester police car drove by, and then stopped in front of the building. The two officers would later testify at the trial that they saw movement inside the vestibule. As the two police officers ascended the steps, we watched our getaway cars glide on by, steering cautiously away from the scene. Through the glass in the doors, the cops could see us crouched in the foyer. They drew their guns and demanded, with considerable agitation, that we open the doors.

Perhaps stupidly, we didn't open the doors. We knew this would be the last few minutes of freedom we'd have for months or years ahead. So we remained sitting on the floor, with our hands in full sight, and we talked quietly among ourselves while the policemen radioed for help. We congratulated each other on a job well done.

Caught or not, the draft records could not be reassembled. We'd ended the draft in Rochester. No one cried. No one was freaked out. We weren't even particularly afraid. This was a moment that each of us had contemplated, and it seemed that each of us was prepared.

Before long, squad cars and cops surrounded the building, and we looked out on a phalanx of *very* angry city, county, state, and federal cops. None of them could find a way into the building, which further fueled their agitation. After a while—ten minutes, perhaps longer—someone backed a pickup truck up against the side of the building so that a policeman could jimmy a bathroom window and then crawl through and gain entrance. Moments later this lone policeman rushed past us in the vestibule and opened the doors, admitting a flood of law enforcement officers.

The jig was up.

In subsequent years various writers conjectured that the arrest occurred because the cops were acting on a tip they'd received about the Rochester draft board raid before it happened. I've never seen anything to justify this claim, and much to disprove it. I don't know where the claim originated, but it seems to have become part of the lore of the raid.

It was suggested by some that Elizabeth McAllister wrote about the planned Rochester raid in a letter to Phillip Berrigan, who was then serving his sentence at the federal prison in Lewisburg, Pennsylvania. This supposed letter was smuggled to Phil by his cellmate, who was a snitch for the FBI. It's true Liz smuggled letters to Phil through his cellmate, and it's true the cellmate, Boyd Douglas, was a snitch. But decades later, when I had a chance to review the letters myself, I couldn't find any mention of the impending Rochester raid.

Others suggested the feds knew about the raid in advance because of a tap on Ted Glick's phone. In a later trial it was revealed that indeed Ted's phone had been tapped, but here too there's no evidence that the feds learned about the Rochester raid from Ted's phone records.

Ultimately, the suspicion that the FBI somehow knew about the Rochester raid before it happened doesn't make sense. If they'd known, they wouldn't have sat idly by all night and let us cause damage to their own offices. They wouldn't have allowed us six unfettered hours inside the Federal Building. They'd have been inside waiting for us. They'd have stopped us before we could have done anything. This was precisely what happened later that fall in Camden, NJ, when an informant tipped

Democrat and Chronicle

Published by Gannett Co., Inc. in Rochester, N.Y., Monday, September 7, 1970

10 CENTS
Sunrise

DRAFT OFFICE WRECKED, POLICE CAPTURE 8 HERE

Quarters Of FBI Also Hit

BY JAMES R. STEAR

Three major offices in the Federal Building were vandalized early yesterday and Selective Service files affecting several thousand young men were damaged or destroyed.

Eight young persons, half of them women, were arrested inside the building by police shortly after 4 a.m. and charged by federal authorities in connection with the crime. One was identified as the son of a college president.

The offices, ransacked in the building at Fitzhugh Street North and Church Street, were those of the Selective Service System, the U.S. attorney and the Federal Bureau of Investigation.

The intruders broke into the arsenal in the FBI's second-floor office and spread wrappers all over the floor, but no attempt was made to take them from the building.

In the Selective Service office, the intruders broke into

Draft records cover the floor of local selective service office after protestors' predawn attack.

...Gerald Jed Hanna, member of draft board 76, and Philip Liebschutz, board 76 chairman, survey damage

Democrat and Chronicle
Rochester, N.Y.
Mon., Sept. 7, 1970

JOE T. GILCHRIST | WAYNE BONEKEMPER | FRANCIS B. CALAHAN | THEODORE J. GLICK | JOAN NICHOLSON | SUZANNE WILLIAMS | JANE DOE 3 | JANE DOE 4

Draft-FBI Offices Ransacked Here, 8 Captured

off the FBI to a draft board raid, and the raiders were arrested while entering the building.

And there's something else. I was there that night, and I know from the reaction of the legion of arresting officers that the raid hadn't been anticipated. Those first two cops were surprised as hell when they found us. Through the closed and locked doors, they did a lot of shouting about guns and bombs, and anyone who knew anything about us knew we'd never act with guns or bombs. The police thought we were Weathermen. Even after the doors were opened and they were inside and they found nothing more dangerous on us than a crowbar, they continued demanding that we tell them where we planted the bombs. They had no idea who we were or what we'd been doing.

That's true of all the cops who showed up that night and swarmed the federal building, and there were easily more than a hundred of them. And what about those who conducted lengthy interrogations following the arrest, far into the next day, after we'd been hauled to the county jail? They too were still trying to figure out who we were and what we'd done.

They'd had no forewarning. We hit them where it hurt the most, and had they known we were coming, they'd have found a way to prevent it. Cops aren't in the business of letting a crime progress all night while doing nothing about it.

That night, while I was downstairs in the Selective Service offices shredding draft records, DeCourcy and Suzi were upstairs raiding the records of the FBI, looking for evidence of illegal activities by federal agents. Hoover's FBI, with the prodding and gratitude of Richard Nixon, had embarked on a nationwide strategy of using the FBI as a political arm of the White House. Anyone who made it a habit to speak out against the war or against Nixon could have told you this in 1970. People were being followed, phones were being tapped, and dirty tricks were being played. But there was little evidence to prove the extent of the abuse of power. A peek at the Rochester FBI surveillance records on political "enemies" of the White House would be most revealing, we hoped.

Unfortunately we were apprehended before the contents of the Rochester FBI files could be examined and revealed. But a similar raid took place six months later in Media, Pennsylvania. The FBI files taken in that raid were later printed in the New York Times in a kind of corollary to the Pentagon Papers of Daniel Ellsberg. Just as the Pentagon Papers showed the level of deception in the military planning for the war, the Media FBI files showed the level of illegal government surveillance, harassment, and entrapment being conducted by the FBI under the direction of J. Edgar Hoover, with the knowledge and encouragement of Richard Nixon.

Anyone who thinks the FBI would have waited patiently outside the Rochester Federal Building all night while we ravaged their own offices inside has never met an FBI agent. The FBI had no forewarning about the raid.

At our trial a few months later, Paul Camping, the officer who first arrived on the scene, testified under oath that if he hadn't seen movement inside the foyer he wouldn't have stopped to investigate. When asked if there had been a tip, if he'd had any prior suspicion there would be any activity at the Federal Building that night, he answered no. The FBI officer who was first on the scene testified he arrived approximately one hour after the initial arrest. He also testified the FBI had no prior information about the raid.

It was really that simple. That night the police were lucky and we were not. If those cops had driven by a minute earlier or five minutes later, the arrest wouldn't have happened.

The Monroe County Jail in downtown Rochester was one of the oldest continuously operating jails in America. The men's wing was shaped like a tight square donut with four tiers of windowless cells on all four sides, topped with a barred glass roof that was so filthy that no sunlight could penetrate it. Every surface was iron or steel. Much of it was coated with layers of industrial-strength paint, and all of it was coated with industrial-strength grime. The bottom level boasted a "common room" in the middle—a narrow, noisy cavern with two steel tables bolted to the steel floor, where inmates vied for a chance to play with the lone chess set. The only other object provided for the inmates' amusement was a black and white television that was set unreachably high, tuned to one random channel, and blasting at high volume twelve hours every day.

Each morning at six a.m., the cell doors slid open and each inmate had sixty seconds to decide how to spend the next twelve hours—either outside or inside his cell. After one minute the cell doors were shut again, and they didn't open again until six p.m., when all the inmates had to return to their cells. Most mornings I joined the mess of inmates in the common room, but some mornings I chose to remain in my cell, opting for a day of relative privacy. It was always a balancing act. Alone in a cell all day with nothing do, one ached for companionship. Crowded in the common room all day, one ached for some breathing room. Neither choice was a good one.

The tables in the common room seated twelve people, but each day there were forty or more inmates in the crowded space. Those who didn't find a seat were relegated to pacing in a mindless circle around the table. The circle went in one direction only—counter-clockwise—at a constant pace that never varied. While pacing, inmates talked with each other, or didn't. No one ever watched the television; intended perhaps for entertaining the inmates, it was nothing more than a torture device.

I circled the common room hour after hour with my three male co-conspirators. Ted Glick and I deepened the friendship we'd begun that summer. We each were inwardly distraught about our prospects, but resigned to them, and both of us feared that our budding relationships with the loves of our lives wouldn't outlive our sentences. Ted and Sarah had been married that summer. Sue and I weren't that far along; she was still waiting for her divorce to come through.

I enjoyed my talks with fellow conspirator Frank Callahan, a genial college student from Pennsylvania. Aside from his concerns about our looming prison sentences, he anticipated the demise of his relationship with his family.

Wayne Bonekemper, our youngest conspirator, was unreadable. On the few occasions when he bothered to leave his cell, Wayne lurked in the shadows of the common room, and rarely spoke a word to anyone. I'd never get to know him. All these years later I still wish I'd made more of an effort to reach him.

During visits inmates were herded together into a dark cage outside the cellblock. Around this cage, set several feet back, was another cage, constructed of iron bars and a fine mesh screen coated with a century of dust and grime. Visitors stood outside the second cage, trying to identify the inmate they'd come to visit amid the shadows and through the opaque screen. Inside the inner cage inmates were bunched shoulder to shoulder, jockeying to find their visitors' faces on the outside. Visits were a shouting match, with one inmate shouting "I LOVE YOU!" to his dimly-seen visitor, while competing with the inmate next to him, who was pushing against his side and simultaneously shouting, "DAMN YOU BITCH, WHY DID YOU BOTHER TO COME HERE?" It was impossible to hold an actual conversation in these conditions. After the first few visits from my mother and from Sue, I asked them not to come again. These horrible attempts to visit were worse than no visit at all.

Sue was justifiably angry at my imprisonment, which is to say, she was angry at me for joining the action. She and I had agreed to start planning a future for ourselves, and now that I was arrested, what kind of future could we have?

My mother was fearful and did her best to be supportive. But so many things were wrong. Her son was in jail and likely to remain there for a long time. She still hadn't found suitable work. Sue had been kind and generous to my mother, but my mother never seemed to take to Sue. There was always a tension between them. Everything was at odds.

Those weeks in the Monroe County Jail are mostly one giant smudge in my memory, a dark and dim stretch of tedium, noise, numbness, and desperation. But a few things stand out: the friendship I struck up with Nestor Mojica—a pockmarked, middle-aged Puerto Rican bank robber who wrote powerful poetry about his crimes, his fears, and his loves; Pete—a frail, young heroin addict whom I befriended during his two-week stay in Monroe County, shielding him from the taunts and threats from other inmates; and, in the cell next to mine on the top tier, an angry, desperate, and muscular young black man, who one night set his mattress on fire and was burned severely before the guards responded to our shouting. They entered the cellblock, lumbered up the four flights of stairs, lumbered back down again to retrieve a fire extinguisher, and eventually returned to extinguish the fire. His inhuman screams and the smell of his burning flesh have never faded from my memory. And yet, as horrible as it was, it wasn't the worst thing I saw in prison.

My bail was set at one hundred thousand dollars, which was a way to make sure I remained in jail until the trial. One week segued into two, then three, and then four. Aside from weekly meetings with my co-conspirators and my attorney, there was no respite from the cellblock.

I agreed to take an attorney. All seven of my co-defendants didn't, opting to defend themselves. DeCourcy and Suzi in particular felt they couldn't morally accept the services of an attorney when so many accused lacked sufficient representation. DeCourcy, Suzi, and Jane Meyerding also refused to accept bail, as a sign of solidarity with the other inmates in the women's wing of the jail.

I thought this reasoning flawed. We were each facing potentially thirty-eight years in prison, if the court decided to give us the maximum penalty for the six felony charges that had been levied against us: two charges of burglary, two of breaking and entering, one charge of hindering the administration of the Selective Service Act, and one of trespassing on a federal reservation. Initially the state also filed multiple charges against us, which pushed the potential sentence for each of us to almost a hundred years; but the state dropped the charges when they conceded they had no jurisdiction over a crime that had been committed on a federal reservation.

However noble I might have thought myself to be, I wasn't noble enough to lie down and roll over while a prosecutor tried to put me away for the rest of my adult life. I wanted a few days or weeks of freedom before my ultimate incarceration, and I wanted an attorney. He might not be able to do much for me, but he'd do more than I could do for myself. A local Rochester attorney, Herman Walz, stepped up to defend me, and by so doing became the unacknowledged defense attorney for all eight of us.

Herm received advice and assistance from several high profile attorneys who'd defended clients in similar trials across the country, including William Kunstler of the Chicago Seven fame. Kunstler visited Herm for several days, and also met with us at the jail. In the end, though, it was simply Herm's calm and pleasant fastidiousness that served us well.

During the sixth week of my incarceration, a Cornell English professor, James Matlock, put up his house as surety for my bail, and I was released. This was an extraordinarily generous and courageous act on Matlock's part. Matlock had a wife and two young daughters who need- ed a roof over their heads. He must have considered the possibility that, despite any assurances I might give him, and whatever my best inten- tions were, there was always the possibility I wouldn't show up for trial. But Matlock never even asked me if I planned to stick around for the trial. He simply and selflessly put up his house.

And who was standing on the jailhouse steps on the morning of my release on bail?

Phil Shuman.

Phil told me he'd heard a radio report of my arrest while he was driving one morning to his job as a mall photographer in Lawrence, Kansas. He'd been paroled from El Reno shortly after I saw him some ten months before. He said he knew I was going to jail for sure this time, and he knew I'd never survive it unless he helped me. He persuaded his boss to give him extended time off and drove to Ithaca, where he found my mother and Sue.

Sue had been offered a room in the home of a friend, Jordan Clark, who went on to an extended career as an actor on the soap opera *Guiding Light*. Jordan had a small cottage on the shores of Lake Cayuga, and Phil was crashing on the floor of the guest bedroom where Sue slept.

Phil's view of the world was infectious. He took great delight in every- thing he saw, everyone he encountered, and every moment he lived. It was Phil's credo that freedom was perhaps preferable to imprisonment, but ultimately it was all the same. Life was a joy, a wonder to be shared and grasped and celebrated. He believed dark moments existed only to the extent you let them. Phil was all about pleasure, and he found no pleasure in darkness.

As Pollyannaish as all of this sounded to me, I also felt it might be the only thing I had to hold onto as I headed to prison myself, so I listened to Phil. In the remaining weeks before my trial, I spent most of my hours in his company, much to the consternation of Sue and my mother, both of whom were skeptical of Phil's utility on the one hand, and jealous of his time with me on the other.

There was one other thing Phil taught me: in prison, never be alone. It made sense to me that an inmate was most vulnerable when he was alone. I'd seen this first-hand during my brief ventures in incarceration. I'd been isolated and alone in El Reno, and terrified that at any moment I'd come under some kind of attack. In Monroe County I'd had the companionship of my fellow conspirators, and I'd reached out to Pete, the young dope addict, for the very reason Phil was expounding. I knew that if Pete had been left on his own he'd have been an easy target for anyone who wanted to mess with him, so instinctively I'd taken him under my protection.

It was really that simple, Phil said. Be happy. And never, ever be alone.

Phil was right. And the way it played out for me during my incarceration in federal prison proved how right he was. Prison could have, perhaps *should* have, been a horrifying experience for me. But it wasn't. It was just life, and life was truly beautiful.

The trial of the Flower City Conspiracy lasted two weeks.

Two years before, in Oklahoma, Judge Bohanon had blocked every de-fense witness my attorney called to the stand. Now, in Rochester, much to the consternation of the U.S. Attorney, our judge allowed us to call any witness we wanted, and he placed no restrictions on the number or character of the questions we posed. His leniency in the conduct of the trial was, even to my biased eyes, somewhat ridiculous. In the end, it worked greatly to our advantage.

Jury selection was instantaneous. We announced at the start of the procedure that we'd offer no challenges to any juror being seated. We'd be happy to accept the first twelve jurors, whoever they were. This course of action embarrassed the prosecution into matching our non-chalance, so the trial proceeded apace.

Judge Harold Burke, born in 1895, was the oldest judge sitting on the federal bench. He was his own man, and he ran his courtroom the way he wanted to run it. In our case, that meant he gave the defendants free reign. We could summon any witness we wanted, and those witnesses could testify about anything we asked. In Rochester, in this courtroom, the war itself would be on trial.

The trial was covered by the national press, attracting reporters from up and down the East Coast as well as stringers for *Newsweek* and *Time*. An article in the Harvard Crimson provided a condensed but accurate record of the course of the trial:

> The Trial of the Flower City Conspiracy
>
> Harvard Crimson, Wednesday, December 02, 1970
> by BARRY WINGARD
>
> THE testimony of Father Daniel Berrigan at the trial of eight young middle-class white Americans here on Friday, November 20, has helped focus attention on a very important yet virtually unreported political trial. The eight people facing possible sentences of up to 38 years are Joan Nicholson, 36; Ted Glick, 21; Frank Callahan, 21; Suzi Williams, 21; DeCourcy Squire, 21; Jane Meyerding, 22; Joe Gilchrist, 21; and Wayne Bonekemper, 17. They are The Flower City Conspiracy, and have been actively engaged in speaking out on the issues of American racism at home and abroad, the conduct of the empire-building war in Southeast Asia, the treatment of prisoners in American jails, and the role of the three government agencies whose offices they disrupted before their arrest at 4:15 a.m. on September 6, 1970.
>
> ...The trial opened in Harold Burke's Federal Courtroom on November 16.
>
> The defendants have been attempting, within the limits set by Judge Burke and the larger legal-political system, to cut through all of the legal jargon and the physical and psychological control of authority in the court-room. When they

refused to enter any plea at their arraignment, Judge Burke entered not guilty pleas for all eight of them. Seven of the eight are conducting their own defense. Their message is a relatively simple one—to open to the judge, the jury, to those in the courtroom and to those beyond, the facts of their lives which led them to feel compelled to take an action against three very oppressive institutions: the Selective Service System, the Federal Bureau of Investigation, and the United States Attorney's Office. They are striving consistently inside the courtroom and out to have people judge both their actions and the reasons that motivated them to destroy government property. It is an effort to go beyond the legality or illegality of what they openly admit to having done. Similar efforts have been made in the past in American courts of law, beginning with the trial of the Catonsville Nine—the priest brothers Philip and Daniel Berrigan and seven other Catholics who burned draft records with home-made napalm at the Baltimore suburb of Catonsville in May of 1968. But something new and different is happening in Rochester's Federal Building, even if the result for the eight defendants is the same as it has been for other defendants in the past—the expected long prison terms.

By presenting a long, technical, dollars-and-cents-of-destruction prosecution the assistant U.S. Attorney has brought to public attention for the first time in a court of law some facts about the operation of the Selective Service System that many people had suspected were true but could not prove. In her testimony for the prosecution Mrs. Emma Hibbard, Rochester Draft Supervisor, was asked about the reason for certain notes that were attached to individual draft files introduced into evidence for the prosecution. Her response confirmed that Special Agent Joseph Cain of the Rochester FBI office had investigated one draft registrant because he was suspected of being delinquent and of having taken part in anti-draft demonstrations. Over the agent's note was one in Mrs. Hibbard's handwriting directing that both notes be removed should the registrant appear and ask to see his file. The file of another registrant, Robert Osborne, had a similar

FBI memorandum attached noting that investigation had turned up the fact that Osborne was a "known draft counselor." Mrs. Hibbard also acknowledged that information on registrants that is received from anonymous sources but considered "relevant" is kept on file "to be removed should the registrant ask for his file."

Judge Burke has allowed extensive cross-examination by the seven defendants who are representing themselves—he calls it giving them some "latitude" when the prosecution objects—and they have made good use of it to ask probing questions. Another FBI agent has been seated at the prosecution table since the beginning of the trial, working closely with prosecutor Walford in formulating questions and making note of certain testimony on the part of defense witnesses. His name is Thomas Moore, and he testified about the damage done in the office of the FBI. Under cross-examination, Suzi Williams pushed him hard about possible FBI investigation into an August 26 National Women's Day demonstration in Rochester, and about FBI surveillance of Radical Women's Groups in general. His plea of "sensitivity" and "national security" to Judge Burke was finally upheld, but ten minutes of dodging Suzi's questions left small room for doubt that Women's Liberation has special significance for Mr. Hoover's investigators.

Across the street from the courthouse, the Presbyterian church serves as a center of community support. On the evening of the second day of the trial, Attorney William Kunstler spoke to a crowd of 700 in the church hall. Of the defendants and their action he said:

"They are the lucky ones. They have found it. They are right and good and clean and strong—and they can live with themselves even in jail. Is it better to be on the outside and live a lie than to be on the inside and live with yourselves? They have made a choice. Others have made it in the past. They will spend their lives—or a portion of them—in a federal penitentiary or go underground and live their lives in perpetual fear of apprehension... They will always be able to say to themselves I hope I was a man or I was a woman, and that I loved my brothers and sisters."

David Dellinger, the following night, spoke movingly of the myth of the fair trial and of the possible years in jail that are ahead for the eight:

"Is it fair that they have on trial the people they have on trial and they don't have on trial the people they don't have on trial? The people who damaged the files, they are on trial, but nobody is asking the draft boards to justify what they do."

THE HIGH moment of the first week, however, was undoubtedly the appearance of Father Berrigan, who is serving a three-and-one-half-year sentence for destroying draft files. Brought from Danbury "Correctional Institute" to testify as a character witness for Joe Gilchrist, who was a student at Cornell during Berrigan's chaplaincy there, the priest was on the stand for three hours. Over the frequent vehement objections of Walford, who was openly outraged that Berrigan should even be there to testify, "Father Dan" forcefully and movingly related to the court the content of frequent conversations he had with Joe during the two years they were together in Ithaca. He told of the experience of seeking shelter underground as protection from a B-52 bombing raid on Hanoi while he was there in 1967 on a mission of mercy to bring back to America three POWs. He spoke of the children he saw in North Vietnam who had been burned with napalm, and of the total destruction of the countryside and food supply of that small nation. He told of his growing concern that Americans were unaware of the things being done in their name by the Johnson and Nixon administrations in Vietnam. He told how he came to believe that speaking out against the war and injustice here at home were not sufficient, that one had to risk suffering and persecution, jail and maybe even death if he were serious about wanting an end to the killing. This gentle man, who has been such a clear and consistent voice against the institutionalized killing which America has promulgated both in Southeast Asia and in the ghettos and on the campuses at home, struck to the heart of what had moved the eight young people to do more than simply speak against injustice. His presentation was soft and he faltered at times. Sounding very tired and drawn, constantly asking for water as he spoke, several times he apologized to those in the courtroom for "not being very sharp today." Each time he tried to explain that he'd been kept in solitary for three days, the judge would silence him and order the remarks stricken from the record. Finally, Dan burst out to tell the packed room that he would neither eat nor drink until he was back in Danbury, as a way of protesting the brutal treatment given to prisoners who are in transit from one jail to another. He had been taken from Danbury on Tuesday, and was not told where he was going or for what he was being taken away. He spent three days and nights either traveling or in solitary confinement, never permitted to mix with other prisoners in the jails where he was kept. It was not until the night before he testified that he was permitted to know where he was being taken.

At one point in his testimony, after a thirty-minute battle between the prosecution and the defendants as to the propriety of entering scripture as testimony, Joan Nicholson introduced into evidence Matthew 5:1-12, from Christ's Sermon on the Mount. This was after the government had objected to entering the Holy Bible as evidence, claiming it to be irrelevant. Judge Burke sustained the objection. The beatitudes were not ruled objectionable, however, and Father Berrigan slowly read through the ancient teachings of Christ. In the crowded courtroom, the old words took on new meaning to those who understood how much the government detests the kind of testimony that men of the church like Berrigan can offer about the effects of national policy. Near the end of the passage he read:

"Blessed are ye, when men shall revile you, and persecute you, and shall say all manner of evil against you falsely for my sake.

"Rejoice and be exceedingly glad; for great is your reward

in heaven, for so persecuted they the prophets which were before you."

THE TRIAL is still going on. After the Thanksgiving recess, five defendants gave closing statements on Monday the 30th of November. Final arguments were presented yesterday, and the case went to the jury. The government has pressed hard to deflate the significance of the raids on the FBI and U.S. Attorney's offices, but their very obvious uptightness has shown through. The defendants have still not issued a public statement as the contents taken from the FBI office were removed from the bags of evidence by FBI agents before they were brought into court. Even a court order for their presence would not produce them. They have been described by the FBI as having to do with "racial relations" and are described as "too sensitive to be the object of public perusal." One thing remains clear here in this affluent western New York city, regardless of the immediate outcome. People here have for the first time had to confront the issues of the war, the draft, and racism, in a way that will not easily be repressed. Eight very serious young Americans are so deeply concerned over the course their nation is taking that it may cost them 38 years of their lives.

Far away from Rochester, and one day before Daniel Berrigan testified in my defense, FBI Director J. Edgar Hoover made an appearance before a Congressional committee, seeking $14.1 million in supplemental appropriations to fund a thousand additional agents and two hundred and two additional clerks. To justify the need for the added manpower, Hoover cited the threat to the country presented by anti-war radicals. In particular, he testified, there was a plot organized by the imprisoned priests, Daniel and Phillip Berrigan, to kidnap Henry Kissinger and to blow up underground heating tunnels in Washington, D.C. Hoover identified the group as the "East Coast Conspiracy to Save Lives," or the ECCSL.

The charge was ludicrous, as anyone who knew anything about Phil or Dan or any of us would surely know. We weren't in the business of kidnapping or bombing. That was Weatherman territory, and we weren't the Weathermen. Our modus operandi was the shredding of paper, or the spilling of our own blood, but not bodily harm to another person. We were adamantly nonviolent. Hoover's claims were outrageous.

Nonetheless, the next morning, newspapers coast-to-coast published on their front pages this alarming revelation by the nation's chief police officer, and that included Rochester newspapers. As Daniel Berrigan was called to the stand to testify in my defense, there wasn't a person in the courtroom unaware of the accusations made by Hoover the day before. The headlines stared out from the folded papers carried in by those attending the trial, and worse yet, were boldly displayed lying face-up on the prosecutor's table, only feet from the jury box. Could all this have been a mere coincidence? Was the timing of Hoover's testimony an accident?

Regarding the name of the alleged conspiracy, the East Coast Conspiracy to Save Lives: There had in fact been such a group—a group very similar to the Flower City Conspiracy. The ECCSL was the name taken by a group of draft board raiders in Philadelphia a year earlier. No one had been arrested or prosecuted for the ECCSL's action. They'd gotten  away clean, taking all of the records from fourteen draft boards with them. The day after the raid, the raiders surfaced in a press conference, claiming responsibility for the raid but never explicitly confessing to having done it. Ted Glick had been a member of that group. Neither of the Berrigan brothers was involved.

Dan Berrigan was named as one of the ringleaders of the alleged kidnapping conspiracy. Ted Glick had already acknowledged in court that he'd been a member of the East Coast Conspiracy to Save Lives—though he meant the real one, not the fabricated one that Hoover cooked up to scare congressmen. Thus when Hoover's words exploded in the media, Hoover made the case in the minds of the jury and everyone else connected with our case that we were not only shredders of paper but kidnappers and bombers as well. This was never explicitly argued in court, but there was no mistaking the presence of this accusation in the courtroom. It was powerfully prejudicial. And there was nothing we could do about it.

After two and a half weeks of testimony, the case was handed off to the jury. We expected them to come back quickly with a verdict, but the first night passed, and then the next day as well. The length of their deliberations made us almost gleeful, if not hopeful. After Hoover's incendiary testimony before Congress, we'd anticipated a quick and certain conclusion to our trial. Frankly, we couldn't imagine what was taking the jury so long. None of the eight of us had ever denied we committed the acts of which we'd been accused. We'd been caught red-handed. We openly acknowledged we did these things, not only claiming responsibility but outright confessing. What could they be deliberating about?

Jon Margolis, writing in the Long Island newspaper, *Newsday*, put the outcome of the trial this way:

> The Flower City Conspiracy trial ended last night after two and a half weeks of testimony and it was hard to tell just who had won. The defendants faced up to 38 years in federal prison as they walked to jail shouting invitations to the jury and receiving the applause of the audience. The assistant US Attorney got the congratulations of the court clerk but he refused it and walked off glumly. The jurors walked out crying.
>
> For the first time in any trial of anti-war radicals, the defense had been able to make an issue of the legality and morality of the Southeast Asia war. The accused questioned witnesses about atrocities in Vietnam, discussed their own political and religious philosophies and introduced into evidence copies of the Declaration of Independence and an essay by French philosopher Albert Camus.

It turns out that during the weeks of our trial we'd gotten under the skins of the jurors. The brutal testimony offered by witnesses who'd been in Vietnam awakened them to the reality of the war. Our own testimony revealed the earnestness of our cause and the innocence of our intentions. Spending eight hours a day for two weeks in the courtroom with us allowed them to get to know us. My seven codefendants defended themselves and were on their feet frequently in front of the jurors asking questions of the witnesses and bantering with the prosecutor and the judge. I was on the stand for two hours in my own defense, and my mother and Daniel Berrigan testified in my defense as well.

Ultimately the jurors got to know us as people not unlike themselves, and they discovered they liked us. They found themselves feeling the way we felt about the war, and wishing they too might be able to do something about it, if not something as drastic as what we'd done. They were hugely conflicted.

The members of the jury knew we were guilty as charged, but they didn't want to convict us. They were torn between their duty to uphold the law, and their remarkable fondness for us.

Although we were not to learn of it until some days after the trial, something happened to end the jury's deliberations. Late on the second day of deliberations, the foreman of the jury sent a note to the judge with the question: "If we convict the defendants, will you be lenient in the sentencing?" Judge Burke sent back a one-word reply: "Yes." Thirty minutes later we were called back to the courtroom to hear the verdict.

Forty-eight times the foreman of the jury, Joseph Palazzo, called out, "Guilty"—once for each of the six counts against the eight of us. And forty-eight times he added the phrase "with a recommendation of leniency." Many jurors wept throughout the reading of the verdicts. We found ourselves in the peculiar position of consoling the jurors as we were taken into custody by the federal marshals and led away to jail.

Judge Burke stayed true to his one-word note to the jury. Four of the defendants received twelve-month sentences, a slap on the wrist for what we'd done. Two received fifteen-month sentences. The remaining two, Ted Glick and I, received eighteen-month sentences. The judge said he based the sentences on extensive background information provided to him by the FBI on each of the defendants. We assumed Ted's longer sentence was added punishment for his involvement with the ECCSL, and that mine was for my previous—but overturned—Oklahoma draft conviction. The judge wasn't obligated to state a specific reason for the differences in sentencing, and he didn't.

We all had been *very* lucky. If this trial had been conducted before any other judge in the country, it'd have proceeded very differently. Seven defendants might not have been allowed to defend themselves. The witnesses we called might not have been permitted to take the stand, and their testimony most certainly wouldn't have been allowed to ramble so far from the specifics of the indictment. Daniel Berrigan wouldn't have been transferred from Danbury Federal Prison to testify on my behalf, and the jury wouldn't have seen for themselves how kind, gentle, and spiritual he was. The jury wouldn't have had any opportunity to get to know us, or to hear hours of testimony about the reality of the war from first-hand observers. And the judge wouldn't have been so lenient in sentencing.

I could do eighteen months. Even with Phil Shuman's generous coaching, the prospect of my doing five years in prison had been devastating, and the genuine possibility of ten, fifteen, or twenty years substantially more terrifying. One year before our trial, a judge in a draft board raid case in Milwaukee had given the defendants fifteen-year sentences, and it was at least that kind of outcome that I'd been anticipating.

Damn, was I lucky! I could do eighteen months.

One other note: Following the Rochester trial, the FBI agent who assisted with the prosecution was reassigned to the Minneapolis office as a punishment for getting too cozy with us, the defendants. Thomas Moore had been an FBI agent in Oklahoma, where I'd first met him. He'd been transferred some months before the Rochester action and assigned, in part, the job of keeping track of me. During the months before my trial, I'd gotten to know Tom well through his many visits and our many talks. He was a nice man—too nice, perhaps, for the FBI.

It's hard to explain how one can be sentenced to prison and be joyful about it at the same time, but I was. I'd get through this. I'd be okay. Life would go on.

That day I didn't need my mother to visit me following the sentencing. If she had, she wouldn't have found me weeping as I'd been in Oklahoma. She wouldn't have had to utter her one word admonition, "Don't." Still, my thoughts turned to a letter she'd sent me while I was locked up in the Monroe County Jail awaiting my Rochester trial, before my bail had been posted.

This is what she wrote:

September 20, 1970

Dear Joe,

I'm sitting at a window directly across from the cemetery. It's quiet— early Sunday morning. The sunshine filtering through these majestic trees create alternate shadow and light giving the place tranquility. As I looked out and watched the night turn into day, things more or less fell into their proper perspective.

My darkest experiences in the past years ended with a knowledgeable light. Each time I emerged with more understanding of human nature and of life itself.

And thus will you grow.

All my love,
Mom

We decompressed in the Monroe County Jail for another two weeks while the Justice Department decided how to parcel us out among the various prisons in the country. The four women—DeCourcy, Suzi, Joan, and Jane—all went to Alderson, West Virginia. It was the only federal prison for women on the East Coast, so like it or not they all got to stay together, and I'm pretty sure they were all pleased.

Ted went to Ashland, Kentucky; Frank to Allenwood, Pennsylvania. I no longer recall for sure where Wayne went, but it was somewhere in the South. After I was deposited for a two-week detour in the county jail in Buffalo for no discernible reason, they sent me on to Milan, Michigan.

The Federal Correctional Institution (FCI) in Milan, Michigan had been built as a geriatric prison in the 1940s, but had recently been repurposed as a young man's prison due to the burgeoning population of that demographic. Evidently in the 1940s the Federal Bureau of Prisons didn't believe that old prisoners had much need for exercise, or much of anything else except bunks, because that's what I mostly found at Milan—lots of metal bunks in large open dorms, and lots of young inmates with too much time on their hands and nothing to do.

Located half an hour south of Ann Arbor, and surrounded by expansive cornfields, the compound consisted of an Escher-like configuration of buildings that came together in a square, with three wings penetrating into one of its sides like spokes. That side was A block—the administration building where the warden, the captain, and the caseworkers had their offices. Also located in A block were the infirmary and dentist office, the "arrival and discharge" (A&D) compound, and the visiting room. The three spokes were: C block—where a limited number of inmates got better accommodations (semi-private cells, which they shared with one other cellmate) and extra privileges after an extended period of "good behavior"; D block—otherwise known as "the hole"; and E block—similar to C block except it was reserved for inmates on study release or work release.

Branching off at a right angles from both ends of A block were B block and F block—where most of the inmates served out their sentences. B block was two stories tall and divided in the middle, making four wings (B1–B4). Each of the wings contained about a hundred inmates crammed into an open room with bunk beds, sharing a communal TV room, open showers, and an open toilet area. F block was the mirror image of B block.

Closing the square was a squat building which housed the mess hall, prison industries, the laundry, and the so-called gym—a gloomy hall that boasted a handful of dumbbells, and which also served as a movie theatre for particularly lame and heavily censored movies on Saturday nights.

Especially favored inmates could make fifteen cents an hour in prison industries making metal lockers for the military, or cleaning the dirty socks and towels of several hundred inmates. These jobs tended to go to the hardcore crooks, generally identifiable by their tattoos, doo-rags and outsized biceps.

My entry into Milan was much easier than my entry into El Reno two scant years earlier. I was older, stronger, and—I hoped—wiser. I started out in B1, a wing reserved for newly arrived crooks and for inmates who were enrolled in a methadone treatment program.

During my first night, just before lights out, an imposing felon who bunked across from me made his way to my bed, sat down on it, and put his gargantuan hand on my leg. He intoned he was going to make me his bitch. I responded by jumping up and making noisy threats which I knew I was incapable of backing up. Anything could have happened, but he got up and went back to his bunk and never bothered me again. I guess my acting lessons in college had paid off after all.

The next day I met George Crocker.

I'd been circling the inside yard after chow trying to get a little exercise before the tower guard, in his distinctively flat voice, intoned "clear-the-yard; clear-the-yard" over the intercom. I was seeking the maximum possible dose of cold, fresh air. I stopped on a sidewalk near the middle of the yard and was looking at a lighted display of the Nativity—baby Jesus, Mary and Joseph, a donkey, a wise man or two. All the figures were about three feet tall, except for Jesus, of course, who was about the size of a fireplace log. The worst offense was that baby Jesus had a light bulb inside his head, in case anyone missed the point that he was holy. It was all too much. I wondered whatever happened to the separation of church and state, and I reflected on the absence of Menorahs lighting up the courtyard.

"Jesus Christ," I muttered to myself.

"Yeah," someone responded from behind me. I turned around and found a tall, thin inmate standing there with a look of disgust on his face that must have mirrored mine. "Merry fucking Christmas," he said.

He said his name was George Crocker, and I told him mine. There followed the inevitable "What's your beef?" and I told him I was in for destroying draft records, which he thought was cool since he was in for refusing induction. He was a Quaker from Stillwater, Minnesota. He also was in B block but in one of the upstairs wings, B3. He'd arrived a couple of months before me. We continued on our way, circling the yard. By the fourth round we were fast friends, and I had the start of a "family."

The next night I sat with George at chow and he introduced to me some pals of his: Frankie from Detroit, whom everyone called Weasel, serving two years for a Dyre Act violation (driving a stolen car across state lines); Jellico, a six-foot-four draft resister whose height was exceeded only by his gentleness; and Joe Saylor, a vet who was returning from a tour of duty in Vietnam when he was busted at Detroit Metro Airport by a German Shepherd that sniffed out an ounce of dope in his duffel bag.

After chow our walk in the inside yard took us by the Nativity scene, and each time we passed it one of the group would comment on how offensive it was—its false cheer, its faux promise of salvation, the reminder that it was Christmas and we were in prison. Then George did something none of us expected. He stepped onto the grass and snatched the baby Jesus from his crib. Then he pulled the plug from the extension cord, extinguishing Jesus's light. He tucked Jesus inside his long army surplus top coat, and when the "clear-the-yard" sounded, he took Jesus to bed with him. The next day, George, who worked as a clerk in the dentist office, took Jesus to work and hid him in the false ceiling above the dentist chair.

That morning all hell broke loose. The inmates were assembled in formation in their units, called back from wherever they'd been working. One by one they were searched, and dispatched to form lines in the freezing yard while the units themselves were ransacked. No mattress was left unturned in the search for our Lord and Savior. None of the inmates knew what the hacks were looking for—except George and me and our buddies. It was sweet. It was better than a real present.

At lunch we could hardly contain ourselves. Jesus had made a clean break, and the guards seemed helpless to find him. Then Frankie had an idea. Frankie worked in the paint room…

Frankie smuggled the paint to George that night at chow, and the next morning, George took Jesus from his hiding place and made a slight modification to Jesus's face. Then he quickly restored Jesus to his hiding place above the ceiling tiles, and by the time George's shift was over, Jesus had dried. George returned to the compound with Jesus once again under his coat. That evening, after chow, we gathered once more around the crèche, and George reunited Jesus with his virgin mother.

It didn't take long for the Black Muslims to notice what we'd done. In the Milan FCI in 1970, the Black Muslims were a small group, numbering less than a dozen and not taken too seriously by anyone. They spent every possible moment in each other's company, which was no more than what I did with the "family" I'd found in prison. But they were quirkily disciplined. Through some connection they had with the laundry, their surplus khakis were superbly tailored, starched and pressed, with perfect creases in their pants. The top buttons of their shirts were always buttoned, and their shoes were perfectly shined. Whereas George and I and our friends casually tripped and strolled around the yard in our crumpled and ill-fitting army surplus hand-me-downs, they marched lock-step in silent formation, a dozen right feet falling together as a dozen left feet were lifted. Other people might not take them very seriously, but they took themselves quite so.

The Black Muslims formed a circle around the crèche and turned their backs to it. They were protecting their baby Jesus—their *black* baby Jesus.

Before long some hillbillies found out what was up with the Nativity, and they were out for blood. Nobody was going to paint *their* Jesus black. A scuffle ensued, but before it could get out of control the guards swarmed the compound, the "clear-the-yard" was sounded, and the fight was stopped almost before it started.

The next morning, Jesus was gone. So were Mary and Joseph and the donkey and the wise men. And so were the tacky Christmas decorations that had been hung on the dorm bulletin boards.

Now this, I thought, was going to be a fine Christmas after all.

At the start of 1971 John Mitchell resigned as attorney general in order to manage Richard Nixon's re-election campaign. Richard Kleindienst, who'd been Mitchell's number two man in the Justice Department, replaced Mitchell. Kleindienst and Mitchell wound up in prison later for their roles in the White House orchestrated break-in at the Democratic headquarters at the Watergate Hotel.

Before his resignation Mitchell authorized a couple dozen federal grand juries around the country, headed up by a special prosecutor named Guy Armstrong. In the winter and spring of 1971, Armstrong crisscrossed the country getting these grand juries going. Each had a different specific focus, but they all had the same ultimate goal: to neutralize the anti-war movement. They wanted to get as many anti-war activists off the street and behind bars as possible, and the peace movement to burn up all of its energy and money in defending itself.

The plan was brilliant. The more the protestors got socked with subpoenas and indictments and trials, the less time they had to attack Nixon or to continue their protests. They couldn't take to the streets if their leaders were all in jail, or about to go to jail. Ultimately it worked. And Hoover was all over this. It gave him one more thing to do with the domestic surveillance money Congress granted him after he broke the story about the alleged Berrigan conspiracy.

In January 1971, one of these grand juries—in Harrisburg, Pennsylvania—returned an indictment charging six people with conspiring to kidnap Henry Kissinger and blow up heating tunnels in Washington, D.C. I'd worked with four of the six on draft board raids: Elizabeth

McAllister, Joe Wenderoth, Neil McLaughlin and Tony Scoblick—one nun, two priests, and one former priest. I'd never met Phillip Berrigan, who was also indicted, since he'd already been in prison before I got involved in the raids. And the sixth person indicted, Eqbal Ahmad, a professor of International Relations at the University of Chicago, I'd met on one or two occasions when he had visited Dan Berrigan in Ithaca, but I'd never had so much as a conversation with him.

Two of the six, Liz McAllister and Phil Berrigan, were also charged with illegally smuggling letters in and out of the federal prison in Lewisburg, Pennsylvania, where Phil was jailed.

It was this last item that bothered me. Liz had always excoriated everybody else about security. Her paranoia about my mother and my fiancée Sue had compelled me to step away from the Delaware action. She was always on everyone's case about who said what to whom, about the need to use safe phones and false names and never to put anything in writing. And now she and Phil were being prosecuted for smuggling letters to each other, supposedly with plans to kidnap Kissinger? This didn't make any sense.

She couldn't have been that stupid—stupid enough to conspire to kidnap the Secretary of State of the United States or, if she had so conspired, stupid enough to write it down in a letter to Phil that she smuggled into a federal prison. If she really did these things, it was a stupendously phenomenal blunder. It was way beyond stupid.

Seven other persons were named as "unindicted co-conspirators"—a kind of no-man's land of federal injustice in which those named are forever accused but not charged, and thus without an opportunity to present a defense. Dan Berrigan was one of the unindicted co-conspirators, as was my Rochester co-defendant, Ted Glick.

Holy shit. Had there really been such a plan? Had any of these people actually considered taking these kinds of actions? I was more grateful than ever that I'd ended my relationship with the Berrigan/Grady/McAllister group when I did. I wasn't looking forward to how this might play out.

Prison was a fluid place, with inmates coming and going. You were never sure if someone you saw today would still be around tomorrow. Inmates disappeared sometimes in the middle of the afternoon or in the middle of the night, and you had no way to know what happened to them. Maybe they were just doing a stint in the hole, or maybe they were transferred to another joint, or maybe they'd hit the big time and made it to C or E block, and thus they weren't seen much, if at all, in the general population. Maybe they were raped in the middle of the night and transferred to the infirmary. In spite of the constant uncertainty, in my first year in prison I had a pretty stable, extremely supportive, and wildly inventive group of prison pals.

Conscientious objectors came and went. When I arrived at Milan, there were four. At the peak, there were fourteen. On any given day it was hard to get the number straight. The Bureau of Prisons was paranoid about allowing us to stay as a group in any one prison for any length of time, so most COs tended to be moved around a lot. I was lucky that I spent most of my time in Milan.

All prisons were not created equal; some were unequivocally worse than others. It took some effort to recreate Milan from the inside as a facility that was safe and creative and nurturing—at least as much as a prison can be. Starting all over in a new prison could never easy for those inmates who were whisked away in the middle of the night.

Imprisoned COs came in various packages. Some were as young as eighteen, and some were in their late twenties. Some were educated at Yale or Harvard, and some had dropped out of high school. Some were religious and some weren't. Some were hale and hearty, and some were frail. Some were political and some weren't.

Some, like Ralph Squire, DeCourcy's younger brother, were "non-cooperators." Ralph had refused to walk into prison, so he had to be carried in. Once in, he refused to eat. While on his hunger strike in Milan, he was held in D block, the hole, and I was able to get permission from the warden to visit with him for half an hour a day. Aside from that daily visit, Ralph had no distractions, since he was allowed nothing to read and no other visitors. He was only in Milan for a couple of weeks before he was transferred to the federal prison in Springfield, Missouri, where he'd be force-fed through a tube inserted down his mouth and throat.

In addition to George Crocker and myself, there were a few other COs who remained in Milan without being transferred: John from Virginia, an energetic ball of humor and constant source of good times; Don from Kentucky, an inventively goofy hillbilly; and Ken from Detroit, a shy kid.

But my pals weren't all COs. The ranks of our family included one bank robber, one kidnapper, several hapless joyriders, and a number of druggies of various descriptions. There were Frankie G and Frankie B—twenty-year-old cousins from a notorious Milwaukee crime family serving identical sentences for a cocaine bust, both of them dashingly handsome and blithely complacent about their sentences. Danny M was a freckled Buddhist LSD peddler from Ohio, a practitioner of yoga and meditation, and a supremely serene soul. Randy Ball was a baby-faced eighteen-year-old blond surfer and artist, who was busted while trying to raise rent money selling pot at a McDonald's in Gary, Indiana. He arrived as terrified as I'd been in El Reno, but we quickly surrounded him with our protection and he, too, served his time without incident.

Whatever the crime, there was just something about a crook that either identified him as belonging or not belonging to our family—something instantly identifiable. We kept an eye out for new arrivals, and when any of us spotted a kindred spirit we quickly brought him into our fold before he could get in trouble or find himself hassled by any other faction in the prison. We took care of each other. We made the time go fast.

My two exes from Cornell, Gretchen and Steve, came for a visit, and they got permission from the Warden to conduct a theatre workshop for a score of my handpicked pals. Out of the workshop came a little underground theatre troop, and that spring I obtained the permission of the warden to conduct an ongoing theatre workshop. We met five nights a week for two and a half hours in the deserted visiting room, rehearsing our own take on Beckett's inscrutable *Waiting for Godot*. The play made immediate sense to us. Long after the rehearsal period, we'd still find ourselves quoting certain lines that spoke to our situation:

VLADIMIR That passed the time.

ESTRAGON: It would have passed in any case.

VLADIMIR: Yes, but not so rapidly

Truer words were never spoken in prison.

Over a period of months I also directed scenes from Harold Pinter's *The Caretaker* and a sweet little prison play called *Gallows Humor* by Jack Richardson. The possibility to perform these plays for an audience was held out to us but never realized. We only performed these plays for ourselves, in the visiting room and in a corner of the yard we claimed as our own. But it didn't matter if anyone else saw them or not. It mattered only that we did them.

Sue and a Cornell writing professor named Gary Esolen got permission to teach a writing workshop to twenty inmates. They were allowed into the prison compound to use a shuttered classroom in what had once been the education wing before the Bureau of Prisons stopped funding education for inmates. This workshop was open to whoever signed up first, and the participants were a wonderfully motley crew of crooks. No great novels or epic poems came out of this workshop, but it provided a day of relief to some needy felons, several of whom hadn't been in the company of a woman in months or years.

Danny practiced his yoga by himself until he noticed a number of us were watching and starting to mimic him. What began as answering a few questions for a few fellow inmates turned into a regular yoga class conducted on Saturday and Sunday mornings. Weather permitting, the class was held in our particular corner of the inside yard. As we contorted our bodies and vocalized our mantras, other inmates gave us wide berth, not knowing what the hell we were doing or why we were doing it. But we knew. It felt good. And it was something we could do together.

Frankie and Frankie—the crime cousins—sunbathed in the warmer months. Somehow they came up with short shorts, which they were able to get for anyone else who wanted them. They stretched out on the grass and slicked themselves down with baby oil, which they got from the commissary, and lay there all day on weekends. We called it "going to the beach," our own private Riviera.

Books were a problem. Milan had no library. There had been one, but it shut down a couple of weeks after my arrival, which didn't matter a lot since there wasn't much in it to begin with. The prison rules allowed each inmate to have two books sent in from the outside, but once you received your two books that was it—no more books for the entire span of your sentence. We weren't allowed to share books. If someone was caught with someone else's book, they both went to the hole.

We were allowed two subscriptions, and I subscribed to the *Atlantic Monthly* and the Sunday *New York Times*, publications with some heft, the reading of which would consume hours. There was no prohibition against sharing periodicals, and every week there was a long string of inmates lined up to read the *Times*. First it went to George, and then to Joe, and then to Frankie and Frankie, and then to…

I was contacted by a professor of religion from Temple University, John Raines. He'd heard about me from people he knew, and he offered to teach me a college correspondence course on the history of religion. I'd have taken a correspondence course on the history of worms, if it meant getting something else to read, so I said yes. He tailored the course to my situation and provided not only books on Buddhism and saints, but also the collected works of Alexander Solzhenitsyn: *The First Circle, One Day in the Life of Ivan Denisovich*, and *Cancer Ward*. These books didn't exactly fit the syllabus for a religion course, but that wasn't the point of my correspondence with Professor Raines. I simply wanted something good to read. The gruesome stories of Solzhenitsyn's sojourn in the gulag made me more appreciative of my advantages in a U.S. federal prison. Comparatively, I had nothing to complain about.

A Cornell writing professor and published poet, Bill Matthews, started corresponding with me about poetry. He sent me sheath after sheath of new poems he was writing for his next book, with discussions of what he thought worked, what didn't, and what was frustrating. In return I sent him my feeble attempts at poetry. I inundated him with jailhouse verse—plaintive odes of love confined, of desire unfulfilled, of innocent youth wasted behind iron bars.

Most of the inmates lacked the funds to spend at the commissary, which was open for two hours a week on Saturday mornings. The commissary had things that made life a smidgeon easier: fresh fruit, decent shaving cream, brand name soap and toothpaste, cigarettes, and candy bars. Each month Sue sent me ten dollars, the maximum monthly amount, to pad my commissary account. And on Saturday mornings I always bought the same thing: as many oranges as I could.

By now you're hopefully getting the idea that I'd absorbed my mother's wisdom regarding lemonade. Bit by bit, with the collaboration of fellow felons, we'd transformed Milan from just another shabby federal prison to a creative playground. We'd done it in increments so small they were nearly undetectable, but when considered together they started to make quite a difference in the day-to-day lives of several young incarcerated men.

I like to think that I was the spark that started this transformation, or rather that my mother was, with her single word, "Don't." That may be too generous a conceit, since the life I shared in Milan with George, Danny, Joe, Randy, Jellico, Frankie and Frankie, Phillips, Ken, and others wasn't exclusively of my own making, nor could it have been. We each contributed to it. But it had to start somewhere.

It probably started the night George stole Jesus. But if I hadn't been receptive, if Weasel hadn't painted Jesus's face, and if that practical joke hadn't led to the next plan to break out of the mental box that this physical box was designed to construct… well, then we'd have just been prisoners. But we were so much more. All of us. And we knew it.

That spring I wrote a letter to a friend, and it fell into the hands of a NY radical rag, *WIN*, published by the War Resisters League. *WIN* printed it in their November 1971 edition. In the letter I rhapsodized how swell things were in prison, a blasphemous conceit to those in the "movement." An editorial comment attached to the letter apologized for my failure to call for the "abolition of prisons" and noted: "Some folks might consider Joe's letter counter-revolutionary." Well, I never did totally fit in with the revolutionary crowd.

The letter ended with this embarrassing poem:

Roses are red

Violets are blue

Life is a trip

Prison is too

Insipid, yes. But also, true.

Food in prison was uniformly tasteless. The meatloaf tasted like the chicken, which tasted like the cornbread, which tasted like the beans, which tasted like the Jell-O. I'll never quite understand how they made all the food taste the same. It tasted gray. Perhaps the correct thing to say is that it didn't have any taste at all. That's why oranges were so important. They tasted orange.

At night, before lights out, I'd sit on my bunk in the cavernous dorm, which smelled of too many dirty socks and too much disinfectant, and I'd hold an orange in my hand. I'd bring it to my nose and smell it. I'd rub it over my lips and cheeks. I'd roll it around in my hands till my palms and fingers started to color. Then I'd peel it slowly, thrilling with each eruption of fragrance from this marvel that was an orange. First, I'd eat the peels. I loved their flavor, their texture, their promise of the fruit yet to come. I could almost feel the vitamins surging into my cells. Then I'd eat the segments, one by one, savoring the first as much as the last.

It was David Harris who'd introduced me to oranges. Oranges had always been there, of course. But I'd never really *experienced* them before. Somehow, on that day in April 1968, when he and Joan Baez took me to the emergency room after I injured my foot, and David handed me that orange, it was like I saw them, smelled them, tasted them for the first time.

I gave away more oranges than I ate. That was my thing in prison. I was the guy who gave away oranges.

Because I could read and write and type, I was assigned a desk job in the office of Colonel Strong, a white-haired World War II vet whose job was to do basically nothing. Unfortunately for him, someone in Washington noticed him on the payroll and gave him an assignment, which was to rewrite all of the OJT (On-The-Job-Training) manuals for the Federal Bureau of Prisons. All the prisons used the same manuals for the inmates who worked in the various shops that kept the facilities running—the plumbing shops, the electrical shops, the paint shops, the small engine repair shops. Some genius in Washington had decided all the manuals needed to conform to a new format, a different arrangement of bullet points and descriptors, which, though maybe not any better, was new. It was the most meaningless kind of busywork. Colonel Strong handed me the manuals and told me to do it, not because he was lazy, which he was, but because he was totally incapable of the task himself. He put his feet up on his desk, leaned back in his chair, and napped, while I revised the manuals.

After two days I quit.

Inmates weren't allowed to quit their assigned jobs, but I quit. I told my caseworker the same thing I told Colonel Strong: sitting in a window-less cinderblock office all day listening to Strong snoring while I revised manuals that didn't need to be revised in the first place was the equiva-lent of locking myself inside a jail within a jail. I said I'd just as soon fester in the hole all day as bide my time in an airless tomb with Colonel Strong and those useless manuals. I told them what I really wanted to do, and was willing to do, was work. Hard work. I wanted to be as-signed a job where I built up a sweat and at the end of the day returned to my bunk tired.

They argued such a job would be wasting my education, and I told them the job with Strong was already doing that. I was fully prepared to be hauled off to the hole, but surprisingly, after conferring with each other, I was assigned to "lawn detail."

The next day I reported to the rear sallyport. A massive iron gate rolled back and admitted me into the no-man's land between prison and the outside world, and then it closed shut behind me. Then the outer gate rolled open, and I walked out of the prison. Bop was there with an idling powder blue pickup, and I climbed into the back of the pickup with other crooks assigned to the same detail, and we drove off to the "Onion Shack"—Bop's tool shed and clubhouse.

In the coming months I spent my days mowing giant lawns, dredging irrigation canals, trimming trees, plowing snow, planting petunias, and driving tractors. I sweated. I got tired. I dug in the dirt and I was out in the elements—the sun and the rain and the wind. And at night, I slept like a baby.

The Milan warden, Chuck Hughes, lived in a big Colonial brick home just outside the prison gates. A long driveway led to it, and it was flanked on both sides with flower beds about a hundred yards long. It was March and I was prepping the beds. I was getting them ready to plant some spring flowers, petunias mostly. It was too early to plant them, but not too early to get the beds ready.

A car drove up. The customary dark four-door sedan. A Ford, naturally. Two federal marshals got out. They looked just like federal marshals always look: dark blue suits, sunglasses, holstered pistols, and spit-shined shoes. They each had broad shoulders and a hint of a belly. Nice manicures. They told me to turn around and put my hands on my head. Then they restrained me (not that I needed restraining) with hand-cuffs, leg-irons, and a waist chain, and they put me in the back seat of their car. I asked what was going on, but I knew they wouldn't tell me. I figured I was probably being transferred to another prison.

We drove all day. We stopped only once, at a McDonald's somewhere in Ohio. One cop went in and got some Big Macs, while the other one kept an eye on me. We ate in the car. Ever wonder what it's like to eat a meal bent over in a back seat wearing handcuffs chained to your waist? Most of the lettuce and tomato wound up in my lap.

I needed to pee. So one officer went in the McDonald's and announced he was a federal marshal escorting a dangerous prisoner, and he cleared a path for me to the bathroom. From the way people looked at me you'd have thought I was Charles Manson.

I was uncomfortable but not particularly scared. Prison transfers happened all the time, for no discernible reason. It was odd how they came for me—outside the gates, in the flower bed—and it was a little odd they were transferring me solo in a sedan. Transfers were usually done with batches of inmates, in vans or on buses. But I still figured it was just a transfer.

That first night they dropped me off in the county jail in Youngstown, Ohio. Prisoners in transit weren't allowed to let anyone know what's happening to them, but someone made a mistake, and that night I talked the jailer into letting me have a phone call. I called Sue and told her where I was. She wasn't aware of anything happening that might prompt them to move me other than just their normal bureaucratic nonsense. She said she'd call around and see what she could find out.

The next morning the marshals picked me up early and took me to Harrisburg, depositing me in the Dauphin County Jail, a brand new jail which wasn't completely open. They led me to a cellblock which held only one other prisoner. I was locked in a cell on the third and top tier. The other prisoner was way down on the first tier, at the other end. I never saw him. I only heard him—all day, every day, and a good part of the night, his nasal voice bouncing off the steel floors, iron bars, and cinderblock walls.

From dawn to dusk and way into the night, my unseen companion warbled the same friggin' song in the same pained falsetto: "Jeremiah was a bullfrog," he wailed. "Was a good friend of mine…"

It was torture. That's why I still break out in hives anytime I hear "Joy to the fishes and the deep blue sea…"

Altogether I was there thirty-three days, locked in that isolated cell listening to that unceasing asshole. Nothing to read. No one to talk with. Nothing to do. Just me in my five by nine cell, and Mr. Juke Box down below providing his one-note entertainment. I got out of my cell only three times during that entire period, aside from a shave and a shower once a week.

The first time out of my cell was ten days after I arrived there. I still had no idea what was going on. I figured there must be some hiccup in my transit, and I was parked in Harrisburg until it was sorted out. Then one morning a guard opened my cell door and told me I had visitors. Great, I thought. Maybe it's Sue. Maybe she's found out what's going on. But it wasn't Sue. It was a tall man with an angular face, wearing a thin tie, a brown suit, and cowboy boots. It was Ramsey Clark.

Ramsey Clark had been LBJ's attorney general. He'd succeeded Bobby Kennedy after Kennedy resigned to run for president. And Clark wasn't alone. There were two other lawyers present, including Leonard Boudin, a prominent Massachusetts activist lawyer I'd heard of but never met. His Weatherman daughter, Kathy, had escaped an explosion in a Greenwich Village townhouse in 1970, and went on to be convicted for robbing a Brinks truck in 1981, for which she served twenty-two years in jail before her release in 2003. The third lawyer was a younger guy named Tom Menaker, from Harrisburg.

They offered to represent me.

"For what?" I asked. One said, "Hasn't anyone told you why you're here?" And I said, "No. I figured I was just in transit." So they filled me in. They told me about Mitchell, Kleindienst, and Armstrong's grand juries, and that one of the grand juries was convened in Harrisburg and was looking into the alleged conspiracy to kidnap Henry Kissinger.

I was numb. It was as if a ton of bricks had fallen on me and I couldn't move or speak. They said I'd be taken to the grand jury room on the following day and asked questions. They told me that so far the prosecutors had asked the same three or four questions with a few variations. All of the questions were vague. They said the grand jury was on a fishing expedition, trying to find evidence to justify the indictments they'd already charged six people with. They said one question the prosecutor would ask me was if I'd ever been to an anti-war meeting, and if so, when, where, and who was there and what was said by whom. The question was ridiculous, of course, since to answer it I'd have to narrate the previous three years of my life. They said they couldn't tell me how to answer, but if I wanted, I could refuse to answer the questions. That seemed reasonable to me. They said they were volunteering their services because they were outraged at what was going on. They said not to worry.

I did worry, but given what eventually happened, I should have worried more.

The next afternoon I was hobbled in chains and led to a waiting car outside the jail, and another set of marshals transported me to the grand jury room in the federal courthouse. As I shuffled through the hallways, the marshals on either side hurrying me along, I passed a few people I knew, including Sue, my mother, and my Rochester attorney Herm Walz; but I wasn't allowed to speak with any of them.

The jurors in the grand jury room reminded me of kids in a high school detention classroom supervised by a substitute teacher. Some were napping or nodding off, some read newspapers or worked on crossword puzzles. A paltry few were paying attention.

Still wearing my chains, I was taken to a chair at the front of the room, facing the jurors. The prosecutor, William Lynch, asked me three questions. The first one was the ludicrous and unanswerable question the lawyers had mentioned, demanding I recount every anti-war conversation I'd ever had with anyone. The other two questions were just as vague and general. No one asked anything about kidnapping, Henry Kissinger, heating tunnels, draft board raids, or anything specific at all. There were no questions about the Berrigans or Ted Glick or any other particular person I knew or might have known. Then I was excused and transported back to jail. A day passed. Then another. And another. Ten days passed in all without any word from anyone about what was going on.

During this period I hallucinated. It's a common side effect of sensory deprivation. Fortunately I knew this—having heard about it from other inmates and having read about it in books by Solzhenitsyn—and I was therefore somewhat prepared for it. I also was a bit practiced in hallucination from two superb encounters with LSD as a Cornell undergraduate, so I accepted the arrival of the spirit world with some relief that the tedium of solitary was about to be interrupted.

In my fantasy world I relived my entire life. Once that was done, I decided to try it again, with some alterations. I changed a few things to see what my life might have been like under other circumstances, had I made other decisions, had other things happened to me.

I spent one intensely satisfying day as a salamander.

It was during this time that I finally understood, at the root of my being, what my mother meant when she wrote me on the day of my Rochester sentencing:

My darkest experiences in the past years ended with a knowledgeable light.

Each time I emerged with more understanding of human nature and of life itself.

That describes what happened to me as a result of my time in solitary in the Dauphin County Jail. What should have been a horrifying experience left me at peace with myself. I'd been given a rare and precious gift. I emerged content with my life as it was, happy with myself and the world. It felt as if I'd walked through a door that had always been there in front of me, and once I walked through it, the tensions, concerns, and worries that had previously occupied my life fell away.

There have been many times in my life when I've revisited those days spent in solitary, when I've relived the peace that I'd found there. In that spare, empty cell I found contentment with myself, and only myself. I learned that anything extra in my life is a gift to be treasured, but not expected. In the end, I am all I have. And I like what I have.

When you're left with nothing but yourself and you're okay with that, there's no darkness anymore. There's no pain too big to suffer, no joy too great to embrace, no love too intimidating to accept.

On the eleventh day following my return to solitary, I was returned to the courthouse, and the judge informed me I'd been indicted for criminal contempt of court for refusing to answer the questions of the grand jury. When the judge asked me how I pleaded, I just laughed. I could think of no other response, and even if I had, I'm not sure I could have uttered it. I was a verbal basket case by then. I'd been in isolation now for three weeks altogether and my mind was oatmeal. I'd had so few opportunities to speak with anyone that my tongue had forgotten how to form words.

Meanwhile the grand jury had been busy grilling more witnesses. I learned later that thirty people in all had been subpoenaed to appear before the Harrisburg Grand Jury. Most of the people subpoenaed were people I'd never met and whose names I'd never heard before. Twenty of those subpoenaed had, like me, refused to testify, and of the twenty, ten of us were singled out for prosecution on the contempt charges. We could never figure what logic the prosecution used in determining whom to charge. I never understood why I was there at all, except as a pawn in a much larger game.

The grand jury had also amended the original Harrisburg conspiracy indictment, confusing further what had already been confusing enough. Instead of six alleged conspirators there were now eight, with the addition of Mary Cain (an ex-nun who was Tony Scoblick's wife) and Ted Glick (my Rochester codefendant). Instead of the original seven un-indicted conspirators there were now five, and Dan Berrigan was no longer listed among them. Dan's name didn't appear anywhere in the indictment, and, thank god, neither did mine. They'd also added a third conspiracy charge, alleging these eight individuals had conspired to raid draft boards in Philadelphia, Delaware, and Rochester. Before the case went to trial, the indictment would be amended once more, and Ted Glick would be dropped from all the charges, which is why the trial eventually became known as the trial of the Harrisburg Seven.

I knew that the third conspiracy charge was bogus. Ted was the only person among the indicted who'd had any involvement in the Rochester draft board raid. Some of the others might have had a hint something was going to happen in Rochester, but they hadn't participated in any aspect of the planning or execution. I also knew first-hand that some of those indicted had been involved in Philadelphia or Delaware, but also that some of them had not. Yet all of them had been charged with con-spiring to do all three raids.

It felt as though the prosecution was just throwing everything into a big pot, hoping something would stick to someone. Maybe the other con-spiracy charges were as flawed in their construction. But I didn't know. I was just glad I had nothing to do with any conspiracy to kidnap anyone or blow up heating tunnels anywhere. These folks were facing potential life sentences.

But then, so was I. Normally a criminal contempt conviction carried a maximum five-year sentence, but I already had six felony convictions stemming from Rochester. If I got another conviction—for anything—I'd automatically get a life sentence.

This was unbelievable.

After I entered my not guilty plea, they took me back to my cell on the third tier of the Dauphin County Jail, where I got to listen to One Dog Night for another couple of weeks. Eventually, the same set of marshals showed up and took me back to Milan. We stopped at the same dismal McDonald's on the way back. I didn't want any food and I didn't need to pee. I'd practically stopped eating.

I arrived back at the Milan FCI in the middle of a workday. The dorm should have been empty, with all the inmates out on their various work details. But as I entered the dorm, there was fellow inmate and pal, Joe Saylor, his arms spread wide and grinning like we'd both just won the lottery. He'd been working the outside yard on lawn detail that afternoon, and saw the marshals pull up with me. He'd got permission from Bop to come back inside and greet me. "Welcome home, brother," he said.

Home.

Yeah, this was home. It was a hell of a lot better than the Dauphin County Jail, and it was starting to look like I might be here a lot longer than I thought, so I might as well get used to it.

Welcome home.

While in prison, I lived my life vicariously through letters—reams and reams of letters. After the "clear the yard" in the evening, I had two hours in the dorm with nothing to do. I preferred sitting on my bunk, tuning out the din of the hundred inmates who cohabited my space, reading the letters that came for me that day and responding to each of them.

All correspondents had to be pre-approved by my caseworker, and I had about twenty correspondents on my list. Most of them were faithful writers. As soon as they got a letter from me they responded, and vice-versa. Two of them, my mother and Sue, didn't wait for my response. They tended to write every day, as I did to them, so that our communication was sometimes jumbled. It was like having a constant conversation with another person in a time-warp.

I kept a log of each letter I received and each letter I wrote. If someone had been delinquent in responding, after a short while I wrote them anyway. I made sure the flow of letters never stopped. It was important to get letters every day and to write letters every day. It meant I wasn't forgotten.

So each night I wrote four, five, or six letters, penciling wings of thought on yellow lined paper. Writing was a lifeline for me, a link to the world outside, to the friends and family I'd left. Often when I was writing, I didn't feel like a prisoner anymore—just a guy having a conversation with a friend—except for when I couldn't get the prison out of my head, and it dripped and skittered all over the page, and the words screaming to get out of my head were little versions of my locked-up self.

After my Rochester conviction my mother had stayed in Ithaca through the holidays, but then she moved to the Catholic Worker. It was a move she'd been contemplating since I'd first introduced her to the Worker and to Dorothy Day. When Dorothy learned of my mother's interest, she invited her to move to the Worker's House of Hospitality on Manhattan's Lower East Side, and Dorothy offered her a bed in Dorothy's own quarters on the third floor.

It was the right decision for my mom. At the Worker she helped staff the busy soup line each evening, and in the afternoons she worked across the street with Barbara Hawkins, whom she'd known in Oklahoma, staffing a storefront that provided used clothing for New York's homeless. My mother was always happiest when she was helping other people, and that was the entire mission of the Catholic Worker and everyone associated with it.

That winter and spring of 1971, she wrote to me of her childhood and her letters were full of energy and light. She wrote me fragments of stories she remembered about "froggy" and "toad," and she sought to gain my collaboration in crafting these stories into a children's book. She sent me clippings from the New York papers of items which had caught her attention. Sometimes her letters went on for pages, and sometimes they were only a sentence or two, but every day she wrote. Twice that spring she boarded a bus at Grand Central Terminal and made the long haul across the northern states to southern Michigan to visit me.

Then something changed. As summer approached, her letters grew shorter, tedious, and less certain. She wrote less often. The energy and hopefulness that had infused her letters in the spring had dissipated. I could sense that something was wrong.

And so it was that I was in prison. And so it was that my mother was at the Catholic Worker. And so it was she fell to her death. And so it was I learned of her death.

I don't know why, exactly, my mother "fell" from the roof of the building. I do know that living with her scars for twelve years had been horribly difficult, and that each year it got harder, not easier. Perhaps she hadn't gotten used to the unceasing stares and the intrusive questions of strangers. In New York she might have found it intimidating to walk down the streets. New Yorkers are blasé about most everything, but my mother's appearance was not easily ignored. Inside she was just herself, and to me she was just my mom, but to the world she was a freak.

The scars themselves became harder to bear over time. Burn scars don't breathe or perspire, and most of the surface of her body was scarred. Hot weather was especially discomforting. And severe burn scars don't get more flexible over time; they get harder, thicker and tighter. They constrict and they crack and they bleed. Then there was the never-ending problem with her eyes. For twelve years she'd had only partial eyelids, which were reconstructed by Dr. Anderson and not complete enough to close her eyes. For twelve years her eyes had been irritated twenty-four hours a day, and she never slept soundly since her eyes were always open.

I know she found friends at the Worker, and I know she found a purpose, but maybe it wasn't enough. I'll never know. But this I know: Her long suffering was finally over. My grief at her death was tempered by my relief at the end of her suffering.

Rose Gilchrist, RIP

On July 15 Rosie Gilchrist died in a fall from the roof of the First Street House. She was a 63-year-old native Oklahoman who had lived at the Worker off and on for a year.

In life and in death, Rosie brings to my mind what Charles Williams called the mysteries of co-inherance and exchange. In his novel, **Descent into Hell**, Williams speaks of our pains, fears, and troubles as "parcels" we must carry, and develops the idea that we are not ultimately so separate from one another that we cannot sometimes pick up the "parcels" of others.

Rosie carried more than her share of "parcels." Her face, hands and arms were terribly scarred in a fire, yet she carried on with the personality of the beautiful woman she had been. She was considered so unstable as to be committed to a mental hospital, yet she was the one who went out of her way to clean and comfort the patients whom the staff of the hospital preferred to neglect because they helplessly soiled themselves. Her son, Joe Gilchrist, was subjected to one long trial for draft resistance in Oklahoma and eventually sent to prison for destruction of government files with the Flower City Conspiracy. Rosie lent her spirit and courage to the many young people who carried on the political work surrounding these actions. At the Worker, though she felt acutely the element of conflict which sometimes underlies the many interactions in our house of hospitality, Rosie was an unfailing folder of papers, sweeper of floors, and nurse to one of the women who fell sick.

Rosie's ability to carry her "parcels," and others', seemed to spring from the courageous openness with which she met people and circumstances, from her recognition that the humanity we share outweighs our apparent separation. Long before civil rights became a popular cause, when most Oklahomans still spoke of black people as "niggers," Rosie worked toward justice for those who were for her just other people. The love she extended to all peoples in the world made her an opponent of war and she acted out her conviction through support of resistance activities and participation in every peace demonstration available. On her way to Washington this April 24, she fell in with the gay liberation contingent and returned to tell me that she had learned a great deal from people whose perspective and concerns she had never met before.

There is a temptation in writing about Rosie to reduce her to one's own neat categories. In fact, she was a lively, complicated individual. Sometimes her fearless openness led her to speak so forthrightly as to offend. Her plans, and her demands on others, were often too grand to be practical, nor would she compromise when she decided what ought to be done. Yet her stubborn determination and impossible dreams were balanced by unobtrusive displays of gentle generosity: cooking for friends of her sons, doing odd jobs on college campuses, coaching a golf team, and finding kind greetings for those about her.

In her last few months, Rosie was working on a scheme to have her scars used as examples in a campaign to help burn victims and people disfigured by leprosy. There were many days on which she was terribly depressed, but then she would rise out of it to tell me that she was glad she had been hurt so much because it had taught her that we simply must care for and forgive one another. In Rosie our co-inherance and exchange were alive. I am grateful to have known her; we miss her.

Jan Adams and Kathy Schmidt.

There's a passage in my mother's obituary that I need to call out:

> On her way to Washington this April 24, she fell in with the Gay Liberation contingent and she returned to tell me she had learned a great deal from people whose perspective and concerns she had never met before.

Wow. That's my mom. Open as always. And ahead of the curve. She was way ahead of me. It'd be more than ten years before I marched in a Gay Pride parade myself.

I never had a conversation with my mother about my feelings for men, but I've always wondered what, if anything, she might have suspected. My brother Gordon once wrote me that he always suspected that "the nerd" (meaning my twin, Jim) was queer, and not me. And I suppose in outward appearances there was never anything flagrant about my predilection. Still, moms have this way of knowing things about their children.

In all likelihood she never had an inkling, but still, this passage in her obituary has always seemed to me like a message from the grave. It's almost as if she's giving me permission to be gay. No. More than permission. Approval. I admit that I take some degree of comfort in that.

At the time of her death I hadn't yet committed to being gay. I had no question about my attraction to men, but I also had an attraction to certain women, and a burning desire to have a family, which, in 1971, would have been impossible with another man. So I chose, for many years, the straight life. But not altogether straight.

My mom. How perfect that even in her obituary she had a message for me.

During the last years of her life, my mother dreamed of helping the lepers of Molokai. She'd always thought her scars and disfigurement mimicked that of lepers. She thought that somehow she could put her image to use on their behalf and become a voice for a voiceless people.

She wrote me letters about her dream. She wrote me how she was seeking support from her doctor in Oklahoma, Dr. Anderson, and how she was trying to get on *The Today Show* to appeal for help and understanding for the lepers. Her dream was far-fetched. It was doomed never to come to anything. No one she reached out to seemed to support it or believe in it with her. But it was her dream.

At the end of July I was notified that the Federal Bureau of Prisons had granted me permission to correspond with Daniel Berrigan. Normally inmates weren't allowed to correspond with ex-cons who'd already done their time, or with inmates who were still serving their sentences in another prison. Over the next few months I exchanged a number of letters with Dan. When I was eventually released, I wasn't allowed to take Dan's letters with me. Presumably Dan's letters to me were destroyed. But Dan was allowed to take all of his correspondence with him upon his release. The following letter is one of many now part of the Berrigan collection in the Cornell University Rare Books Manuscript Collection:

July 31, 1971

Dear Dan,

The day ends as it began—with a slow, soft drizzle—muffling sounds, cooling the air, infecting even the most boisterous inmate with a certain calm. Walking in the rain has become something of a ritual, whose meaning reaches beyond the obvious symbolism of cleansing, to touch upon other universal needs. To walk in silence alone—or better with a friend. And then to separate, shower and bed down with a cup of coffee, pen and paper. Not a bad way to end the day.

I was informed yesterday that the Bureau had given permission for me to correspond with you, in reaction to a request from Sen. Mark Hatfield. I was genuinely surprised. It doesn't sound like the Bureau we all know and love. And I was unaware that such a request had been made. And so I begin this first letter to you, not knowing if it will actually reach you and knowing better than to hold my breath.

I hope that you are well, and that the physical discomforts of confinement aren't severely compounding your recent illness. Like many others, I had unrealistically hoped for your parole. (I once held such illusions for myself.)

It has been two weeks now since the death of my mother and the gathering of friends in NY in gentle celebration of her life and spirit…

I recall that when you testified in Rochester in November, my mother told [your brother] Jerry that you had taught me more than she. It's pointless to argue one way or the other about that, but she believed it, and loved and respected you for it.

I've been working as the prison gardener since April and all the carefully planted seeds have become fully flowering plants. My days are spent with the sun, soil and wind—a perfect solitary setting for meditation and reflection. All in all, I've few complaints about my imprisonment (although many against imprisonment per se). It has provided a quasi-monastic environment for intensive introspection, and some much-needed growing up. Not to be neglected are the benefits of learning to play the guitar (finally) and disciplining myself to write—poetry, songs, stories—and an abundance of correspondence.

Summer passed. Fall arrived.

Our lawn crew created a new garden outside the prison gates where minimum-security, short-time inmates could now picnic with visiting family members on the weekends. I was still limited to two visits a month—except for visits with Trudy, which miraculously didn't count—but now those visits could take place outside on a picnic ground. Most wives visiting their husbands in prison didn't bring their children, especially small children, because of the trauma of passing through the sallyport, the humiliation of the pat-downs, and the discomfort due to the strict rules of the prison visiting room. But here, outside the prison, the nearby gun tower seemed to disappear, and the grim-faced guards casually strolling between the tables took on the appearance of park rangers. Kids frolicked. Faces brightened. And overflowing baskets appeared choked with fried chicken, fresh fruit, and homemade pies and cakes. Each table was the scene of its own private gathering, but the grounds as a whole had the feeling of a community celebration or a church social, as slices of pie and jugs of iced tea or lemonade were passed from table to table.

That fall Bop got permission to take a crew off-campus to do a day's worth of volunteer work at the Ann Arbor Botanical Gardens. When we got there he put the other inmates to work, and then he took me to a remote clearing where I found Sue sitting on a blanket with a picnic lunch spread out before her. I didn't get any work done that day.

On another occasion, Trudy just happened to ask to see the warden at precisely the same time Bop was seeing him on another matter. She told Warden Hughes she'd come across four tickets to a Cobo Hall concert in Detroit, and she was wondering if there were a few inmates who deserved a road trip, who had minimum security status, and who could be trusted to behave. Bop spoke up that he had just the right combination of deserving inmates under his command on the lawn detail. So a few nights later I sat with Bop and three fellow crooks—and Sue, who had a fifth ticket of her own—listening to the Moody Blues. This was the music Sue and I had played when we'd first met. As I sat there, holding Sue's hand and drinking in "Nights in White Satin," I reflected on how lucky I was.

During my final fall and winter at Milan, Trudy got permission to escort me to church services outside the prison once a month, which meant attendance at the Friends Meeting House in Ann Arbor, followed by a lunch at Trudy's home. Occasionally services were held at a campsite owned by the Quakers on a small lake outside Ann Arbor. By the end of summer, Sue had moved to Ann Arbor to be closer to me and to look for work. Going to church with Trudy meant spending time with Sue.

I've recorded here some pleasant moments and the pleasant thoughts that accompanied them. As fortunate as I was in my imprisonment, it wasn't all fun and games. When occupied on my work detail or engaged with my friends I was able to forget, for a while, that I was locked up, but during the long nights in my bunk, I ached for release.

I was sick to death of playing cards or chess, of walking in circles around the inside yard, of being awakened each morning by that damn toy xylophone played over the dorm loudspeakers. I was tired of the humiliation of lining up for "sock call" every night, when I exchanged one pair of dirty, thin, white cotton socks, which I'd worn that day, for a clean pair I'd wear the next. I was tired of my number showing up on a list every two weeks ordering me to report to the barber shop. I was tired of being a number. I was tired of showering in a group and shitting in an open room. I was tired of posturing inmates and intractable guards. I was tired of my idiot caseworker. I was tired of lifting my balls and bending over for the strip searches that followed each visit. I was tired of visits.

I longed to wear real clothes, to eat real food, to live my life in the company of women and children and old people and dogs. I wanted to stretch my legs on a jet-black night and see stars in the sky again. I longed for the freedom to read anything I pleased and to write letters free of censors. I wanted to swing on a swing and climb up a tree. I wanted to have sex at night before I went to bed and again in the morning when I awoke, and again in the afternoon if I wanted. I wanted to sleep past noon, to paddle a canoe, to break two eggs in my own frying pan. I wanted to lie on a beach, to walk down a street, to drink a cold beer in a tavern, to play Frisbee with a dog. I wanted to ride a bike, to go for a run, to take a nap by myself. I wanted licorice and pretzels and chocolate and blackberries and honest-to-god maple syrup. I longed to be free.

Book Three:
The Chains of the Skyway

MY FRIENDS FROM THE PRISONS,
they ask unto me
HOW GOOD,
how good does it feel to be free?
AND I ANSWER THEM MOST MYSTERIOUSLY
Are birds free from the chains of the skyway?

BOB DYLAN

In February 1972 I completed my prison sentence for my Rochester convictions, sans parole as expected. Instead of simply walking out of the prison, as I'd hoped to do, I was shackled once more and driven to the federal courthouse in Detroit, where I had a bail hearing on my Harrisburg contempt indictment. To my surprise and relief, the judge granted me bail on my own recognizance. I was released, and went home with Sue.

That same month the Harrisburg conspiracy trial started. I read about it from afar. The prosecution and the defense battled each other for four weeks just to agree on a jury of twelve, plus three alternates. There were predictions there might be as many as ninety-five witnesses called; one journalist predicted two hundred witnesses. In the year since the conspiracy indictment had been handed down by the grand jury, the defense had spent more than three hundred thousand dollars to prepare for trial, and the prosecution spent three times that. The trial promised to be a full-blown circus, with the government throwing everything they had at the defendants, and the defendants pushing back just as hard.

Upon my release I took a job in Ann Arbor as a childcare worker at a group home for delinquent teenage boys—court kids. I thought maybe I could use my prison experience as a tool to help these kids go straight and stay out of trouble, and perhaps occasionally I did. My fiancée, Sue, was teaching in a private school run by the same agency. We rented a small, one-bedroom apartment near the University of Michigan football stadium. We drove a beat-up old Studebaker. We shopped flea markets for used furniture and dishes. We planted a small vegetable garden in the backyard. We got a cat. We ate lots of oranges. We invented new ways to make love.

On April 1 Sue and I were married at Cornell in Anabel Taylor Chapel, the same chapel that had been firebombed in the days following Martin Luther King's assassination in 1968. Our wedding was the first event held in the chapel following its restoration, and it was overflowing with people we knew, and some we didn't.

The service was an open-agenda, Quaker-style ceremony. Aside from our vows, which were short and which we wrote ourselves, we hadn't planned anything, and it turned out we didn't need to. Our friends sang songs, told stories and jokes, and read poetry they'd written for the occasion. A dance troupe performed. George Crocker, who'd been released from Milan a couple of months before me, passed out oranges.

The FBI was there, unapologetically taking pictures as everyone arrived and as they left, and they joined us at our reception, which was held on the farm of Jack Lewis, the head of CURW. As we cut the cake and stuffed pieces into each other's mouths, an intrepid agent leaned out of a hovering helicopter to film the scene below. A few defendants from the Harrisburg trial were among the celebrants.

The Harrisburg trial was on break. The prosecution had ended their lengthy case the week before, and in a stunning and unexpected move, the defense had rested its case without presenting any witnesses. The powerful defense team was satisfied the government hadn't proven their case, and that the defense had successfully pointed this out to the jury during the prosecution.

When it came time for the defense to call witnesses, Ramsey Clark, speaking for the several defense lawyers, stood up, turned to the judge and jury, and uttered one simple sentence: "The defendants will always seek peace, the defendants continue to proclaim their innocence, and the defense rests." That was it. That was the entire defense. Seventeen words.

It was brilliant and it was enough. After seven days of deliberation, the jury remained deadlocked 10–2 for acquittal on all three conspiracy charges. Liz McAllister was convicted on three charges of smuggling letters into a federal prison, and Phil Berrigan was convicted on four charges of smuggling letters out. They'd each be handed nominal sentences for this relatively minor infraction.

It'd be decades before I had occasion to read those smuggled letters for myself, and when I did, I was appalled. These peaceful and thoughtful people had actually contemplated the kidnapping of Henry Kissinger.

It never got to the planning stages, but it'd been discussed. Thank god they came to their senses before the plan took shape.

Sure, they'd given up on the idea before Hoover ever complained about it to the Congressional Appropriations Committee, and yes, that appears to be why a majority of the jury felt their discussion never reached the definition of "conspiracy," but to my mind, that's splitting hairs. Kidnapping and bombing are tactics that should never have been considered—not even for a minute. Such an extreme escalation of action would have violated everything all of us had stood for. I was, and still am, greatly mortified it was ever contemplated.

What follows is a portion of a letter Elizabeth McAllister smuggled into prison to Phillip Berrigan, and which was made a part of the formal indictment of the Harrisburg Seven. It's hard to reconcile this letter with the earnest, mild-mannered nun I knew. I went through an intensive three-day retreat with her at Iron Mountain, and I bivouacked with her in Baltimore and Delaware. I was (and like to think I still am) her friend. But I must not have known her as well as I thought I did. The woman I knew could never have written the following, nor could the people she names in the letter, most of them also friends of mine, have ever considered the proposed plot:

> This is in utter confidence and should not be committed to paper and I would want you not to even to say a word of it to Dan until we have a fuller grasp of it. I say it to you for 2 reasons. The first obviously is to get your thinking on it, the second to give you some confidence that people are thinking seriously of escalating resistance. Eq called us up to Conn. last night along with Bill Davidon....Eq outlined a plan for an action which would say—escalated seriousness—and we discussed pros and cons for several hours. It needs much more thought and careful selection of personnel. To kidnap—in our terminology make a citizens' arrest of—someone like Henry Kissinger. Him because of his influence as policy maker yet sans cabinet status, he would therefore not be as much protected as one of the bigger wigs; he is a bachelor which would mean if he were unguarded he would be anxious to have

*unguarded moments where he could carry on his private affairs—
literally and figuratively. To issue a set of demands, eg cessation of
use of B52s over N. Vietnam, Laos, Cambodia and release of political
prisoners. Hold him for about a week during which time big wigs of
the liberal ilk would be brought to him—also kidnapped if necessary
(which, for the most part it would be)—and hold a trial or grand jury
affair out of which an indictment would be brought. There is no pre-
tense of these demands being met and he would be released after this
time with a word that we're non-violent as opposed to you who would
let a man be killed—one of your own—so that you can go on killing. The liberals would also be released as would a film of the whole
proceeding in which hopefully he would be far more honest than he is
on his own territory.*

Had someone asked me, as a lark, to sit down and write down a farcical
and exaggerated course of action for an anti-war group to take during
this period, I wouldn't have been able to come up with anything nearly
as asinine as what is proposed in this letter. It's scant relief they figured
this out themselves before they acted on it.

The end of the Harrisburg conspiracy trial should have been the
ignominious end of it all, but it wasn't. The government could have
retried the alleged conspirators on the deadlocked indictments, but it
never did. By 1972 a fatigue seemed to have set in across the nation,
shared by the peace movement and by the government alike. The peace
movement was in disarray, and the government, after Watergate, had
other things on its mind.

A few months after the jury deadlocked on the conspiracy charges, the
federal prosecutor in Harrisburg announced there would be no new
trial. But nothing was said about the ten of us who were still under
indictment for refusing to testify before the Harrisburg grand jury. I remained under a very dark cloud, still facing a possible life sentence. The
prosecution wasn't giving any hint of what they intended to do with
us—the remnants of the celebrated Harrisburg trial—who remained under indictment for contempt. Would the failed conspiracy prosecution

of the Harrisburg Seven prompt the government to drop the contempt charges, or would they seek some measure of retribution by coming after us anyway? We had no idea what to expect.

In case I was tempted to forget my tenuous status, the FBI was there to remind me, in the form of James Riley, Special Agent, of the Detroit office of the FBI. Before I'd even been released from prison, Riley visited my anticipated employer—my immediate boss and my boss's boss and all of my co-workers—and attempted, with various measures of success, to recruit them to keep tabs on me. During the first week of my release, he visited my landlord and my neighbors and made sure they were apprised of just how dangerous this ex-con was. Every day during the first month of my freedom, Riley was parked outside my house, ready to follow me to work or anywhere else I might go. He made sure I was aware I was being followed.

Then he and a partner came to see me. I agreed to meet with him in a neutral place—a café. I was irritated and I was curious what this was all about. I wanted the harassment to stop.

Riley wanted to turn me, to recruit me to spy on an Ann Arbor group of hippies who called themselves the Rainbow Coalition. I'd never met any of them, I told Riley, who didn't seem to believe me but ultimately didn't care. His message was simple. If I wanted to "clear my name," I needed to cooperate with the FBI, and that meant working for them as a snitch. I told him the only thing I wanted was to be left alone, but he wouldn't leave me alone. He kept calling me, visiting my neighbors and co-workers, and trying to set up an appointment to see me again. He was like a bulldog that wouldn't let go of its prey once it'd sunk its teeth in.

I turned to my Rochester attorney Herm Walz for help. Herm helped me craft letters to the FBI in Washington to get them to call off their dogs. I have since obtained, under an FOIA request, nine hundred pages of my FBI record, in which there is correspondence from Hoover directing Riley to desist. I'd finally be left alone.

In June 1972, Ted Glick, one of my codefendants in the Rochester draft board raid case, won his appeal. The appellate court ruled the judge had acted illegally by holding private conversations with the jury without the knowledge of the defense. It held that the judge's one-word answer, "Yes," to the jury's inquiry about his disposition toward leniency was likely a factor in the guilty verdicts, which were rendered within minutes of the jury receiving the judge's answer.

Ted Glick was summarily acquitted of all charges stemming from the Rochester draft board raid. The other seven of us, however, remained convicted. None of us had filed an appeal, and the deadline for us to do so was long past.

When Ted had filed his appeal, I'd been asked if I wanted to join him, and my answer was firmly, "No." I wanted to serve my time and get it all over with. I didn't want to delay it while an appeal, which I thought had no chance, wound its way through the courts. Ted himself had never hoped to win. He'd appealed only because he wanted some time out of prison to try to save his marriage, which was collapsing under the pressure of his imprisonment.

Now the U.S. Attorney in Rochester had the option to retry Ted. After a brief period, the federal prosecutor announced his office was dropping the matter. It remains a mystery why the case was dropped instead of retried. Perhaps it was because a new trial would have been hugely expensive—the ordeal of rounding up the dozen prosecution witnesses, re-interviewing them, and prepping them for the trial; the task of recovering and inspecting the boxes of evidence and the reams of transcripts from the first trial; the likelihood that a new trial would consume the attention of the court and the U.S. Attorney for weeks or months.

The assistant U.S. Attorney who prosecuted the case, Wolford, hadn't seemed to enjoy the task the first time. Could it be that the decision not to prosecute had something to do with his own attitude toward the war, the draft, and the defendants? Had Wolford, like the jury, grown marginally sympathetic to the actions of the Flower City Conspiracy? Or was he just tired of it all? Perhaps it was simply the onus of conducting the trial itself that was the deciding factor.

Was the decision to drop the case made in Rochester, or was it made in Washington? If it came from the Justice Department, perhaps the Nixon administration had decided they'd simply suffered enough publicity from these pesky draft board raiders. Perhaps the disappointing and embarrassing results of the Harrisburg trial inspired them to refrain from another lengthy prosecution.

We'll never know.

In 1973, Sue gave birth to our son, Jordan. It was the best day of my life.

In the summer of 1974, after three years under the cloud of a federal indictment, I received a notice in the mail that my indictment for criminal contempt of court for refusing to testify before the Harrisburg grand jury had been dropped. It was over. I could get on with my life.

Jordan Gilchrist, age two.

And so ended my career of "resistance"—not with a bang but a whimper. The world had become no less polluted with causes for protest, and I possessed no less faith in the healing power of the American tradition of civil disobedience, but for me the wind had gone out of my voice, the strength from my muscles, the stridency from my heart. Over the next four decades, I sought, selfishly no doubt, something other than the tumult of the public soapbox or the privations of imprisonment.

My life had been in turmoil throughout my childhood and my young adulthood, and now I wanted a normal life.

I transferred to the School of Education at the University of Michigan to complete my undergraduate degree. I had only one semester remaining at Cornell, but Sue and I had no desire to return to Ithaca. Ithaca was our past, and we were intent on building our future. In order to better accommodate my class schedule, I took a management job with a restaurant chain. It doesn't get any more normal than that.

In 1975, after three years of marriage, I finally figured out what I should have known from the start. I'm at least an eight on the Kinsey scale. From practically the time we met, Sue had been aware of my attraction toward men, so my decision to separate was not a shocking surprise to her. And as she knew, I'm not incapable of loving a woman. During our marriage, Sue and I had had a good and healthy relationship, and I was and still am truthfully in love with her.

But ultimately, my happiness lies in being with a man. My marriage with Sue never devolved into something sordid or miserable or ugly, but it never evolved into what either of us wanted. In the summer of 1975 we separated. She kept the house, the car, and virtually all of our joint possessions. I took my clothes and books. I granted her custody of our son. As a six-time felon, I wouldn't have been successful had I fought her for custody, and her home was likely the better one for Jordan anyway. I wasn't worried about her standing in the way of my relationship with my son.

We both had come from broken homes, and we both had experienced the foulness of fathers who used their children as weapons in a never-ending war against their wives. We vowed never to do that with Jordan, and we further vowed that neither of us would ever say anything negative about the other in Jordan's hearing. It was an easy promise to keep.

Something else happened in 1975—something that would change the rest of my life. I was camping in the Gros Ventre Range of the Wyoming Rockies, just east of the Tetons. The majestic Tetons are well known but few people pay attention to the more humble Gros Ventre Range, and that's precisely why I was there. The Tetons in the summer are as packed with tourists as Disneyland—and that wasn't my idea of a vacation. The Gros Ventre Range, on the other hand, is empty, hundreds of square miles of empty, and it boasts what is likely the best view of the Tetons from across a broad, fertile valley.

I'd taken to backpacking frequently since prison. I exalted in sleeping under the open skies and walking empty trails. I camped in the wild as often as I could, in the remotest regions I could find. Most often I took Jordan on these trips, usually inviting a buddy of his along as well. Frequently we were joined by Phil Shuman and his two boys. But on this trip it was just me and Randy Ball. Randy and I had continued our friendship after prison, and he was now working for me in Ann Arbor.

On the last day of our week-long adventure, as we were coming down the mountains, we met a fellow hiker who was going up. We learned he was out of coffee, and he learned we were out of marijuana. We fired up my Sterno and brewed up a pot, and he fired up a joint of his "Maui Wowie." He said he was from Hawaii. I told him my name and asked for his, and he said "Damien." "Damien *what*?" I asked. "Just Damien," he said. And then the ridiculous happened.

I felt the earth move. The heavens parted. The sun rained down. Birds sang in harmony and wove intricate patterns in the sky. The wind whispered my name.

For years, ever since the day I'd walked out of his house, I'd wanted to get rid of my father's name. When Sue and I had been married, we discussed inventing a new last name for ourselves, but we never decided on anything. From time to time I considered changing my name to "*something* Coleman" or "Coleman *something*"—some combination with my mother's maiden name; but as stupid as it sounds, I never found the right combination.

It'd never occurred to me that, like Damien, I didn't need two names. One would do just fine. I could just be "Coleman." At the instant Damien introduced himself, I knew this was my new name. Randy and I raced down off the mountain and we drove straight back to Ann Arbor without stopping except for gas and a quick bite—a journey that took more than twenty-four hours. Before going home, I stopped at the courthouse and filed the papers to change my name legally.

A few months later, I became Coleman. It felt great then, and it still does.

In 1978, while I was living and working in Chicago, I received an unexpected phone call from Esther Pahlka. I hadn't heard from her for ten years. During all of that time I'd respected the decision she and Harlan made to sever all ties with me when I refused induction in Oklahoma. I'd stayed in occasional contact with their sons, but I'd left Harlan and Esther alone.

Esther said she was in Chicago, staying at the Hilton Hotel. I met her for lunch. She told me she and Harlan had come to the realization that I'd been right about Vietnam, after all, and they wanted me back in their family.

I was ecstatic. I didn't care what opinion they ultimately held about the Vietnam War, or even about my draft resistance. I was simply glad to be back in their flock. That summer I traveled with Jordan and Jordan's new little sister, Whitney, to Oklahoma—my first trip back home in ten years. It was great to have a family again.

One day in 1980 I answered my doorbell, and my older brother Gordon was standing there with all of his possessions in a battered suitcase. Things hadn't been going well for him. He'd lost his job. He was behind in child support. In fact, he was wanted by the law in two states for not meeting his court-ordered obligations to his children. He had no money and no home. And he was drunk.

Of course I gave him a place to stay. I'd missed him and Jim. I hadn't been in touch much with either since our mother's funeral. It'd bothered me that neither of them had visited me in prison, but I'd tried not to let it get under my skin. I knew in my gut that if it'd been the other way around—if either of them had been in prison instead of me—I'd have written and visited faithfully. Nothing could have kept me from going to see them. But they weren't me, and I wasn't them. Life is complicated, so who knows why they never made the effort. I was simply glad to see Gordon again.

Ever since my mother's funeral, Gordon had been carrying a burden—a secret he'd never shared with anyone. A few nights after he arrived in Chicago, he sat me down and leveled with me. "Here," he said, passing a box across the table. "This is Mom. She's your responsibility now."

When Mom died in 1971, Gordon had been living in Shreveport. After her funeral, he flew back to Shreveport, and at the first opportunity he embarked on a road trip to Texas to place my mother's ashes in the Coleman plot in the cemetery in Vernon. Before driving to Vernon, he planned to visit his children, who were living with their mother in Arlington, Texas. But in Arlington, he stopped for a drink at a bar. His car was broken into and Mom's remains, along with Gordon's golf clubs and luggage, were stolen.

Three years later Gordon's phone rang. It was the Dallas police department. They'd broken up a burglary ring, and among the loot stashed in a forlorn garage they'd found Mom. Through the serial number on the

container, they'd been able to trace her remains to the mortuary in New York, and from there they'd tracked down Gordon. The cops placed Mom in a small cardboard box, wrapped the box tightly with packing tape, slapped on a bunch of stamps, and mailed her back to my brother. For seven years she'd remained sequestered in that box on a shelf in Gordon's home.

Together we laughed at the story. It was so, well, "Mom." Nothing was simple in her life, so why should the disposal of her remains be any different? Now she was in my hands, and I had to decide what to do. In the meantime, I placed her on a shelf in my closet.

Gordon's arrival in Chicago heralded new opportunities for both of us. For more than a decade, I'd felt that I carried little, if anything, of my family with me. I'd carved out a new, independent, and reasonably successful life, and I'd achieved my life-long goal of living a life of happiness and sharing.

I don't think I knew how much I missed him until Gordon came back into my life. But he was a mess. He was so besotted he was hardly capable of doing anything for himself. And he didn't have a dime to his name.

Being Gordon, he was able to charm his way into a job selling mattresses. It was a lousy job, but it was income and it gave him something to do outside the house. When he failed to show up for work one day, and then another, he lost the job. Then he lost another job. And then another one.

By this time in my life I was working at the American Hospital Association as manager of education, responsible for a staff that coordinated their three hundred annual conventions and meetings. I worked hard, I loved my job, and I was good at what I was doing.

The AHA encouraged volunteer work, and I joined the board of the new and struggling Howard Brown Memorial Clinic—a storefront clinic serving the needs of Chicago's gay community. It happened that I joined at the very moment that the first cases of AIDS were appearing on the East and West Coasts. The number of cases quickly skyrocketed, and Howard Brown became an important player in the effort to battle AIDS.

At one point, when the clinic's executive director had to resign for health reasons, AHA gave me a six-month leave of absence to step in and perform the job. It was during this period that the clinic obtained its first AIDS research contracts with the NIH and the Centers for Disease Control, and today the Howard Brown Health Center, in a shining new facility on Chicago's north side, remains an international leader in medical treatment and research for the LGBT community.

Although things were going well in my professional and social life, my home life sucked. Coming home to Gordon had become seriously unpleasant. As much as I wanted to be with and assist Gordon, he was greatly interfering with my quest for my own happiness, and he certainly wasn't doing anything for his own.

One night I turned left instead of right, entering the door to the bar across the corner from our house on Racine Avenue. In Chicago (in case you didn't know) there's a bar or two on nearly every corner in every neighborhood, and it was this particular bar in our neighborhood that had become Gordon's home away from home. He spent more time there than he did anywhere else, and sure enough, he was there that night. I grabbed him and told him he needed to come home with me right now. He knew I meant business.

I told him he had a decision to make. I'd arranged for him to enroll in a thirty-day, in-patient treatment program for alcoholics. Either he could admit himself that night, or he could pack his bags and sleep on the sidewalk, for all I cared. I told him I loved him and I wanted to live with him, but that I couldn't abide his drinking anymore. So it was his choice. What did he want to do?

He chose treatment.

Dry, Gordon became my wonderful brother again. We lived together for four years, until we each knew it was time for us to renew our separate lives. He moved just two doors down from my apartment. He was doing well as a manager of a computer store. He was starting to date, he'd lost a lot of weight, and he was sober.

And I was starting my own business. At the AHA, I'd written software for my staff to manage the myriad details of our many meetings (the registrations, the money, the speakers, the hotel arrangements, the travel, the scheduling, etc.). At this early stage in the PC revolution, no one else was doing this, and I saw a business opportunity. Gordon was my first employee—but he was more than that, really. He was my partner. I handled sales and client relations and did most of the programming. Gordon kept the books and managed the operations, and he frequently cleaned up my programming. We worked together for five glorious years.

Later Gordon would falter again. Many times. He married a wonderful woman, who loved him beyond endurance. His weight ballooned past four hundred and fifty pounds. Several times he'd begin drinking and then quit. Again and again his health would fail and then recover. He almost died a dozen times. He was in and out of various hospitals.

Gordon renewed his relationships with his children, somewhat successfully. Though they had no reason to, they seemed to forgive the way he'd abandoned them years earlier.

He retained through all his ups and downs his sense of humor. Ultimately, however, his twin addictions—eating and drinking—killed him

Jim has done well in life. I wish we were closer than we are. The rift we experienced when we were eleven, and which widened when I left home and he stayed behind, has never quite healed. We have no disagreements with each other. We are simply, unfortunately, strangers.

Jim married just out of college and he and his wife have two amazing children. Jim chose a career in academics, sticking with his love of Speech and Communications. This specialty, which my father told him would never amount to anything, afforded Jim a tenured position at Western Michigan University, where he now works as CIO.

As for me, I never lost my lust for theatre. After prison it seemed an impossible dream. I married Sue. We had Jordan. I was determined to provide for him, and I saw no opportunity to make money in theatre.

I floundered for a while in jobs that weren't quite right but that I none-theless enjoyed. I managed a restaurant in Ann Arbor, managed the Dining Room at the new Ritz Carlton hotel at Water Tower Place, and cooked in a swanky French restaurant on Chicago's Rush Street while working nights a few doors down as a bouncer at a gay bar. Then I cre-ated a job for myself as general manager of a new thousand–seat, glitzy Chicago cabaret called the Park West. It wasn't exactly theatre, but it was close, and it more than satisfied the itch that needed scratching. I stayed at Park West for five years, welcoming artists ranging from Bette Midler to the Rolling Stones to Count Basie to the Village People. It was a great gig. But after five years, I needed desperately to get out. It was the 1980s—the cocaine years—and I saw many friends and colleagues ruin themselves and their lives while living in the fast lane of late nights, free booze, and rock and roll.

In 1981 the American Hospital Association hired me, and as I've men-tioned, it presented a propitious opportunity for me to remake myself, and it paved the way for me to open my own software company in 1985. By the 1990s, most of my clients were in Europe, and for more than ten years I was out of the country more than I was home.

In 1988 I met John, the love of my life. Ten years later we moved to rural Wisconsin. I continued to consult internationally in custom software development until a few years ago when John, who is ten years younger than I, gave me the gift of early retirement. I then built a new outdoor theatre at a local non-profit arts center, and I'm finally doing what I wanted all along. I write plays, I act, I direct, I design. After five years of devoted work, I gave up my role as artistic director, and now I freelance as a writer, performer, and producer.

In 2004 John and I were married in San Francisco during the first wave of gay marriages, when Mayor Newsome defied the law and instructed his city clerks to issue licenses to gay couples. Our marriage, along with those of four thousand other couples, was annulled by the California Supreme Court a few months later. But we are persistent.

That same year I campaigned against a heinous constitutional amend-ment banning gay marriage in Wisconsin. I headed the anti-amendment campaign in four counties in the southwest region of the state. Regrettably, the amendment was passed, as were similar amendments in many other states. I'm happy to report that at least our rural county voted against the amendment.

In 2009 John and I were married a second time, this time in nearby Iowa, but that marriage has legal status only when we happen to be in Iowa. In 2010 we took advantage of a new opportunity to become "domestic partners" in Wisconsin, granting us at least a handful of the rights that legally married couples take for granted.

We live in this strange new world. I'm astonished that gay rights have come so far. At the same time, I'm livid that they have not come further. It perplexes me that my legal relationship with the man I love changes depending on which state we happen to be in at the moment—which brings me back to my disaffection with all things religious. Just how can it be considered Christian for people to want to keep my relationship with John extra-legal? What's Christian about denying us the opportunity to care for each other?

But that's a subject for another book.

The milestones in my mother's life were by and large tragic, but I don't want to leave you with the impression that it was these events that defined her.

My mother was as filled with love as my father was devoid of it. In my presence, she always exuded a calmness, a rock-solid peacefulness that demonstrated that while she might not have been living in the best of conditions, she was at ease in the world.

Her focus was rarely on herself. She was a curious woman—curious about the world she lived in, about nature, about politics, about baseball, and most of all, curious about the life and needs of whoever was in her presence. Without exception my friends loved her and gravitated to her, largely because she was so interested in them and because she genuinely cared about other people.

My mother didn't judge others. She was a careful listener and she remembered what people said to her. If you had a meaningful discussion with her and then met her a year later, she'd recall the details of that discussion. If you'd ever told her the names of others in your family or life, she'd remember them.

After her visit to Cornell in 1967, I found that she often knew more about my friends than I did. I, unfortunately, tend to take my friends for granted. Once someone enters my life, the particulars of their origin aren't always a priority for me to know. But my mother was inquisitive and always wanted to know as much about the people she met as she could. Often when my mom and I were having a conversation, she'd mention someone I'd long since forgotten, and then she'd share some detail of that person's life I'd never known.

My mother never cared about material possessions. She never aspired to have a big house, a fancy car, expensive jewelry. In the end, she was more comfortable living out of a suitcase that held everything she owned in the world, with room left over. Today my mother would probably look askance at my oversize house and my plethora of things. She'd want to know why I need all this stuff, and I wouldn't know how to answer.

My mother wasn't given to standing on soapboxes. While she set high standards of behavior for herself, she wasn't preachy or unforgiving to others. If she preached at all, she preached by example. When someone she met needed something that she might be able to provide, she stepped in to help, never seeking gratitude or recognition. For her, helping is just what one does. If she herself didn't have the resources to provide the help, she tried to find the resources somewhere else. That was the pattern of her life. She had the impulse to be helpful.

How then do I reconcile these memories of my mother's character with the two fateful and horrific moments when she sought to take her own life?

I don't have an answer to that question. My mother wasn't a victim of depression—at least not the long-term sort of depression that one carries on one's back hour upon hour, day after day. To the contrary, she was a bona fide optimist most of her life, seeing the good in the bad, the silver lining in the dark cloud, making lemonade from lemons. This was true before the fire, during her recovery, during her incarceration, and throughout the scant three years of freedom that followed.

What, then, caused her on that dark day in 1959 to attempt suicide by immolation, and what caused her in 1971 to leap from the roof of the Catholic Worker?

I'll never know, but I can't help but conjecture the reasons.

Jim, Gordon, and I all bear our own scars from my father's cold temperament, so it's not hard to imagine how much worse it was for her. She shielded us, as much as she could, from his anger, his abuse and his meanness—and took it upon herself. The more my father was away from home, the more my mother found her own way in the world, through her volunteering, her friendships, and her charities. Each attempt at independence she undertook resulted in an escalating rebuke from my father. She was desperately unhappy in her marriage.

It was the shortcoming of the times as well as the shortcoming of my mother that she saw no other way out but her own death. Why she chose such a dramatic means of accomplishing it is a total mystery, one that I'll never solve.

After the fire she survived for twelve hard years, and she did so with extraordinary grace. I can't imagine myself behaving as nobly under the same circumstances. She demonstrated resilience beyond my understanding, and she laughed her way through all of it. My mother loved to laugh, to smile, to chuckle. Life amused her. After her many operations she always covered her mouth when she laughed. Perhaps she didn't like the way her smile looked, the way the scars on her face pulled at her lips and cheeks. But nothing stopped her from laughing.

It's remarkable that she progressed from bedridden invalid to Civil Rights crusader in a few short years, that she subordinated her own tragedy to right grievous wrongs against others. Even more remarkable is how she bore the punishment of her witness. Perhaps it's only because she'd experienced something far worse—her own immolation—that she was able to abide with grace the five long years of confinement in a state mental institution.

But ultimately her optimism failed her. Did something happen at the Catholic Worker that triggered her demise? Or was it just the weight of all those years of living in a scarred and battered body? Was it loneliness that drove her over the edge, or the pointlessness of trying to live a life of meaning when she felt she had so little to give herself? And I have to ask, how did my own incarceration figure into things? I suspect it bothered her more than she expressed to me. To me she was strong and courageous, and by example she coached me to be the same. But did she lose courage in the face of the imprisonment of her youngest son?

A half century has passed. How do I feel about all that has happened?

I remain immensely proud of my mother—of her commitment to Civil Rights and her generosity of spirit. I am eternally sad that I was not smart enough at the age of fifteen to speak up in her defense, and that it took me five long years to obtain her release. I am regretful that I was not there to do more to ease her re-entry into the world.

I remain mostly satisfied with my role vis-à-vis the war and the draft. To the question, "Would I do it all over again?" the answer is, "Yes."

The Vietnam War was a horror, an unnecessary and stupid war that killed more than fifty thousand of my generation. Few of those killed were among the privileged of our nation. The draft was rigged that way. The sons of the underclass were deemed expendable. I'm glad I wasn't silent; that to whatever extent, I put a spoke in the wheel of Nixon's war machine.

I am glad I didn't flee to Canada or Sweden or elsewhere. In 1977 President Jimmy Carter fulfilled a campaign promise and issued a pardon to the hundreds of thousands of young men who never registered, or who fled the country rather than face conscription. The pardon didn't extend to Mennonites like Pete Washek or Quakers like Pat Vaughn—religious pacifists who'd been improperly denied CO status by their draft boards and sentenced by judges to five years in prison for following the dictates of their faith. It didn't extend to any of the more than two thousand young men who served time in federal prisons for draft resistance during the Vietnam War. Carter pardoned only those who fled. We who stayed behind and took our medicine remain convicted felons. I can't speak for the other two thousand, but for me, that's okay. I'm proud to be a felon—a "felon for peace," as my friend and fellow felon Jerry Elmer puts it. That's a stripe I earned.

I'm aware that I live in a hyper-patriotic country, and that this hyper-patriotism tends to overwhelm, from time to time, the possibility of rational thought or discourse. This uber-patriotism is pervasive, but never so much as on every Memorial Day, Fourth of July, and Veterans Day, and on these occasions I crawl inside a shell. I believe that I'm as cognizant as anyone else of the sacrifices soldiers have made for our country, but there's this itch at the base of my skull, where my brain won't stop asking questions.

Why do we as a nation celebrate only our soldiers, and never our peacemakers? Why is there a war monument in every town square in every crossroads town in America, but not a single acknowledgement anywhere of the sacrifices others made in the name of peace instead of war? Yes, we celebrate the birthday of Martin Luther King, but only as a Civil Rights leader. No one seems to remember he opposed the war in Vietnam.

But more than that, why do we keep churning out more wars and more soldiers and more damaged veterans? As Pete Seeger asked, "When will they ever learn?"

Recently, a new friend asked me if I was a veteran. I said "Yes." Then I said "No." Then I said, "Yes." True, I was never in the military. I never went to war. Instead, I fought against a war that should never have been waged, a war that cost tens of thousands of American lives and hundreds of thousands of Vietnamese lives. I served just under two years in a uniform—a prison uniform—and subsequently I have passed some forty years as a felon. I knew the risks going in. That's the lesson penned by Thoreau and ennobled by Gandhi. Civil disobedience comes with risks, and one must be willing to accept them.

It also has its rewards. I am unabashedly proud of my role in the 1960s and '70s. And that is reward enough. It will have to be.

From time to time I'd feel a bit guilty that Mom was still in the box. Now and then I'd bring her out of the closet and give her some air on a mantelpiece or a coffee table, but eventually she'd find her way back to the closet.

The truth was I liked her close by. The other truth was I didn't know what to do with her. It didn't feel right to take her to Vernon to her old family plot, and every other place I considered—and there were several—didn't feel right either. So I kept her. I liked her being around.

In 2002 a light bulb went off in my head. Molokai. My mother dreamed of Molokai. Helping the lepers in Molokai was her unfulfilled and final dream. I would take her remains to Molokai.

In 1865 the King of Hawaii, Lot Kamehameha, issued "An Act to Prevent the Spread of Leprosy" which branded all lepers criminals. During the first year islanders were chased down, inspected, arrested, and herded into cattle stalls on boats for the fifty-eight-mile journey across choppy waters from Oahu to Molokai. The ships didn't even pause to drop anchor at the base of the tallest sea cliffs in the world, which rise more than thirty-three hundred feet. Instead, the exiles were thrown off the ship into the water to make their own way to shore or drown. Their possessions were thrown in after them, to float either toward Kalaupapa, the inhospitable shelf of land beneath the cliffs, or out to sea.

Those who reached the land lived in caves or in crude shelters patched together with gathered sticks and driftwood. There was no potable water other than what might collect in pools from rain. There was no edible vegetation.

The exiles were declared civilly dead. They were automatically divorced from their spouses. Their wills were executed as if they were in the grave.

Seven years after its founding, a Belgian priest, Father Damien, arrived with supplies. With the support of the faithful from around the world, he built houses, churches, schools, and coffins. He provided medicine and food and clothing and books. He built a hospital. Visitors rarely made their way to Kalaupapa, but two well-known writers did. Robert Louis Stevenson wrote that it was a "prison fortified by nature," and it certainly was that. But perhaps Jack London's description rings more true: "The pit of hell... the most cursed place on earth."

In 1898 America annexed Hawaii and the decree remained. In 1959 Hawaii attained statehood and still the decree remained in force. It wasn't until 1969 that the largest medical segregation in history was finally ended. Today the leper colony at Kalaupapa on Molokai is a National Park. The last few survivors of the leper colony still live there.

The more I learned about the leper colony on Molokai, the more suited it seemed as the place to distribute my mother's ashes. It was the site of an egregious wrong—a wrong unacknowledged for more than a century. Kalaupapa represented my mother's last dream, an unfulfilled aspiration to help others who'd suffered in ways not unlike herself.

And there was that other weird business: The eight thousand lepers exiled to Kalaupapa were rescued from chaos, anarchy, and poverty by the Catholic priest Father Damien. Was it just a coincidence that the mysterious hiker from Hawaii—the one I'd met on a mountain in Wyoming and who inspired me to change my name—had also been named Damien? I'm not a person who believes in "signs," but if I were, I'd surely been given a sign.

January 25, 2002

For three days I've been relaxing in a thatched-roof shelter on a beach on the northwest coast of Molokai. This remote resort and its sparkling beach are remarkably empty of tourists, and I've had this splendor and luxury to myself. I have snorkeled alone in a crystal-clear bay, picked up shells from a beach free of footprints, built fires with twisted driftwood. At night I lounge outside under a billion stars, listening to the roar and the shush of the ocean. And as the sun rises, the last day of my trip arrives. I'm ready to let go of my mother.

I climb into my rented pickup and drive a short distance to a parking lot on the edge of a dense forest rimming the high sea cliffs of Molokai. I enter the forest, and giant ironwood and eucalyptus trees immediately overtake and soar above me. A hazy morning mist blows in from the sea, and the air between the trees is suffused with a ghostly, otherworldly glow. The deep cushion of the needles and leaves mutes all sound. I am alone, totally alone. This, I think, may be the single most peaceful place on earth.

I climb up and down the rills and rifts of the sea cliffs, wandering closer and then farther away from the edge in the soft silence of the forest. After a while I stop at a promontory that overlooks Kalaupapa, the site of the Hawaiian leper colony. I balance on the edge of the world's tallest sea cliffs. More than half a mile below me, waves pound a rocky shore. The sea recedes to infinity.

Somewhere in me a valve opens.

I exhale the weight of the sixty-one years of her life and the thirty-one years since her death, and I breathe in the cool, fine mist that blows up into my face from the turbulent Pacific Ocean. At last I have brought my mother to her final resting place.

But something tells me the journey isn't quite over yet. Just a bit farther, it tells me. This place is so quiet, so private, so peaceful—but what could be farther on?

And so I continue my trek deeper along the sea cliff. With each passing moment, this intensely private place seems to become even more intimate, more eternal, and more peaceful. I come to another promontory and this, that something tells me, is the place. I pull the container from my backpack and sit with her briefly. I empty my thoughts.

There is nothing in the universe but this place, myself, and my mom's remains.

I open the container. It seems as if she leaps out of my hands to rush down the cliff. I sit—peaceful and jubilant, tearful and joyful, alone and one with the world.

☼

Acknowledgements

Thanks to: John Fetters for yelling at me for twenty-five years to write this book and for supporting me as I did; to the Wisconsin Arts Board for a Literary Artist Fellowship that funded my research; to Dean Bakopoulos, Marcia Jablonski, Matt Rimer, and Jeanne Lambin for support of a different nature altogether; to Danielle Trussoni for getting me started on this project, to Frank and Sandee Beaman for the friendship and advice.

Special thanks to Dean Bakopoulos, a terrific writer, teacher, and friend.

Thanks also to: Susan Gilchrist, Mollie Daniels, Clara Luper and Calvin Luper, The NAACP Youth Council Freedom Center of Oklahoma City, Harlan and Esther Pahlka, Bob Pahlka, Trudy Huntington, Jerry Elmer, Jane Meyerding, Milo, Dallas, and the good folks who maintain the Oklahoma Historical Society and the Cornell University Rare Books Manuscript Collection.

Thanks also to my publisher, Kristin Mitchell and the staff of Little Creek Press, and my editor, Carl Stratman.

This book is not a work of fiction. People named actually lived and to the best of my knowledge did the things they are described as doing in this work. I have tried to be as accurate in the reporting of names, dates, and occurrences as my research and my memory and my personal collection of memorabilia have permitted. Any errors or omissions are strictly my own.

About the Author

Coleman is an author and playwright, and co-founder of Peddler Creek, which produces events and workshops in the literary and performing arts. He lives in rural Wisconsin.